Monitoring Business Performance

The idea of using models to inform business practice seems appealing, as it suggests the abstraction and control of a large, complex subject by means of a smaller, easily manipulated mechanism. In reality, however, many models prove inadequate when translated into business methods. *Monitoring Business Performance—Models, Methods and Tools* elucidates how the assumptions and perceptions that guide performance assessment are often based on models that are poor interpretations and descriptions of reality.

In this book, the author scrutinizes the models underlying a number of well-known business methods and tools and sheds light on the assumptions and subjective perceptions that undermine their effectiveness. In doing so, he offers a unique criticism of accepting business models without questioning their relevance and applicability, and he highlights the need to treat models as hypotheses, rather than as certainties.

Per Lind is Professor in Industrial Economics and Management at Uppsala University, Sweden. He received his doctoral degree from Royal Institute of Technology, Stockholm. He has experience with management in industry (production, marketing) with IBM and Logica, and he has developed business monitoring systems for UNIDO. He is author of *Computerisation in Developing Countries* (Routledge, 1991), *Small Business Management in Cross-Cultural Environments* (Routledge, 2012) and about 60 other publications in English, Spanish and Russian.

Routledge Advances in Management and Business Studies

For a full list of titles in this series, please visit www.routledge.com

Monitoring Business Performance

Models, Methods and Tools

Per Lind

Routledge
Taylor & Francis Group

LONDON AND NEW YORK

First published 2015 by Routledge

2 Park Square, Milton Park, Abingdon, Oxfordshire OX14 4RN
711 Third Avenue, New York, NY 10017

Routledge is an imprint of the Taylor & Francis Group, an informa business

First issued in paperback 2018

Library of Congress Cataloging-in-Publication Data

Lind, Per, 1940–
Monitoring business performance : models, methods, and tools /
   by Per Lind.
      pages cm. — (Routledge advances in management and business
studies ; 60)
   Includes bibliographical references and index.
   1. Management.   2. Performance.   3. Management science.   I. Title.
   HD31.L473   2015
   658.4'013—dc23
   2014004832

ISBN: 978-0-415-83670-8 (hbk)
ISBN: 978-1-138-61797-1 (pbk)

Typeset in Sabon
by Apex CoVantage, LLC

This book is dedicated to
Eva, Mattias, Peter and Johanna

Things are almost never what they seem to be.

Contents

Tables

Figures

Boxes

Preface

This is a reflective, rather than a how-to, book about models and model application in monitoring business performance. The discussion objective is to illustrate how assumptions about reality are translated into models and, from there, into tools and methods, observing that assumptions are sometimes relevant and lead to useful models, and sometimes they create overly simplified and less useful models. This book is not an overview of models and tools for business monitoring per se, but rather a selection of descriptive circumstances where the model concept can be illustrated.

Many approaches to business monitoring have been developed, extensively reported and examined in research reports and other documents where each technique has been analysed in its own framework. The approach in this book is to look critically at the underlying assumptions found common for all approaches—for example, where vital parameters can be identified and analysed and where the future is predictable based on historic data. This book challenges some of these fundamental assumptions.

In places, the text may appear abstract to the reader and references to philosophy and history may seem far-fetched and distant from the context of business monitoring. Debate in recent years, however, about narrow-mindedness in theorizing management and organisation has triggered a new interest in management studies from a critical perspective with the ambition to broaden the study and emphasise its part in a broader social context. This is also the ambition of this book, which has grown out of my interest in organisational behaviour and, in particular, how perceived and interpreted facts influence behaviour. The first reason for my interest was a study of computerisation in the vehicle industry in Egypt. The study led to observations and reflections about what happens when models developed in one context and for a specific purpose are transferred between different socio-economic and cultural contexts. The question that attracted my interest was to what extent the models, translated into computer solutions, can maintain their explanatory power when transferred from the context in which they were originally designed and developed to another setting with different conditions.

I realised that the transfer of models across space has similar implications as the transfer across time. Models and methods are developed in response to organisational or other needs, and they tend to become normative, in spite of the fact that the conditions that prevailed at the time of design may have changed; new conditions may require other kinds of solutions and methods. The French philosopher Jacques Derrida even suggested that the connotations of words change with time, which justifies the question: To what extent can earlier models and theories make sense at a later time?

Models do not develop by themselves; they are the result of inquiries into matters of interest and importance, and since both inquiries and models emanate from human interaction (based always on somebody's interpretation) they can never claim to be objective. The language philosopher Ludwig Wittgenstein—his notion that we create pictures of facts that become models of reality—has influenced my thinking. By this, Wittgenstein wanted to say that models can never be objective but are always based on interpretations of reality. The model itself cannot tell whether it is true or not; neither is it possible to make an *a priori* assumption about a model's relevance. The model as a picture or image of reality, rather than reality itself, is the fundamental idea throughout this book.

A model as a mapping of reality is therefore closely linked to the concept of probability, as characterized in the questions, "Is it probable that these variables are significant for the design of the model?" and "Can the model predict a future stage with any significant probability?" Maynard Keynes alleged in *A Treatise of Probability* that part of our knowledge we obtain direct and part, by argument. The theory of probability is concerned with the part we obtain by argument and it treats of the different degrees in which the results so obtained are conclusive or inconclusive. Lack of understanding about fundamentals of probability may contribute to the problem encountered when a model turns out to be a poor image of reality.

What do we mean by a model being a poor image of reality? Basically, this statement is about the cause-effect assumptions: The cause is not well defined or articulated, or it can be described in different ways, making the model ambiguous. The model can also be coloured by the interpreter through wishes and subjectivity. Emmanuel Levinas, known for his deep distrust in readymade theories about what characterises a good human being or a good society, claimed that the treachery of such theories is that they too easily persuade man to be standing on the side of the Good, creating a biased model. Michel Foucault, like Levinas, rejected theories, and instead suggested the discourse as the primary unit of analysis.

As subjectivity is always a weak point for models and theories, alternative models may emerge through a discourse. Foucault quotes a passage from the Argentinian writer Jorge Luis Borges, purportedly taken from a Chinese encyclopaedia that divides animals into different categories: (a) belonging to the Emperor, (b) embalmed, (c) tame, (d) sucking pigs, (e) sirens,

(f) fabulous, (g) stray dogs, (h) innumerable, (i) drawn with a fine camelhair brush, (j) et cetera, (k) having just broken a water pitcher, (l) that from a long way off look like flies.

Models used in organisational contexts are primarily for explaining or predicting cause-effect relationships. Prediction looks forward from what is to what will come, whereas explanation looks back from what is to what went before. For example: What predictions are possible about future demand if there is an increase in price? Why have conflicts occurred in an organisation during a change process? In monitoring performance, there is an interest in inquiring into and researching these and similar questions. The difficulty here, which is a part of the problem of models in social science, is the interaction with human beings. Explaining a cause-effect relationship in a natural science, such as physics or chemistry, is different from accomplishing the same in a social science because explanation in the latter situation also must involve *understanding*. As real understanding also involves empathy, the model is not just about the observer making a picture but also about the interaction between observer and the observed.

In Part 1, Models and Theories, the introductory section and Chapter 1, Monitoring Business Performance, are followed by four chapters dedicated to discussion about models; the model concept; its background; and the links between models, theories, hypotheses.

Part 2—Methods and Tools—looks in more detail at methods and tools to assess and analyse business performance. Measuring tools like indicators and the use of information systems are presented along with discussion of the general problem of measuring what is sometimes not measurable as important aspects of business monitoring.

Many people have contributed directly or indirectly through their views on and discussions of models, and I wish to place on record the following colleagues who have forced me to think, re-think and finally take the step of tempting Fate by writing this book.

Robert Gasch—In your kitchen in Berlin, after you went out to buy bread early in the mornings for our long breakfast discussions (that lasted well beyond lunch time), topics varied from philosophy via literature to politics, but models and interpretation of reality were never far away. Thanks for letting me share with you your deep knowledge and wisdom.

Bengt Sandkull and Peter Westerholm—Our colloquia dedicated to discussions about models that have taken place regularly for a couple of years have been highly inspiring and elucidated many aspects of modelling from which I have benefited greatly. I place you on my record for our stimulating discussions and for sharing with me your experience and knowledge.

Owe Ronnström—From your background as an ethnologist, you widened my rather narrow view of models by introducing narration and metaphors as kinds of models. It taught me to look beyond the self-imposed setting of boundaries around concepts like models.

During the preparation of this book, I have been most indebted to Richard Koehler for his valuable support as a reviewer of the contextual language, and also for his valuable comments based on his long professional experience in international business.

For the text in the following pages, and for any misconceptions, obscurities and doubtful conclusions, I carry the full responsibility!

Per Lind
Landsort, Sweden
February 1, 2014

Part I

Models and Theories

Scholars in the empirical sciences have views about theories and models and tend to have a never-ending discussion about their sequence—whether a theory leads to a model or whether model and theory are interacting and inseparable. The view in this book is that a model is a picture created from assumptions about facts, and a theory is a form of insight facilitated by the model, a way of looking at the world rather than firm knowledge of how the world is.

A model is a reduction of reality in the sense that a phenomenon is explained by a limited number of facts that have been considered relevant and representative for the phenomenon. Reduction thus means that certain facts of reality have been deliberately omitted and the fundamental model problem concerns those facts: Would they have augmented the explanation power of the model if included? Or alternatively, are there facts that are characteristic for the phenomenon but not recognized by the observer and, therefore, not included in the model?

Reduction makes the model an incomplete and fragmented picture of reality and, therefore, also reduces the ability of the model to describe, to explain, to understand, to predict, to change, to prescribe, or to organise completely. The reduction means that a picture of the phenomenon is created but the reduction is not reciprocal—the model does not lead back to the reality it maps simply because we do not know about those facts that may have been omitted through the mapping process.

Ludwig Wittgenstein, the language philosopher, formulated the concept of a model as follows:

> We make to ourselves pictures of facts—the picture is a model of reality.
>   In order to discover whether the picture is true or false we must compare it with reality.
>   It cannot be discovered from the picture alone whether it is true or false. There is no picture which is a priori true (1922, 38–43).

The purpose of the model is to explain, to describe how something is; the purpose of prediction is to prescribe and to intervene. The metaphor is another kind of reduction that does not predict but describes, not by mapping but by comparing with something that is well known. While the metaphor does not have predicting power, the model can both describe—a model *of*—and predict—a model *for*. This dual meaning of the word *model* sometimes has a confusing effect because the distinction is not always obvious, depending on the language. A model *of* something corresponds to what in the German language is described by the word *Abbildung*. A model *for* something may depict something that is worth copying. A school or a hospital showing exceptionally good results may be referred to as a model school or hospital for other similar institutions. For this, the German language has the word *Vorbild*. Confusion in the English language with implication for how the model concept is treated is bound up with the lack of distinction between these two meanings of *model*. For students with academic textbooks in English, the lack of distinction does not stimulate critical thinking about models and their applicability in social science.

In this volume, Chapter 1 introduces the concepts of monitoring and performance in organisations (with specific focus on business organisations), and Chapters 2 through 5 have their foci on models from other realms.

Chapter 2 has a detailed discussion about models as descriptions of reality with limits in eternity that no model can grasp. A small model with few parameters may be capable of mapping a small part of reality, while a model with more (relevant) parameters may be capable of mapping a bigger part. The more a model encompasses, the more parameters and boundary conditions must be known and understood while, at the same time, the model becomes complex and less reliable.

In Chapter 3, models in social and natural science are compared. Model design starts with the identification of parameters that describe the problem and highlight the cause-effect relations. The primary question is how to identify the parameters, how to measure, how to discover relations and how to interpret the findings. Even if problem definition is similar in natural and social sciences, the identification of parameters may turn out to be most different, which is an important observation because natural science has been 'a model' for model building in social science. The chapter illustrates the difference between these models with an example.

In Chapter 4, the question is raised whether models and theories are transferable between different contexts. For natural science, the answer is yes, at least in general. In social sciences, such as in organisation and management theories, the answer is more doubtful, as illustrated by several studies of cultural impact on organisational behaviour that show that values, traditions and social patterns are sufficiently different in different parts of the world to not justify the adoption of one uniform organisational theory.

In Chapter 5, models are discussed from a broader perspective with linkages to knowledge development and the theory of ideas.

REFERENCE

Wittgenstein, L. (1922) Tractatus Logico-Philosophicus. London, Routledge & Kegan Paul.

1 Monitoring Business Performance

INTRODUCTION

When a well-known international company in the mining business a few years ago announced that one thousand one hundred and fifty employees had been discharged worldwide because of decreasing demand, the company shares soared on the international stock markets. Financial journalists reported that the financial market jumped with joy and predicted a prosperous fortune for the company, at least within a short time frame, owing to lower operating costs. Shareholders were certainly among those who cheered at the prospect of promising dividends, as did other stakeholders, such as equipment suppliers to the company who would benefit by the prospect of increased sales as reduced labour costs would boost up the need for additional equipment and machinery.

A group with less reason for enthusiasm was probably those employees who were laid off and their families. The loss of jobs was certainly a setback also in those places where the company had offices or factories and where new job opportunities were scarce. Business performance is thus a relative concept because of different perspectives, and different stakeholders can be identified: Shareholders are happy when financial returns are satisfactory and owners are happy when their company expands and grows. Customers appreciate good supplier performance when the company delivers products and services at compatible price and quality levels.

Employees are happy when the company provides safe job opportunities and competitive benefits with career opportunities. Governments are happy about tax incomes from profitable companies and managers are happy when the business is performing well and results are improving. Researchers and consultants are happy when performance improvements can be related to research and consulting activities. Each of these stakeholder categories thus has its own views and criteria when judging a company's performance. There is also a wider aspect of business performance that goes beyond the firm itself and its closest stakeholders, referred to as Corporate Social Responsibility. CSR emphasises that companies should have responsibility not only for business development but also for the firm in its relation to environmental factors, to gender equality and to ethical and moral issues. Monitoring the company's performance from a CSR perspective requires a broader set of measures than what is provided through the accounting system. Ethical and moral aspects are generally not features of the average company's performance measures, but they belong to the CSR concept.

BOX 1.1 MINI-ENCYCLOPAEDIA: CORPORATE SOCIAL RESPONSIBILITY (CSR)

For a number of years, management theorists and corporate strategists have been addressing the question of what should be the company's role in society. While most now agree that its role extends beyond the purely economic dimension, there is much debate on the extent of this expanded social role and how social performance can be measured. Adding complexity to the discussion is the reality of global companies that operate in a number of different societies. Theories that attempt to define the company's responsibility to society are generally grouped together as theories of corporate social responsibility (CSR).

A strong strategic approach to CSR is found in the work of Carroll (1991), who has devised a model of CSR that takes into account economic, legal, ethical and philanthropic dimensions. The model places the economic obligations of the company at its base, recognizing that the business must be economically profitable in order to survive. Above economic activities are legal responsibilities. Legal obligations cover many areas, including employment law, environmental law and health and safety regulations. Of course, the law sets minimum standards, which may differ from country to country. A firm with a strong CSR policy will aim to go beyond minimum legal standards. Carroll's model sees this exceedance of minimal legal requirements as an aspect of ethical responsibility, along with respect for ethical norms in the society in which the firm operates. The last element is philanthropy, such as charitable giving, which, while desirable, is less important than the other three—the icing on the cake. Carroll stresses that the model does not posit an inherent conflict between making profits and being socially responsible: For the manager, all four dimensions of the firm's responsibility should be central to corporate strategy (Morrison, 2006).

Corporate social responsibility has recently developed into a widespread and important concept that calls attention to the fact that small enterprises share responsibility with the rest of society for social fairness and human rights, similar to the recognition of shared responsibility for environmental concerns, which has nowadays turned into a business asset. Social entrepreneurship is developing in a similar way.

The concept of social entrepreneurship gained international recognition when the Nobel Peace Prize was awarded to the Grameen Bank and its founder, Muhammad Yunus, in 2006. The bank is a lender of small loans as start-up capital to poor individuals and communities in Bangladesh for entrepreneurial activities in the rural areas. The Grameen Bank started in 1976 as a social entrepreneurship with the objective to facilitate the capacity for poor villagers to invest in a cow or a hand loom and thereby generate an income. Preference was given to women as loan takers, and, of the total number of eight million loan takers, about ninety-seven per cent are women.

A variety of social entrepreneurship schemes has emerged in different countries since 1980; the concept was first coined in 1981 when Ashoka, a global association of the world's leading social entrepreneurs with the aim of addressing the world's most urgent social problems by using market driven business models, was founded.

MONITORING AND PERFORMANCE

Monitoring and performance are associated with assessment and evaluation and are two sides of the same coin: Monitoring is a process taking place while things happen; performance cannot be determined until things have happened and results are being evaluated. Monitoring is the supervision of an ongoing task to determine whether progress seems likely to meet the objectives that have been set in accordance with pre-formulated targets. Performance shows to what extent the task has been accomplished measured against the same pre-set target. What to be monitored, how to monitor and when to monitor therefore depends on the kind and nature of the task and the parameters that have been defined to characterise the task. Monitoring customer service can hardly be accomplished unless *customer service* has been defined and characterised with the help of suitable parameters that have been identified and constitute a model for customer service. In the same way, performance of customer service cannot be determined unless parameters and perspectives have been established and agreed upon as a standard.

While stakeholder perspectives determine what criteria are to be applied for selecting a monitoring model and performance references, the established standards are determined by the prevailing epistemological view (or *Zeitgeist* in German) that dominates for a time period by highlighting specific aspects of reality. The common designation for this *Zeitgeist* in social science is the *paradigm* concept, defined by Kuhn (1962) as a universally recognized scientific approach that for a period brings together a community of researchers by addressing problems and solutions with a joint attitude, such as *what* is to be observed and scrutinized, what *kind* of questions are supposed to be asked and probed for answers in relation to this subject, and *how* these questions are to be structured. Management and organisation theory refers to five paradigmatic periods in the last hundred years. In the following chapters, the five paradigms will be discussed in some detail. The present period is referred to as the current paradigm.

The view about performance is linked to theories and norms that have been developed within different economic and political models. In plan economic models, performance has been measured by how well production meets the production plans, while market economic models set their focus on the market and its actors, such as customers. The view of the customer is important as a measure of good or bad performance. Shareholders and owners measure performance and performance changes with the help of financial instruments that have been designed to work on accumulated company data and to present various scenarios as the basis for decisions about investments and strategies. Employees seldom have access to the same measuring instruments as shareholders and owners, and their assessments about how the company performs must therefore be based on more general or subjective measures. In both situations, the underlying models for measuring financial performance and how an organisation is structured have decisive impact on the perception of performance.

The meaning of business performance monitoring and what is considered satisfactory performance therefore depends on the current management paradigm but also on the perspective—owner, manager, employee, etc. Since the 1980s, there has been a strong focus on individuals such as customers and employees that characterises the current management and organisation paradigm. The perception about what constitutes an efficient organisation has therefore led to partly new monitoring and measuring models and tools. Monitoring business performance has thus shifted focus from earlier views that highlighted internal factors, such as an unequivocal compliance with goals and strategies, enforcing budgeted cost levels, and maintaining organisational stability even at the sacrifice of necessary change in the organisation. The current paradigm focuses on external factors, such as complying with change, being sensitive to customer requirements, and creating dynamic working conditions that support creativity and individual initiatives. In the current paradigm, there is emphasis on the distinction between customers as human beings, sometimes irrational and unpredictable, as opposed to the rational construct of the market.

Figure 1.1 illustrates a major shift in focus that has gradually emerged during the management paradigm period referred to as Organisational Culture, starting around the 1970s, with an emphasis on individuals and groups and their relations in organisations. Organisational Culture, with views and ideas partly borrowed from anthropology, was a reaction to the previous paradigm period, with its predominantly rational view in which the focus was on technology as a driving factor to reach organisational efficiency. The internal efficiency paradigm emphasised stability and control in the organisation and compliance with top management aspirations and norms; the manager's professional performance was measured by the ability to meet cost budget goals. Changes in strategies, both in marketing and product design and development, were the responsibility of top management, and decisions were primarily of the top-down nature (Johnson, 1992).

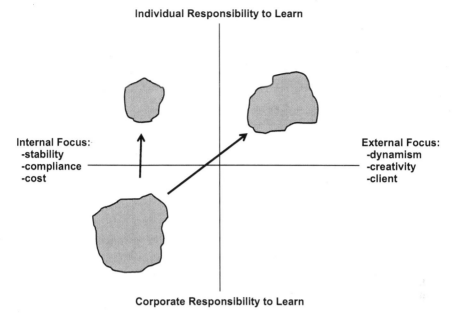

Figure 1.1   Change in focus of organisational priorities (Lind, 2012)

WHEN IS MANAGEMENT IN CONTROL?

The purpose of monitoring business performance is to distinguish discrepancies between planning and result. If discrepancies are noted, management can execute control in order to handle the situation and put things in order. Organisational capital (financial and non-financial assets) and organisational core activity domains (product, technology and market) are cornerstone concepts in executing management control. Chandler thus comments in one of the concluding remarks in his historical exposé of American enterprises that the success or failure in the allocation of funds, facilities and skills provides a useful test of the performance and ability of American industrial executives (Chandler, 1962).

It is generally accepted (Rumelt, 1984; Levinthal, 1991) that an organisation ceases to exist when its stock of organisational capital reaches zero. This may be a *sufficient condition* for liquidation. But is it also a *necessary condition?* There are studies claiming (e.g., Haveman, 1992) that organisations may fail to survive even with a non-empty stock of organisational capital. This may happen if changes in the environment lead to, or require, extensive modifications in a majority of the organisational domains.

Assuming such modifications to be initiated by management, they are subject to line manager perception and understanding of forthcoming situations. But regardless of interpretation, the manager's range of choice is conditioned by the company's culture and history. Strategic decisions in response to external changes should therefore not be made without consideration of the company's historical sediments. This requires that significant events in the company's history be identified in order to map out the characteristics of the company. For such analysis, focus needs to be shifted between management and leadership with regard to the company's activities (Danielsson, 1986).

Organisational Change, Age and Mortality

Ecological organisation theory suggested (Hannan and Freeman, 1989) that organisations tend to resist change due to a strong inertial power. In an attempt to identify this inertial power, Haveman (1992) has proposed a number of constraints that organisations can mobilise to withstand internal and external changes. Such constraints are, for example, investments already made in equipment or production and in marketing personnel, specialised for a particular type of product. Organisational history can also have a constrained effect on changes. It has thus been noted that changes in organisations are much less frequent than changes in their environment. When, however, changes do occur, they tend to divert resources from operating to reorganising, thereby reducing the efficiency of organisational operations (Haveman, 1992).

The question of age dependence in organisational mortality is the feature of organisational ecology that has been most extensively examined empirically. The basic empirical regularity that emerges is that the risk of mortality tends to decline with organisational age (Levinthal, 1991). Different reasons have been suggested as explanations—for example, that organisations tend to become more effective with age (cf. the learning curve) as they accumulate skills and knowledge (Nelson and Winter, 1982). Hannan and Freeman (1989), on the other hand, argue that selection processes eliminate organisations with low reliability. Such reliability can be improved through the development of highly standardised routines, forming the basis of continuity in organisations' behaviour over time (Nelson and Winter, 1982).

Thompson has also argued that standardisation is a way of coping with organisational uncertainty in organisations that exhibit not overly complex internal functional interdependence. When, however, organisations become more complex—for example, through more advanced production systems—interdependence assumes new patterns. As interdependence becomes sequential and reciprocal, planning and mutual adjustments (feedback), rather than standardisation, become more useful to reduce uncertainty (Thompson, 1967). The question of standardisation as a means to preserve continuity and to retain the organisational capital for improved reliability is therefore related to the organisation's level of complexity, in Thompson's sense.

Organisational Capital and Organisational Domains

The term *Organisational Capital* (Prescott and Visscher, 1980), which stands for both financial and non-financial assets, has been used (Levinthal, 1991) to describe when an organisation ceases to exist: A business fails to survive when it can no longer meet its financial obligations to debt holders, employees or suppliers and resorts to or is forced into bankruptcy or liquidation. Conversely, a firm may be buffered from failure if it has a strong market position, a vast manufacturing infrastructure, technological capabilities and a good management. But, as suggested by Hambrick and D'Aveni (1988), a firm's failure in a given year is not due solely to poor performance in that year; it is likely to be associated with an erosion of its competitive position over a period of time. Changes over time in a firm's organisational capital, therefore, reflect a variety of organisational decisions and environmental factors (Levinthal, 1991).

Organisational capital is a somewhat loosely defined concept. From its original meaning (i.e., capital as financial assets), it has undergone a transformation to include a variety of non-financial assets. The basic idea is that the organisation, together with its capital, adds up to more than the sum of the two: a total company resource that cannot be easily imitated and, therefore, counteracts competition and forms the uniqueness of the company. The non-financial part of organisational capital is a form of collective knowledge—that is, the sum of individual cognition that accumulates over time as experience and reflections and that can be shared by a group.

The organisational capital operates on the origination's domains. Thompson (1967) suggests that the domains have three dimensions, viz. products sold, clients served, and technology employed. Changes in domains involve changes in the organisation's formal structure, in patterns of activity and normative order, as well as in stated goals and forms of authority (Hannan and Freeman, 1977, 1984). Change that affects two or three dimensions may thus require such substantial modifications that the company may find itself in new fields of activity that require different competences and profiles. Monitoring business performance can be both operational and strategic with different time perspectives.

CHANGING MONITORING ASPECTS

As aspects and perceptions of what is crucial for organisational performance have changed, the result is increased focus on social aspects (groups, individuals) in the organisation in addition to common organisational and economic aspects. Table 1.1 illustrates how today's business performance model is based on both social and economic parameters. Social aspects have their focus on individuals and groups, their interaction and their roles in the organisation, and they are predominantly internal; their impact on performance stems from the importance of creating creative and harmonic working conditions. The economic aspects, on the other hand, are primarily concerned with the formal and measurable performance of the organisation in its external context defined by beneficiaries, customers and owners.

The principles of business monitoring are more varied and encompass more aspects today than in earlier periods of organisation theory. Tables 1.2 and 1.3 show how organisation and management principles have alternated between a focus on people and a focus on technology.

This implies that in periods where the social aspects are salient, the models developed for business monitoring need to be more varied and designed to capture both social and economic aspects. Traditional accounting systems,

Table 1.1 Aspects of organisational performance (Kaufman and Kaufman, 1996)

Social Aspects – focus on	Traditional Aspects – focus on
• Perception	• Pricing
• Motivation	• Income
• Interpretation	• Profit / Loss
• Learning	• Costs
• Structuring	• Investments
• Conflict	
• Collaboration	
• Culture	

Table 1.2 Evolution of contemporary organisation theory (approximate time periods)

	1900–1930	1930–1960	1960–1975	1975–
Systems perspective	Closed	Closed	Open	Open
Type	Rational	Social	Rational	Social
Central theme	Mechanical efficiency	Human relations	Contingency designs	Power and politics

Source: Robbins (1990).

Table 1.3 Normative and rational shifts in management paradigms

	1870–1900	1900–1923	1923–1955	1955–1980	1980–
Normative	industrial betterment		human relations		organisational culture
Rational		scientific management		systems rationalism	

Source: Barley and Kunda, 1992

for example, were for a long time the primary instruments for monitoring performance and executing management control. With the new management ideology emerging that puts increased emphasis on responsiveness to customers and overall quality awareness, there is, however, a radical shift from treating financial figures as the foundation for performance monitoring to regarding them as one among a broader set of measures. The shift implies that traditional tools need to be complemented by non-financial measures in which the monitoring of a company's business operations comes into the foreground. Overly inwardly oriented companies lose their competitiveness, as stated by Johnson (1993, xi):

> If companies are to compete effectively, they must remove accounting information from their operational control systems and relieve their accounting departments of responsibility for providing information to control business information. In a globally competitive organisation, everyone understands that long-term profitability is achieved by improving customer satisfaction; not by trying to sell the largest possible quantities of what the accounting system says are the highest margin products.

Performance monitoring is thus closely linked to evaluating and hence also to determining what tools are to be used as measures. Monitoring must therefore assume that activities and results can be measured. It is not unusual that the possibility of quantifying the result of an activity determines the scope and objective of the activity—a shift from purpose to measure. A common view is that what cannot be measured cannot be known, but what needs to be known cannot always be measured! The mechanism behind the causal connection between cause and effect makes us interested in performance monitoring, either how one event leads to another or what may be the effect in the future of an activity taking place now. The means we have adopted to facilitate understanding of the mechanism are the models and theories that are fundamental tools of research. The overall quality of a model lies in its capacity to be a purposive mapping of reality but also in its ability to facilitate statements about the future.

Management practice has its roots in business reality as well as in the concepts and ideas conveyed through management training. The influence is, however, bi-directional, as management training is also based on theories and models from codified management practice. The calculation of product costs is an example of a practice that has gradually developed in response to the need for improved pricing of products. This practice, codified into accounting principles and models at the beginning of the previous century, still constitutes the basis for cost accounting.

The second source of management training is based on concepts and models that have emerged through assumptions and observations about organisational behaviour and the interaction between organisations and society. Such concepts and models are derived from changes in society but also from the academic discourses and debates taking place in an ongoing process. The discourses and debates may take place within one discipline but can also be interdisciplinary with contribution from philosophy and other disciplines such as sociology, psychology and anthropology. Once adopted, such models tend to remain influential on management behaviour for relatively long periods as paradigms that thoroughly penetrate management training.

Both the codification of management practice and current management ideology thus has impact on management training, which in turn influences management practice. Figure 1.2 suggests that organisations are units that can be observed in a context characterised by traditions and history, by values and norms, and by employees and leadership style. Values, norms and traditions may constrain employee behaviour but may at the same time facilitate competitive opportunities. Historical sediments limit the degrees of freedom of the organisation, as do various forms of contingencies that constitute the business reality of organisations and enterprises.

Management practice develops in response to challenges and business realities. Management practice may, for example, develop from the obligation to cope with legalisation and accounting principles. Such management practice is interpreted, analysed and codified into management theories and models and, in the next step, into models and theories used in management education and development programmes. Organisational behaviour and business practices are observed and analysed by researchers and others who have a professional interest in organisation and management development. The ambition is not primarily to codify practice but rather to describe, understand and analyse, with the ambition to contribute to new theories and models. The tentative theories and models suggested and developed lead to discussions and debates.

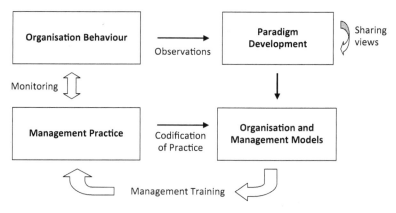

Figure 1.2   Observations and codification as background to management models

Observations and Monitoring

Observing organisational behaviour is also what happens when business is being monitored, albeit on a different time scale. While monitoring refers to supervising tasks to determine whether they seem likely to contribute to meeting objectives, observations in this context are about tasks and their relevance and importance in organisational behaviour. The time perspective is long-term and the ambition is to increase understanding about organisations, their behaviour and their development. While business monitoring is done within the firm and refers to activities within a firm, observations by outsiders may focus on several firms with the ambition to form a consensus view about key aspects for organisational research.

As a result, these discussions may gradually converge towards a joint viewpoint where there is consensus, and the various views may become unified into a coherent theory or paradigm, challenging the prevailing theory (which previously emerged from a similar process). Paradigms developed in such processes tend to last for long periods.

PARADIGMS

Paradigm development shows similarities to the evolution of organisation theory as suggested by Robbins (1990), who refers to the two underlying dimensions in the evolution of organisation theory: the first dimension, in which organisations are perceived as systems, and the second, in which the theory tries to characterise the organisation in terms of how it achieves its objectives. Prior to 1960, organisations were seen as essentially autonomous and sealed off from their environment (i.e., the closed system perspective; Robbins, ibid.). The closed approach was followed by the view that organisations are exposed to and influenced by external events and processes. The second dimension took two opposed positions: The rational perspective argued that the organisational structure is essential to achieve objectives, and the social perspective argued that structure is essentially the result of conflicting forces seeking power and control.

The contemporary evolution of organisation theory as suggested by Robbins (ibid.) can be divided into periods, as indicated in the table above. For each period, organisation theorists have sought to identify central themes that characterised the period.

The table shows that prior to about 1960, organisation theory tended to be dominated by a closed-system perspective in which organisations were seen as essentially autonomous and sealed off from their environment. Beginning around 1960, however, organisation theory began to take on a distinctly open-system perspective, with emphasis on external events and processes as opposed to the primarily internal focus of the closed-system perspective. In the four periods of Table 1.2, the perspectives of organisation theories tended to shift between taking a rational and a social stance to organisational behaviour. The rational perspective claimed that the organisation is a vehicle to achieve specific objectives, whereas the social perspective suggested that the organisational structure is the result of conflicting interest seeking power and control. The central themes of the four periods can be associated with a particular name that is representative of each of the respective theories—namely, Frederic Taylor, Elton Mayo, James Thompson and Jürgen Habermas.

An alternative, but similar, view on the development of management paradigms was suggested by Barley and Kunda (1992), who referred to the American management discourse as moving through five different phases or paradigms during the last hundred years. With minor local deviations, the same development process took place in most countries in the industrialised world, in particular as American management principles were the guiding principles for a vast majority of countries, both directly and indirectly through management guidelines and textbooks.

Barley and Kunda (ibid.) identified five management paradigms, or ideologies, from the late nineteenth century until today. The authors characterise each paradigm as normative or rational if its focus was on human or technological aspects, as when a technological breakthrough happened that required and led to structural changes in organisations. The five paradigms are described in Table 1.3.

Each paradigm tends to have a beginning and an end, although there is overlap between paradigms, and older paradigms tend to remain as sediments in later paradigms. The beginning of a paradigm appears to be related to growing criticism of the previous paradigm for not providing adequate or satisfactory grounds for problem definitions and research approaches. From these aspects, the five paradigms are briefly described below.

Industrial Betterment

The beginning of the paradigm may be linked to some big infrastructure projects in the United States towards the end of the nineteenth century—primarily the building of the railway line from the American East Coast towards the West. The project created job opportunities that immigrants, who were arriving in large numbers during those years, particularly welcomed. Harsh working conditions seriously jeopardised the project and difficulties in speaking and understanding among the many ethnically and culturally different workers created labour problems.

Attempts were made to improve the situation, and it was assumed that better working conditions would lead to higher productivity. Initiatives in this direction were taken by well-known organisations such as Pullman Inc., but also by organisations like YMCA, the Young Men's Christian Association, to organise work with a focus on improved working conditions.

The changing attitude in favour of a more pronounced social and worker-supportive approach came, however, to a halt after severe labour strikes at Pullman Inc., a company that had actively supported better working conditions. The reaction to the Industrial Betterment paradigm lead to a shift in view that scientific rather than social methods in labour relations would be more effective.

Scientific Management

The name irrevocably associated with the next paradigm is Frederic Taylor, an engineer at the Ford Automotive Company who had interpreted events taking place within the previous paradigm in his own way—i.e., that 'workers are only interested in money and feel no responsibility for the work they are doing'. Taylor thought that the best way of organising work was to copy military organisation in combination with scientific methods. Such scientific methods should be based on time studies along the production line.

Production of automobiles at the Ford factories was organised along conveyer belts on which the car, the T-Model Ford, was gradually built from the first production step to the final step with the complete car. Along the belt workers were placed, each worker having a well-defined, specific, mostly simple operation to perform. By determining the exact time for each operation, the time study man would know the total production time for a car. This information came to be of paramount importance for increased efficiency and productivity in the production of automobiles.

With escalating political unrest in Europe and as the global economic recession set in during the latter part of the 1920s, the need evolved for newer views on work organization based in part on the Russian revolution, which created anxiety in the United States about the risk for severe labour conflicts. There was a growing concern among the unions that the introduction of scientific models and the prospect of applying military-style command structures in work organisations would seriously impair the workers' situation. The response from the challenged worker unions was therefore to call for a changed view where workers should be considered assets to the organisations rather than merely problems.

Human Relations

As the world entered into the Great Depression during the 1930s, attempts were made to come to grips with labour and political conflicts. On macroeconomic levels, the model suggested by John Maynard Keynes was intended to reduce unemployment through active State involvement by initiating infrastructure and other labour intensive projects. On the micro level, studies in individual firms showed how more attention to employees and their working conditions would have a significant impact and improve labour productivity. The studies at General Electric's plant in Hawthorne in the United States showed the importance of a two-way information flow between management and the shop floor. Good leadership and communication of goals and strategies would make employees feel loyal to the company and committed to work plans.

Towards the end of the 1930s, war production led to new priorities in organisations, and during the Second World War there was no room for paradigmatic evolutions. After the war, technical innovations that had been developed for war purposes gradually began to infiltrate civil life and found adequate use in factories as well as in administration. In particular, there was a strong focus on computer and information technology. A growing belief in technology and a rational approach to organisations led to new questions about whether happy workers really led to higher productivity. More emphasis on technology and natural science rather than social science became the platform for organisation studies during the years that followed the war. New research in systems theory came to serve as an interdisciplinary bridge between different disciplines and had significant impact on organisation development.

Systems Rationalism

The geopolitical tensions that dominated during the post-war era encompassed many aspects, including the technological race. The launching of the first satellite in 1957 by the Soviet Union marked a technological breakthrough of much importance and triggered a focus on technological development in many countries. Technology alone was, however, not enough, for advancement and organisation efficiency was required to cope with the new technologies developed. Systems theory now became an important instrument to foster more efficient organisations.

Systems theory introduced mathematics on a large scale in organisation studies, which therefore required that not only machines and hard technology, but also humans in the organisation, should be regarded as systems components. A new discipline, cybernetics, was introduced, with emphasis on control through adaptation and regulation.

The reaction to viewing human beings as systems components coincided with the postmodern approach that began to dominate social science and organisation theories and which gradually led to the decline of the paradigm. Alternative ways to organise work in hierarchical systems were found in the network with its open and more flexible approach. A growing awareness about the systems model as too simplified and too rational to describe organisational behaviour resulted in a search for a more realistic approach. New observations and research findings about non-linearity and chaos theory gave new impetus to theories about organisations and the firm. The new approach that emerged was considerably less rational and suggested that the future of organisations involving people cannot be predicted based on the past.

Organisational Culture

The study of large firms had revealed that business success could partly be ascribed to strong internal cultures that strengthened organisational unity and solidarity. Symbols and narratives about founders and the history of the firm contributed to describing firms as special, each with its own culture. The thus-developed paradigm borrowed much of its theoretical background from anthropology, with the result that focus has been shifted from *systems thinking* (which characterised the previous paradigm) to the *individual*—customers, suppliers, employees, stakeholders. The new paradigm, in addition, accepts the interdependency between actors in society and that no organisation can be seen as a closed unit, but rather must be considered in exchange with the rest of society. The focus on the individual strengthens the empowering of employees, who are expected to lead to individual creativity and higher efficiency. The control aspect has been played down in favour of collaboration and consultation between leaders and employees.

The change in opinion towards a more external focus gradually emerged in the 1970s and 80s partly because of dissatisfaction with the rigid and mechanical view of the organisation but also in response to growing demand for a pronounced customer focus (Johnson, 1992). Growing global competition led to new ways of thinking about business as international trade grew and international financial flows were facilitated. Change in the environment required continuous learning by every member of the organization, and *learning organisations* became a mantra.

Learning implied that every person in every process should have the freedom to observe and to identify changes and have the power to recommend opportunities for improvement. Such freedom and power requires that employees have command of the information coming from their own work processes, the key to organizational learning. Having command of information means that the work process must be observed in such a way that performance can be easily measured and that performance trends can be assessed.

Why Paradigm Changes?

The paradigm changes we can observe from Industrial Betterment through the present Organisational Culture seem to have alternated between focusing on human and focusing on technological resources with a rational bias. While Industrial Betterment maintained that improved working conditions should have a positive effect on job performance, the following paradigm claimed that scientific methods in combination with new production techniques would improve productivity. Improved relations between management and employees would have a positive psychological impact on working conditions, according to the Human Relation paradigm. Systems Rationalism had a predominantly rational and scientific approach to organisational efficiency, whereas the current Organisational Culture again holds that performance is closely related to human elements in the organisation.

In Figure 1.3, the paradigms are shown as alternations between normative (focus on the individual) and rational (focus on technology), with a simplified regularity that does not exactly correspond with paradigm shifts. The diagram seems to suggest that there is no overlap between paradigms; one is replaced by the following. In reality, however, paradigms remain as sediments in subsequent periods.

Attempts have been made (e.g., Barley and Kunda, 1992) to explain why shifts between paradigms happened as they did. One explanation refers to changes in the world economy due to major technological breakthroughs, such as the automobile and the computer. Changes in the world economy vary between contractions, denoted by C in Figure 1.3, and expansions, denoted by E. The diagram indicates that paradigms with a technological focus seem to coincide with the breakthrough of new technologies. The following explanation has been suggested.

When the breakthrough of a new and potentially promising technology like the automobile coincides with economic expansion, there is scope for exploitation of the new technology. Resources like roads, petrol stations, service organisations and shops, as well as a variety of other facilities, are needed to

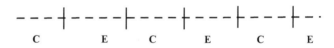

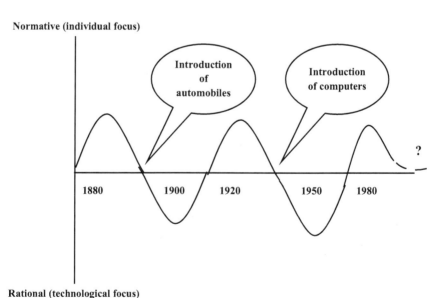

Figure 1.3   Paradigm shifts and fluctuations in world economy

serve the new technology and to facilitate its spread. Techniques and technological aspects are in focus during the introduction phase, during which organisations and organisational learning will have to comply with these needs.

A similar and analogue situation happened when computers were introduced and required new types of facilities, such as peripheral units, specific stationaries for computerised administration, and service technicians. The substantial economic potential of these two innovations forced organisations to focus on rapid implementation and accommodation of the new technologies within their organisational structures and processes. Adaptation between technology and individuals would come later.

As the new technology was established among organisations and firms and the competitive advantages derived from the new technology levelled off, it became essential to obtain maximum advantages and to draw on the potential from efficient human-machine collaboration. With regard to the automobile, skilled service personnel, qualified drivers and new professions developed, which required a focus on humans and how to motivate individuals for the new technologies. Analogue requirements occurred as computer technology passed its initial phase in organisations and firms, and as the mutual adaptation between technology and employees became crucial to maintain competitiveness derived through the new technology.

MENTORSHIP

A concept that has attracted increasing attention within the current paradigm is mentorship and the need for managers to act as mentors. Since performance is assumed to be improved by employee involvement, the new role of the manager as a mentor becomes important. This requires new attitudes and skills in managers—i.e., to understand-interpret-explain and to be endowed with empathy. The new skills also imply that managers must be able to distinguish between valuing and assessing performance. Valuing performance takes an over-all perspective where several aspects are involved, whereas assessing is based on a pre-set goal.

A manager needs to realise that high-performing organisations require high-performing people, and the manager can contribute towards high-performing employees by adopting the mentor role. The mentor role presumes that people have endless resources and capabilities, but they must be mobilised and activated. Furthermore, it is expected that people want to do a good job and to be appreciated, but management attitudes and traditions in many organisations do not live up to such norms. People are social creatures who are driven by their feelings, which may be difficult for managers who have a predominantly rational approach to accept. Regardless of all this, dealing with people is one of managers' principal tasks!

Figure 1.4 illustrates the two manager roles: boss and mentor. As a boss, the manager makes use of resources to achieve the objectives or goals of

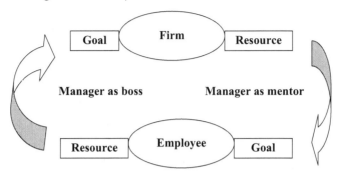

Figure 1.4   The manager's two roles: boss and mentor (Lind, 2012)

the firm. The manager's role is here to plan, schedule, execute and evaluate operational activities that require different resources—for example, human resources. This is the traditional manager role. The additional role as a mentor has not been explicitly formulated in earlier paradigms but is now considered essential in successful organizations. As a mentor, the manager is assumed to have a dialogue with each employee under the manager's direct supervision. Being aware of the employee's ambitions and wishes, the manager tries to determine if the firm is a resource from which the goals or objectives of the employee can be achieved. The firm can, for example, finance language training for the employee that will qualify him or her to negotiate with overseas suppliers or customers. This is a win-win situation, both for the firm and for the employee.

BOX 1.2 MINI-ENCYCLOPAEDIA: MENTOR AND MENTORSHIP

Mentorship has its roots in Greek mythology, as Odysseus appointed his good friend Mentor as a foster parent for his son while Odysseus undertook his extensive travelling at sea.

In mentorship, the mentor conveys his or her knowledge and experience to an adaptable younger person as a step to personal and professional development. The mentor is an experienced, knowledgeable and appreciated senior person offering guidance and support and a role model. Mentorship is a goal-oriented interaction that is characterised by mutual openness, confidence and familiarity. The goal of mentorship is to assist the less experienced person in his or her personal development by asking questions, trying answers and making choices. The mentor shares his or her own experiences and knowledge. Mentoring is reflective and avoids being too objective-focused. In organisation contexts, the mentoring ambition is to make a good manager and leader.

Mentoring is not coaching, but they share some similarities. Coaching is about change and making change work. Coaching is action-oriented and more objective-focused. The ambition of coaching is to make a good professional.

CONCLUSION

Monitoring business performance is a process by which business activities, such as serving customers, retaining a competitive quality in products and services, and complying with budget frames, are administered. Monitoring requires, however, that the most relevant and important aspects for supervision have been identified and selected for the monitoring process. A crucial management task in any organisation is thus to distinguish the vital few from the many less important events and incidents that happen.

Assessing performance is where the monitoring objectives are established. Assessing is done by scrutinizing the business process, and various methods, such as benchmarking and others, have been developed for this purpose. A detailed discussion about assessing business performance follows in Chapter 6.

Solutions developed for a company's financial and organisational problems tend to remain more or less intact for a very long period. Such solutions settle in layers and become sediments. If one wishes to become acquainted with how companies function from a financial perspective, one will encounter great difficulties if expecting to find a logical chain of arguments and assessments, starting from a well-defined point of reference. When this logical chain cannot be found, one may try to build such a chain. The main issue is that there are no such standard solutions that are related by logical chains (Danielsson, 1983).

REFERENCES

Barley, S. and Kunda, G. (1992) *Design and devotion: Surges of rational and normative ideologies of control in managerial discourse.* Administrative Science Quarterly, 37.

Carroll, A. (1991) *The pyramid of corporate social responsibility: Toward the moral management of organizational stakeholders.* Business Horizons, 34 (4).

Chandler, A. (1962) *Strategy and Structure.* Cambridge, MA, MIT Press.

Danielsson, A. (1983) *Företagsekonomi—en översikt* (in Swedish). Lund, Studentlitteratur.

Hambrick, D. and D'Aveni, R. (1988) *Large corporate failures as downward spirals.* Administrative Science Quarterly, 33 (1).

Hannan, M. and Freeman, J. (1977) *The population ecology of organisations.* American Journal of Sociology, 82 (5).

Hannan, M. and Freeman, J. (1984) *Structural inertia and organisational change.* American Sociological Review, 49 (2).

Hannan, M. and Freeman, J.(1989) *Organisational Ecology.* Cambridge, MA, Harvard University Press.

Haveman, H. (1992) *Between a rock and a hard place: Organisational change and performance under conditions of fundamental environmental transformation.* Administrative Science Quarterly, 37 (1).

Jonson, T. (1992) *Relevance Regained—From Top-Down Control to Bottom-Up Empowerment.* New York, The Free Press.

Kaufman, G. and Kaufman, A. (1996) *Psykologi i organisation och ledning* (in Swedish). Lund, Studentlitteratur.

Kuhn, T. (1962) *The Structure of Scientific Revolutions*. Chicago, University of Chicago Press.

Levinthal, D. (1991) *Random Walks and Organisational Mortality*. Administrative Science Quarterly, 36 (3).

Lind, P. (2012) *Small business management in cross-cultural environments*. London, Routledge.

Morrison, J. (2006) *The international business environment*. London, Palgrave.

Nelson, R. and Winter, S. (1982) *An evolutionary Theory of the Firm*. Cambridge, MA, Harvard University Press.

Prescott, E. and Visscher, M. (1980) *Organisational capital*. Journal of Political Economy, 88 (3).

Robbins, S. (1990) *Organisation theory—structure, design and applications*. New Jersey, Prentice Hall.

Rumelt, R. (1984) *Strategy, Structure and Economic Performance*. Boston, Harvard Business School Press.

Thompson, J. (1967) *Organisation in Action*. New York, McGraw-Hill.

2 Models as Descriptions of Reality

INTRODUCTION

The general population has shown growing concern in recent years about economic recession, even in the most affluent parts of the world, and economists reveal bewilderment when trying to explain and predict the global economic system with models that have long ago proved to be irrelevant or misleading; this is no coincidence. During a visit to the London School of Economics in 2008, the British Queen is said to have asked, 'But why did no economists predict the crash?' A comment on the Queen's question was, 'That was the wrong question. Why do economists predict anything, and illegitimately claim prescience for luck' (Pixley, 2012). It is no wonder that ordinary people get confused and worried about what happens to their financial savings, to their houses, and not least to their jobs. World unemployment has passed the record high of 200 million workers after the years of economic crisis, and that in a world of increasing automation where few of the lost jobs will return permanently. In the view of Martin Wolf, chief analyst of the *Financial Times*, a British newspaper, there is need for an alternative model for the global economy. A complicating factor is the lack of consensus among economists, as well as politicians, on what such a proper model should look like.

But not only does the global economy seem to be in need of an alternative model. The uncertainty about an adequate and more relevant model for the public sector has also spread, as concepts like New Public Management (NPM) continue to have an influence on policy makers and politicians. With its strong focus and priority on measurable economic results, NPM pledges to render the public sector more effective with the assistance of borrowed models from industry and the private business sector. Examples from public sectors like social insurance, education systems and public transportation bear evidence of shortcomings because the models tend to ignore or pay less consideration to those factors that are difficult to measure. Such parameters include, for example, individual perceptions of health care quality or aspects related to human values. Critics of the New Public Management concept give prominence to the fact that there are fundamental differences between the complex social systems serving the public and the private business market principles (Dunleavy, 2006). Further aspects of NPM are discussed in Chapter 10.

The last years have therefore witnessed a growing uncertainty, not only about the existing economic models, but also about how management models based on simplified and rational assumptions have permeated the thinking and decisions among policy makers. In response to critical questions related to this uncertainty and to the appropriateness and relevance of the adopted models, concepts such as Critical Management Studies have emerged that question the prevailing management paradigm, looking for an alternative approach to the current leadership and organisation and management practices. Critical Management Studies is first and foremost a criticism of conventional management and organisational theory and has been characterised as broadly left, pro-feminist, anti-imperialist, and environmentally concerned, as well as expressing certain distrust for conventional positivist formulations of knowledge within the social sciences. Among the pioneering writers who have contributed to formulating the critical management view are Morgan (1986), Hassard and Parker (1993) and Alvesson (1993).

While the relevance of the established economic and organisational models are being discussed and also criticised with the purpose of bringing forth more adequate and better justified models, the literature used for academic teaching in economic and organisation theory does not, in general, reflect these critical discussions. The attitude is rather traditional and stereotypical, with limited or no discussion about the underlying models. A common text book in economics for undergraduate levels at Swedish universities (Eklund, 1999) thus presents the model concept as a "kind of simplified description of reality, and for the model to serve its purpose it has to be simpler than the incredibly complicated reality; therefore the economists generally, when constructing their models introduce simplified assumptions" (19). In the same textbook one can also read that

> the simple supply-demand model has been the core of the macroeconomic theory during the last hundred years. The reason for this is not that it would exactly reflect reality but that the model in a simple and cogent way leads us to intelligible conclusions which can be applied in the analysis of economic problems in different ways. Of course these simplifications are unrealistic in the sense that reality does not look like the models. (57)

What is noteworthy here is that the author leaves the remark about models without any further discussion or comment. What the reader—in this case, a student—should expect is some reference to the weaknesses of models and the impact that such weaknesses may have on the model's explanation power. Quotations similar to the one above have been reported from other international student textbooks (see, for example, Baumol and

Blinder, 1994) and justify the question, "If the models, as suggested by the authors, are unrealistic and cannot claim to be reasonable representations of reality, how much can we then benefit from them? And moreover—what do they then represent?"

THE MODEL CONCEPT

The reference to models and how the model concept is presented and discussed in this book is drawn from the language philosopher Ludwig Wittgenstein, who suggested that we create pictures of facts (or states of things) and that the pictures become models of reality (Wittgenstein, 1922). In other words:

Reality—picture of reality—model.

BOX 2.1 MINI-ENCYCLOPAEDIA: LUDWIG WITTGENSTEIN (1889–1951)

Ludwig Wittgenstein was born in Vienna and studied aerodynamics in Berlin before he came to Cambridge in 1911 to study philosophy. During the First World War, Wittgenstein served in the Austrian army on the Russian front, where he began work on his major research that was published in 1922—*Tractatus Logico Philosophicus*. In this book, Wittgenstein first formulated his thoughts about language, which was the main stream of his philosophical activities until his death.

The book is constructed around propositions presented both in German and English. A central theme is that "propositions are pictures of reality", from which follows that "a proposition is a model of reality as we imagine it". Wittgenstein was one of the most influential language philosophers, and the concept of models as pictures of reality was important in his philosophical work. His view was that philosophy is in reality a critic of language, and there are things that cannot be put into words. They make themselves manifest. They are what is mystical (Proposition 6.53). The last proposition that follows has become a well-known citation: "Whereof one cannot speak, thereof one must be silent" (189).

Wittgenstein was professor in philosophy in Cambridge from 1939 to 1948, when he withdrew from the chair due to poor health. He was succeeded on the chair by Georg Henrik von Wright, a famous Finnish philosopher. A recommended biography is Ray Monk's (1990) *Ludwig Wittgenstein—The Duty of a Genius*.

Creating the picture requires an observer who can confirm that the model is a good-enough representation of reality for its purpose and that the simplification of reality that comes with every model can be accepted.

The underlying assumptions that are the basis for the model can, however, be problematized because of their subjectivity and implicit subjectivity to mainstream thinking that may obscure the uncertainty embedded in creating a model. This aspect was noticed by David Ehrenfeld, who suggested in *The Arrogance of Humanism* that the word *hypothesis* might be more relevant and appropriate than *model*.

> I do not entirely understand the sudden and enormous popularity of this word [model] in such disparate fields as behaviour, political science, ecology, biochemistry, and medicine. It has nearly displaced the older terms "hypothesis" and "possible mechanism." But I can see that the idea of a model would appeal to the humanist mind—it suggests abstraction and control of a large, complex subject by means of a smaller, easily manipulated, and totally fabricated mechanism. The term also seems to dissociate the author from complicity in the model in the likely event of its failure; "model" somehow does not carry with it the sense of human involvement and responsibility that is conferred by the partially synonymous "hypothesis". (Ehrenfeld, 1981)

On an uncertainty-certainty scale, the perception of *model* has turned out, as Ehrenfeld (ibid.) intimates, to be more towards certainty than the perception of *hypothesis*. But this bias regarding certainty-uncertainty has also a semantic dimension; the perceived certainty of a model makes it more of a prescription than a description. The English language does not make a distinction between the two meanings of *model*, as opposed to German, for example, in which *model* has two lexemes: "Vorbild" (something worth imitating) and "Abbildung" (picture). The domination of English in research and academic literature therefore leads to ambiguity about whether the model is a description or a prescription! Models may be in a premature state and thereby closer to working hypotheses, but as soon as they appear in formal contexts such as in an academic textbook, they tend to become prescriptions in the reader's eye. This lack of distinction (in the English language) has led to confusion in the use of *model* and has had a hampering impact on the teaching of subjects in the social sciences like organisation theory and economics. An example is the ethnocentricity that appears when management or organisation models developed and used in a Western context are applied in a third world context (see Davies, 1989). Clashes between value systems, different perceptions of time, and varying approaches to work organisation are just a few examples in which cultural and socio-economic differences have impacts on the applicability of models.

The root of the ambiguity in the meaning of model can be traced back to ancient Greece, where Nature was seen as the yardstick for a good life. Nature was superior to man, and by imitating Nature man was guaranteed a good life. Any attempt by man to violate the laws of Nature resulted in *hubris* as Nature struck back, and the balance could only be restored if man stepped back in line, *nemesis*. Nature thus became a model for man, pre-scribing how to live the right life by imitating its laws.

Learning from Nature to increase understanding of natural phenomena gave a new meaning to *model*—to map reality, or part of reality, into a simplified image. The two meanings of *model* are fundamentally differ-ent and can be referred to as prescriptive (or normative) and descriptive (explorative).

MODELS—A BRIEF BACKGROUND

Imitating good examples is not new, and the meaning of *model* as a map-ping or picture of reality can be traced back to the seventeenth century, when the thought of making experiments was born (von Wright, 1986). Francis Bacon, an English philosopher and scientist, suggested that knowl-edge about Nature was a way to predict the future; he may have formulated this idea as "Knowledge is Power". The question of how to interpret the sentence has been debated ever since (Nordin, 1996). One interpretation is that knowledge facilitates the acquiring of power, another that power facilitates the acquiring of knowledge. Von Wright (ibid.) refers to original sources by Francis Bacon that say "Human Knowledge and Power Coin-cide" (*Scientia et potential humana in idem coincident*). If man understands how to methodically inquire into Nature and to elaborate on the answers, he will also be capable of ruling reality and controlling Nature, in com-pliance with her plans and wishes. The inquiries into Nature become the experiments; the answers become the laws of Nature.

Although the Renaissance refers to the rebirth of Ancient Greece (but with a very different overtone), the view was no longer how man should live in balance with Nature. The emerging new view that developed as the result of new science was rather how man should be able to conquer Nature and gain control (Nature was cruel and constituted a threat). Natural science offered methods to exploit Nature and its resources in the service of man, starting from making experiments with Nature. Experimenting with Nature thus became a method to inquire into natural phenomenon like gravitation (Isaac Newton) and planetary movements (Johannes Kepler). The experi-ments, in turn, led to theories from which models were constructed and new theories of the natural world were built on previous theories by incorpora-tion of what worked and what did not work (Pagels, 1988).

While experimenting with Nature would have been strange to the Greek mind, the new knowledge derived from experiments marked another step towards a refined world view. The process was, however, not without ambi-guity, as became evident in the example of Galileo Galilei, criticised and imprisoned for his controversial and heretical ideas about the earth not being the centre of the universe, as had been preached by the Church. The method of working with experiments as a way of understanding reality, foreign to the Ancient Greeks, now came to characterise the Western ideal of knowledge.

The use of models in social science led to a strong bias towards a kind of rationality that one may call *instrumental*; it is goal oriented and technical. This kind of rationality may, however, be inappropriate when confronted with the human values that legitimate the goals. The risk becomes obvious as human aspects are omitted in the model, partly because they may seem irrational, partly because they are too complicated to map into a model, or perhaps because they are not even known *a priori*. As a consequence, the respect for the individual is reduced in formal contexts, and new forms of oppression reappear in those societies that are becoming increasingly rational.

The successful prediction of planetary movements by Kepler and the discovery of gravitation by Newton and others doing experiments created pictures of reality. The thus-created models served the ambitions of the natural scientists, and the news about the discovery of the planetary movements, and, in particular, how a new planet was identified with the help of scientific models, encouraged enthusiastic comments like the one by Mme de Staël, a French lady of considerable influence in political circles in Europe at the time who exclaimed "the moral powers are decided by the same positive laws as the physical powers. If we had complete knowledge of these we would by means of the cause-effect process be able to foresee all life's events in the same way Kepler and Newton measured the movements of the Earth". And somewhat later, Auguste Comte, a French philosopher, claimed, "Science constitutes the ground to predict future events; progress is built from Science, and Science will help us to build the perfect society". The step from models in natural science to their use in social science was not farfetched.

The creation of models from whence further inquiries were asked laid the foundation for the further development of natural science. At the early stage of social science, the concept of models was imitated from natural science, in spite of the fact that problems and the realities from which problems originated differed significantly, as did the identification of parameters. A common question for all models, in both natural and social sciences, is to what extent the model is a reasonable picture of reality or to what extent reality can be mapped into a model.

MODELLING REALITY

Returning to the earlier reference to Wittgenstein and his conception of a model, he also proposed that a picture, being a model of reality, represents what it represents, independently of its truth or falsehood, through the form of representation. It cannot be discovered from the picture alone whether it is true or false (Wittgenstein, 1922).

It is therefore not meaningful to discuss whether a model is relevant or not with respect to its purpose since the underlying assumptions or theories determine how the model has been formulated. Accusing an economic model of not being a good description of the economic reality, or an infrastructure model for being too simple and with too few relevant parameters, is therefore pointless. A model for making prognoses about the future can never be more accurate than the underlying assumptions about what influences the change from now till then.

Wittgenstein (ibid.) therefore remarked that in order to discover whether the picture is true or false, we must compare it with reality. The remark is, however, ambiguous because comparing with reality would assume that reality is completely known, which is rarely the fact and the reason why we resort to using models! Since the picture (or model) is intended to be an image of reality, it is merely a subset constituting a set of parameters assumed to be adequate for the purpose. Comparing the picture with reality, as suggested by Wittgenstein (ibid.), in order to assess the rightness of the model cannot be done unless the model is repeatedly tested for reasonableness and adjusted by incorporating additional relevant parameters. But even with additional parameters, the model will still be a simplification of reality. According to the Law of Requisite Variety formulated as *only variety can absorb variety* (Ashby, 1956), the effort to reduce the complexity of reality by implementing simplicity cannot be done because reality cannot be mapped onto something that is less complicated than reality itself while preserving the same properties. If the ambition is to resemble reality, the crucial question becomes which aspects of reality are to be included in the model.

Creating a model or making a picture thus means that parameters are identified and selected based on somebody's perception of reality and the assessment of relevant or necessary parameters to be selected. If all possible parameters are known to the observer, the question is which ones to select. Alternatively, some parameters may not be known, and some may be neglected because they are not perceived as important or relevant enough. Some parameters not known to the observer might, however, have significant importance for the creation of the model and therefore ought to have been included in the model. By omitting relevant parameters, the explanation or prognostic value of the model will be limited.

The model is not just a picture of facts but also of interactions between parameters. Making pictures of interactions introduces a dynamic dimension to the model that increases the complexity immensely when viewed from a generic perspective. The model describes by means of the picture what is happening in the pictured reality.

The following example illustrates the essence of Figure 2.1. Reality in the example is behaviour in relation to customers. Assumptions and theories which are partly coloured by the prevailing management paradigm have identified a set of parameters considered most relevant to establish good customer relations. Such parameters are, for example, reliable customer deliveries (delivery in time, in right quantity, etc.) and denoted by **a** in Figure 2.1. Other parameters, such as **b**, are known but not considered

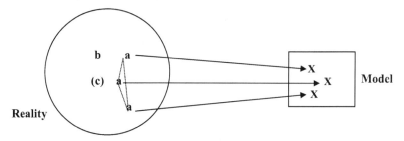

Figure 2.1   Creating a model

important enough to be included in the model. Some parameters, like (c), are not known by the observer. These parameters could be of relevance in formulating the model and might have significant impact on the model design. A (c) parameter is, for example, a customer's previous experience of poor service quality and strong reaction thereto. The final model will hence be designed based on parameters denoted by **a**, which have been considered most relevant. Parameters **b** and (c) will not be included in the model.

From this it can be concluded that reality cannot be described starting from the model, or, in other words, the creation of a model is not a reversible process because the model is a simplification of reality. The three parameters that were selected, eliminated and overlooked for the model in Figure 2.1 are not enough for a complete understanding of the reality of customer behaviour vis-à-vis a supplier. The following three examples are meant to illustrate how assumptions of reality are decisive for the formulation of models. If the assumptions are incorrect or based on misleading information, then the model will not be well adapted to its purpose.

Three Examples of Model Creation

The following three examples describe three different situations in which reality was interpreted and a number of factors perceived as the most relevant and important were translated into models. As it turned out, the models described in the following cases were not good enough pictures of reality!

Deregulation/Liberalisation/Privatisation of Postal Service

Deregulation of the postal sector was decided by the EU member states in 1997, followed by the suggestion to open their postal market to competition. The ambition was to offer service and prices that better reflected customer needs through commercial freedom to private operators. Private shop keepers are today the providers of basic postal services, such as selling stamps and collecting parcels sent by post. In order to make this basic service readily available to customers, tobacconist's shops were considered suitable for this service, as they were to be found in many places.

Since then, however, the anti-smoking campaigns have been intensive in most EU countries and with unexpectedly positive effects. As a result, the tobacconist's shops have experienced shrinking market demands for tobacco products, and the number of tobacco shops is in decline, in Sweden from 2425 shops in the year 2000 to 1300 shops in 2011, a reduction of 46 per cent (Tobaksfakta, 2011). The example shows how the design of the new postal service model did not take into account significant changes in the distribution network that counteracted the expected easy access to postal service. With reference to Figure 2.1 above, the model did not include parameters **b** and (**c**).

Airline Check-In

A majority of airlines today allow on-line check-in; a boarding card can be printed prior to passenger's arrival at the airport. For the handing-in of luggage, special counters are available. The goal of this new passenger handling system was faster check-in at the same time as a reduction of staff at check-in counters—hence, costs could be saved. But while the earlier queues in front of the conventional check-in counters have been significantly reduced, there are new and mostly equally long queues in front of the printing stations for luggage tags, as well as for the counters for baggage-drop. As many passengers are also at a loss as to how to proceed with luggage check-in, airline staff has been allocated for passenger service in the self-check-in areas in airports.

One must therefore conclude that the on-line and self-check-in model is based on the highly rational assumption that passengers are well informed and have understood the procedures for on-line check-in, and that cost-saving by reducing staff while maintaining a reasonable passenger service level is difficult. As in the previous case, the model did not include parameters **b** and (**c**) from Figure 2.1.

Infrastructure Investment

Lake Vänern is the largest lake in Sweden, third in Europe and at a height of 44 meters above sea level. The lake is in a highly industrialised area with several significant export industries of importance for the Swedish economy. Export and import is mainly by ship through the canal linking the lake to the sea. Due to the level difference between sea and lake, there are numerous canal locks necessary for the ships travelling on the canal. Due to wear and tear of the canal facilities, a major investment programme will be necessary within the next few years to secure safe and efficient ship transport for the years to come. The Swedish Maritime Board has therefore been requested to make an investment analysis and to form an opinion about the public value of such a significant investment.

The performed analysis for making a decision has been based on a calculation model used by the Swedish Transport Administration and enjoined by the Swedish government for investments in infrastructure projects. Earlier submitted reports within the same context have emphasized the problem of knowing which parameters to be included in the model—in particular, those parameters that reflect the impact of an investment on industry, regional growth and job opportunities.

With reference to the model used for calculating the future value of the investment, the Maritime Board concluded that the investment could not be financially justified and hence advised against future ship traffic on Lake Vänern. The analysis method is based on the traditional Net Present Value model (NPV), a simple mathematical formula calculating values of investments and revenues backwards in time during a project's life span, utilising a pre-defined discount rate. The Net Present Value thus obtained is used to compare the value of future investments and revenues. The most critical part of the Net Present Value model is the applied discount rate and to what extent it can be estimated for a long project period such as fifty years. The discount rate determines how financial benefits and costs are valued for each period (year) during the lifetime of the investment. An investment calculus for shipping on Lake Vänern should not be shorter than fifty years, and the costs arising today will be compared with benefits that accrue during the next fifty years, a time period of which one can hardly form a reliable opinion. The Swedish government has decided that the discounting rate be 4 per cent for infrastructure investments in order to make different investments comparable. For this project, even small variations around 4 per cent can make the difference in determining whether an investment should be made or not.

A model of calculation is, like all models, a simplified picture of reality. The credence given to models is based on a rational way of thinking: measuring and forecasting. Human tendencies, such as reprioritising goals or rethinking because the world around one is changing, are considered irrational and too complicated to be mapped into a model. Therefore the model of calculation used in this example and being recommended by the government, which has turned down the improvements necessary to secure future ship traffic on Lake Vänern, is not only doubtful because the underlying data is doubtful but also because we can never be certain that the model used is a good enough picture of the actual situation. The question about future ship traffic has an immense significance for the industry, for the region and for the people in the region for a very long time, and it cannot be decided with reference to a model of calculation that is incomplete and which is based on speculations about the development of society and the economy for a long time into the future.

MODELS FOR PREDICTION

Predicting the future, trying to see what lies ahead or just looking for some guidance about dealing with future events, has always been of interest to humans, and history carries ample examples of more or less primitive models for looking into future. In an essay, the British economist Ely Devons pointed out that in primitive societies, magic decided whether hunting should proceed in one direction or another, whether the tribe should go to war, or who should marry whom, giving clear-cut decisions in situations that might otherwise be open to endless wrangling (Devons, 1980). With our definition of models as pictures of reality, we may claim, with support from Bronisław Malinowski, founder of modern anthropology, that magic has parallels with science through its observations of nature and dependence on nature's regularity. Both magic and science develop procedures that must be followed to accomplish specific goals. Magic and science are both based on knowledge; magic is knowledge of the self and of emotion, while science is knowledge of nature (Malinowski, 1954).

During the Renaissance, as thinking about humans and their relation to Nature entered a new direction, the notion matured that knowledge of the causes of events is fundamental for understanding and prediction and can be investigated by means of experiment with models of reality. Even if rational thinking and scientific knowledge thus came to replace magic, the sociologist Zygmunt Bauman suggested that science and magic have many things in common—for example, incantation (Bauman, 2006).

With the simplified picture of reality provided by the model, a presumed cause-effect understanding is created, revealing the mechanisms between causes and effects and what may be concluded about the future. Since prediction and understanding are the two main purposes of models, prediction is the most controversial and uncertain of the two. For example, research in meteorology has revealed that prediction about the future is not only difficult, but under certain conditions, not even possible, according to the meteorologist Eric Kraus (1974), who gave three ample reasons. Firstly, we can never know the present completely, partly because language is not capable of correctly describing complex situations, which also means that models cannot describe realities correctly. Secondly, we are not able to make errorless deductions from what we know—i.e., how, for example, could one ask a question about something that has never happened? And thirdly, our limited imaginations may prevent us from asking the right questions about the future.

Heinz Pagels, an American physicist, gave another example of the difficulty of predicting: One cannot predict the exact position of a ball after two or three rebounds from the walls of a squash court. Even if the initial movement of the ball is well known, the friction coefficients at each touch point are different and uncertain, so the uncertainty of the motion amplifies more and more. Unless one knows the starting values to infinite accuracy (which is in practice impossible), one quickly loses all ability to predict the future values—just like weather prediction (Pagels, 1988). Uncertainty is a fundamental concept in modelling.

A basic feature of uncertainty is blurred cause-effect relationship. Even if one knows that a certain event is going to happen, the range of possible effects caused by the event creates uncertainty. The understanding about cause and effect may, however, vary, as illustrated in Table 2.1.

Coping with uncertainty tends to be more successful the lower the degree of uncertainty. And the reverse is also true: The higher the degree of uncertainty, the more difficult it is to link causes to effects between variables of any organisation model. In organisations exposed to genuine uncertainty, which occasionally happens in the more developed countries but more often happens in less developed countries, the use of information systems to cope with uncertainty is mostly unsuccessful because of the limited or non-existent possibility of predicting future events. In such situations, uncertainty can only be dealt with in an ad hoc manner—i.e., no particular rules apply but situations have to be attended to case by case. As IMF (the International Monetary Fund) and OECD (Organisation for Economic Co-operation and Development) make prognoses, they do not know how big the margin of uncertainty is. Hence, certainty is simulated in areas of genuine uncertainty, and the application of mathematics for simulating future scenarios does not provide any solutions but is rather part of the problem (Orrell, 2010).

Pixley (2012) claims in a discussion about uncertainty in the finance sector that the unknowable cannot be calculated despite everything the finance sector does and says. A bank's aim is to 'beat' uncertainty, but rational calculations can only be made about the past, and the sector clings to and pays huge sums for predictions. Albert Einstein realised there are limits to what calculation can do to grasp the essence of reality: As far as the laws of mathematics refer to reality, they are not certain; and as far as they are certain, they do not refer to reality (Einstein, 1921).

Why is, then, model building of social activities so complicated? Hofstadter (1980) suggests an explanation by asking: What sorts of rules could possibly capture all of what we think of as intelligent behaviour? Certainly there must be rules on all sorts of different levels. There must be many 'just

Table 2.1 Four degrees of uncertainty (Lind, 2012)

Degree of uncertainty	Cause-effect understanding	Possibility to predict
Low degree of uncertainty	Single cause-effect understanding	Future can be relatively well predicted
Moderate degree of uncertainty	Multiple cause-effect understanding	Future possible to predict as one of more alternatives
Relatively high uncertainty	Range of cause-effect understanding	Future possible to predict within a range of scenarios of equal weights
Genuine uncertainty	No cause-effect understanding	Future not possible to predict

plain' rules. There must be 'meta-rules' to modify the 'just plain' rules; then meta-meta rules to modify the meta-rules, and so on. In some situations, there are stereotyped responses that require 'just plain' rules. Some situations are mixtures of stereotyped situations; thus, they require rules for deciding which of the 'just plain' rules to apply. Some situations cannot be classified; thus, there must exist rules for inventing new rules . . . and on and on.

LIMITS OF MODELS

With reference to the previous discussions, the point of view is that models are artificial in the sense that they are not reality, but rather they are images of reality. The French philosopher Henri Bergson thought that the crucial question is to know whether those natural systems we refer to as reality are in fact the same as those artificial systems that science applies to reality, or if they can never be compared with the natural systems that constitute the whole of universe:

> *L'unique question est de savoir si les systèmes naturels que nous appelons des êtres vivants doivent être assimilés aux systèmes artificiels que la science découpe dans la matière brute, ou s'ils ne devraient pas plutôt être comparés à ce système naturel qu'est le tout de l'univers.*
> (Bergson, 1907)

Clearly models have limits, not only with respect to parameters identified (refer to Figure 2.1), but also with respect to how much of reality is to be represented by the model. Reality has limits in eternity that no model can grasp. A small model with few parameters may be capable of adequately mapping a small part of reality, while a model with more (relevant) parameters may be capable of mapping a bigger part. The more a model seeks to encompass, the more parameters and boundary conditions must be known, understood and included in the model. On the other hand, if the part of reality that is to be modelled is not adequately understood or is too uncertain, which is analogue to a problem that has no solution, then the model must be empty.

The problem to be addressed and the questions asked about the problem determine the scope of the model and, hence, the parameters to be identified and included in the model. A model for price elasticity (i.e., the response in market demand to a change in price) is defined as relative change in the quantity demanded divided by the relative change in price. The model may give an accurate value and useful information for a good or a service in a village with a homogenous and predictable customer base. In a city with various customer groups and with different buying patterns, and with product demand that varies with the season, the simple model would not be able to provide practical and useful information. The ambition of modelling a

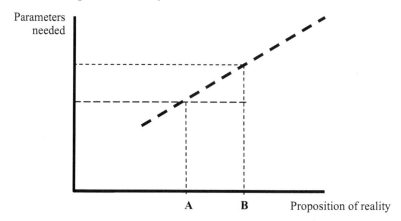

Figure 2.2   Model parameters versus scope of proposition

global development scenario would generally require so many parameters that the resulting model would be useless. Nevertheless, the last fifty years have seen various development models, many with the ambitions to guide the rich countries in directing their development aid to spur economic and social development in the most urgent areas. In hindsight, the strategies that were developed based on various models have been highly disappointing in the results achieved (Moyo, 2009).

The diagram in Figure 2.2 is an attempt to illustrate how the number of required model parameters is related to the proportion of reality (A) that is to be pictured. If the proportion of reality (B) is bigger than (A), then additional parameters will be needed to make the model more reliable and accurate. As the positions of A and B cannot be explicitly determined, both accuracy and degree of representation of the model are in practice not possible to determine *a priori* but can only be assessed after the model is tested.

It is possible that the *explanation power* of the model can be increased with additional parameters, but with more parameters the complexity between parameters will increase as well. Interaction between parameters creates various forms of mutual dependencies that may add to the complexity.

Models as Instruments of Power?

The French philosopher Michel Foucault has criticised modern science, and in particular social science, by suggesting that the combination of knowledge and power is a means that authorities use to maintain a dominating perspective by monopolising the interpretation of reality (Foucault, 1971). The State and politicians infringe on the citizens to regulate their lives by means of social engineering combined with information technology. The authorities have access to and collect huge amounts of data needed for the regulations, and theories in behavioural science are used to structure data into information as basis for decisions. Models become the instruments by which the theories justify political decisions. By attributing scientific principles to a model, decisions can be justified against counter-arguments that can be labelled non-scientific.

The example given earlier in this chapter of an infrastructure investment project may be used to illustrate how an ill-founded investment model labelled as scientifically grounded removes the responsibility of authorities to apply common sense and basic logic when a decision is to be made. As long as the relevance of a model is not questioned, while its scientific status gives it credibility, the model in reality becomes a demonstration of power.

Communication in modern societies is predominantly low-context oriented and based on verbalization of abstract concepts, in contrast to high-context societies where communication is less verbally explicit, with more internalized understandings of what is communicated. Low-context communication therefore requires that abstract words and concepts be 'translated' through models in order to become intelligible. Abstract words like *democracy, crime,* and *development* are basically model concepts that require a considerable number of parameters to make the model a reasonable mapping. The preference of particular parameters in this context can be a deliberate choice to exert power over minds. *Democracy* is a good example of such political control.

Political Goals and Plans

Goals and plans are formulated as directives to be followed by the authorities in charge of public institutions and public service. Goals are determined in compliance with the underlying models that have been recommended by policy makers or consultants or made available from appropriate theories. New Public Management is an example of such a model; it is currently in vogue among politicians and public decision-makers. Figure 2.3 shows how directives are delegated to executing bodies with responsibility for carrying out the plans. The mechanism can be described as a control system with open and closed control.

When control involves the setting of objectives and formulation of plans and references, the term *open control* is used. *Open control* thus includes the setting of goals and the formulation of control plans, whereas *closed control*

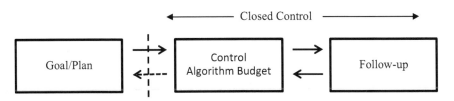

Figure 2.3   Open and closed control in the political hierarchy

accepts the goals and plans that have been set and are carried out accordingly. The primary control algorithm in the political closed control system is the budget, and follow-up is therefore mostly done by measuring costs. The dotted boundary between the closed control and the setting of goals indicate that there is no automatic feedback once the directives have been issued. Since the time frame of the political control system is often extended, the follow-up of political decisions is far from always taking place; thus, it has difficulty influencing the original goals through feedback. *Learning by doing* is therefore not a typical characteristic of political control.

The process of forming goals can make for confusing reading, as illustrated by the Swedish Agency for Economic and Regional Growth and its suggested system for the formulation of goals, follow-up and evaluation of the regional service programme 2010–2013 (Swedish Agency for Economic and Regional Growth, 2013). "The three goal levels differ from each other by when they are expected to be achieved and the possible impact an effort will have on the goal. The following description of the different goal levels is taken from the *System for the formulation of goals, monitoring and assessment of the regional service programme 2010–2013* (Swedish Agency for Economic and Regional Growth, 2013):

- *Activity goal*: a goal for activities that are carried out through the effort, for example number of approved licenses;
- *Result goal*: the result of an effort. The result goal is often divided into different activities and describes the achievement of the effort. For example increase in fuel stations offering alternative fuels.
- *Effect goal*: direct and indirect effects as a result of an effort. An effect goal can give the answer to the question 'what was the intention of the effort?' The effect goals can be defined in the short or long time frame. The effect goals are not within control of the effort."

The *result goal* is semantically as well as from a content point of view an incomprehensible concept where the present and the future coincide as the future hypothetical outcome rather than the actual starting point determines the goal. With the *result* and the *goal* being the same then the outcome is always achieved, a self-fulfilling prophesy! The *result goal* thus reduces the need for knowledge about the process as it intentionally defines a priori how to measure a successful outcome.

Finally, a related example from a Swedish local government, in a public report (Swedish Agency for Economic and Regional Growth, 2013):

> With the strategic goals and requirements of the local government as a starting point the government has formulated 17 result goals. At year end 9 of these have been assessed as fulfilled, 3 goals have not been fulfilled and 5 goals partly fulfilled. The evaluation therefore shows that 14 goals have been fully achieved.

In the previous sentence the word *assessed*, which accentuates a degree of uncertainty, has been omitted! All of a sudden, in the political rhetoric 14 goals have been achieved, whereas in reality only 9 met that criterion. The political language, therefore, needs to be carefully scrutinized in pursuit of dubious and hidden messages!

LANGUAGE AS A MODEL

Wittgenstein (ibid.), to whom we make references throughout this volume, suggested that the logical picture of facts is the thought. The thought is the significant proposition and the totality of propositions is the language. Language is thus a mapping of thoughts about the facts, but not a model of facts in itself. As we formulate a perception of facts, we also form the concepts of mind. Model and Thought are not the same, and even if the collection of thoughts forms the language, it does not imply that language is capable of translating all thoughts into words. Thought is not the same as language (Pagels, 1988) and Wittgenstein therefore claims that "whereof one cannot speak, thereof one must be silent" (1922, 189).

Figure 2.4 is an attempt to illustrate how the communication between A and B by means of language starts with a thought, T_1, being the logical picture of Fact$_1$ translated into a word, W_1, that, in addition, reflects the context, C_1, that influences A's world-view (through a cultural value system, language, and socio-economic and technological context). The same word, W_1, is now transmitted to B through the language, but it may give rise to a different thought, T_2, because of the influence of B's differing

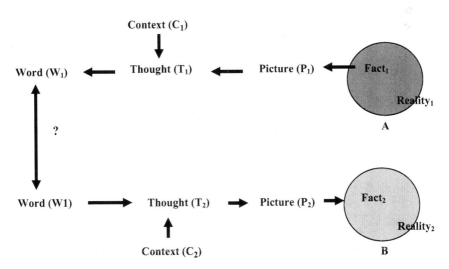

Figure 2.4 Thought and language (Lind, 2012)

context, C_2, and thus may create a different picture, P_2, that refers to a different fact, F_2.

By perceiving the world as a collection of independent fragments or facts, our minds tend also to be fragmented. With the structure of language into subject, object and predicate, an activity starts with a subject having impact on an object considered different and separate from the subject—i.e., language supports the fragmentation (Bohm, 1980). A sentence based on the predicate (verb) represents movement and therefore unites the fragments, rather than separating them. Krishnamurti, the Indian philosopher, emphasised the problem related to our distinction between analyser and that which is analysed, the thinker and the thought, the observer and the observed, and to what extent the division between observer and observed is real in the sense of being a fact and not something theoretical (Krishnamurti, 1972).

Language illustrates the irreversibility of models. The logical picture of a fact does not necessarily lead back to the same fact, as shown in the following examples where there has been a transformation of meaning: A *cleaner* has become a *household technician* or a *sanitary technician*. *Hunting* has become *game preservation*. These examples are euphemisms that may be expressions of political correctness or indicators of improving images that have been patronizing or condescending. A *spade* can be used as an anecdotal example; it was presented in one catalogue for gardening equipment as a *manually operated recreational eco-unit maintenance tool*.

The alternative meanings of words in the examples illustrates the irreversibility of models. A *household technician* is not automatically associated with a *cleaner* when the word is used for a traditional meaning. The reason is that not enough parameters have been involved as we have created the picture that constitutes the model. *Game preservation* is different from *hunting* and a *manually operated recreational eco-unit maintenance tool* as a twisted word for a *spade* shows clearly how the reader's or listener's thought may go in an unexpected direction rather than toward the writer's or speaker's thought and picture of reality.

MODELLING COMPLEXITY

Social systems are constantly undergoing change, or evolution. Changes in society are inherent in society itself and organisations adapt or try to adapt to such changes or to other determinants in society. In organisations, as well as in society at large, changes take place on different levels, leading to different outcomes, reinforcing each other or straightening out or counterbalancing the effects. Several examples can illustrate such effects, such as increasing wealth in parts of the world at the same time that economic growth has stagnated in others; or advances in medical research leading to better health conditions worldwide. Such examples show the difficulty in modelling complex systems because the change taking place makes generalization hazardous.

In social and economic systems, the question of stability is of interest. A stable society and a stable economic situation are attractive starting points from which change can be initiated. Such change can be described by the classical equation called the *logistic equation*. The equation describes the evolution or growth of a population that can be people or animals, but also shops in a city or trucks in a road network. The equation describes the change in number of individuals under constraints characterised by a carrying capacity—in an example of people or animals, these constraints would be food availability and birth- and death-rates with effects on the carrying capacity. The logistic equation can be formulated as a continuous function but also as a discrete equation:

$$X_{n+1} = X_n (1 + \alpha^* X_n) \text{ for } n = 0, 1, 2, \ldots, X_0 \text{ being the initial stage.}$$

X_n and X_{n+1} are stages during the change process.

The parameter α is related to the carrying capacity determining the nature of the change process. The remarkable feature of the seeming simplicity of the model allows a bewildering number of solutions, as noted by Prigogine and Stengers (1985). For values of α between 0 and 2, the process strives towards equilibrium. When α has a value greater than 2 but less than 2.57, there is no equilibrium solution, but the process oscillates in a periodic way between two extremes. When α assumes values greater than 2.57, the final solution cannot be distinguished from a random number, which means that the situation is described as chaotic.

Prigogine and Stengers (ibid.) point out that in spite of its simplicity, the model succeeds in showing some properties of the evolution of complex systems, and in particular the difficulty of governing development determined by multiple interacting elements. Each individual action or each local intervention has a collective aspect that can result in quite unanticipated changes. There is therefore very little understanding of how a complex system is likely to respond to a certain change. For example, new buildings attract a larger number of people into the area, but if there are not enough jobs for them, they remain poor and their dwellings become even more overcrowded. A programme for slum clearance may therefore result in a situation worse than before.

For the design of a model to cope with a complex situation, the principle of requisite variety ("only variety can absorb variety") has important implication for the design. Figure 2.2 indicates that the more complexity in a situation, the more parameters that will be required to create an adequate and relevant model; at the same time, the increasing number of parameters contribute to increasing complexity.

CONSEQUENCES OF INCOMPLETE MODELS—EXAMPLE TRANSPORT SYSTEMS

A cost overrun problem is one of the most important challenges in transport planning. According to literature, the cost estimates used in transport planning are systematically and significantly misleading (Flyvbjerg 2009; Singh 2009). Cost overrun problems seem to be a global phenomenon and are found not only in transport projects but occur in other kind of projects, such as water projects, power plant systems and urban and regional development projects (Jenpanitsub, 2011).

Decision makers want to improve the returns from limited budgets, and models have been developed for cost estimates, for simulation of projects and for cost-benefit analysis, the latter having been an important tool for evaluating and ranking transport investments for several decades. Cost-benefit analysis is based on the net-present value model utilising cost and benefit forecasts. However, large-scale projects spanning over long periods make forecasts about costs and projected benefits hazardous and lead to benefit shortfall problems.

In recent years, there has been an increased focus on cost overruns in transport projects, and new methods have been developed to improve cost estimates and cost calculations. These methods are intended to lead to a better command of costs as well as better cost-benefit models and a more adequate control of public investment budgets. However, strong emphasis on decreasing cost overruns may induce incentives to adapt in both desirable and undesirable ways (Jenpanitsub, ibid.). For example, adding reserve funds to projects may lead to heterogeneous assessments and deceptive representations of relative merits of projects. Such reserves may, in turn, induce lead risks for inefficient designs and overspending. Good incentives in the planning phase are therefore important to reduce or eliminate undesirable effects, such as:

- Undesired reductions of quality: With too much emphasis on reaching cost targets, projects are likely to be constructed below the intended standard levels. Some elements for implementing projects, such as environmental and safety aspects, risk being compromised or even being removed. In such cases, the real costs can become higher because the deficiencies have to be corrected later. Real costs could become legal and liability costs associated with intentional failure to implement high profile project components, such as safety and environment.
- Incentives to postpone the construction of secondary contractual objectives, such as environmental and safety.

The definition of the cost overruns or inaccuracies in cost forecasts is measured as actual cost minus forecast cost as a percentage of forecast cost. An inaccuracy of zero shows that the forecast cost for the project is correct and thus equals actual cost. Forecast cost is the estimate made at the time of decision to build, or as close to this as possible. Actual cost is the output of construction cost measured after the project is completed. All costs are calculated in constant prices or inflation-adjusted currencies.

Flyvbjerg (2008) and Priemus, Flyvbjerg and van Wee (2009) found in their studies of transport projects (based on a sample of 258 transport projects in 20 countries on 5 continents) that

- 9 out of 10 projects have cost overruns;
- Overrun is found across 20 nations and 5 continents;
- The average cost overruns are 45%, 34%, and 20% for rail projects, bridges and tunnels, and road projects, respectively;
- Overrun is constant for the 70-year period and cost estimates have not improved over time.

Many transport projects have thus experienced cost overruns. To mention only a few:

- The Channel tunnel, the longest underwater rail tunnel in Europe, connects France and the UK. It opened in 1994. The construction cost was 80% over budget and revenues were half of those forecasted. An economic and financial ex post evaluation of the project concluded that the British Economy would have been better off had the Tunnel never been constructed"
- The Danish Great Belt rail tunnel, the second-longest underwater rail tunnel in Europe. It opened in 1998. The construction cost was 120% over budget and the project proved nonviable even before it opened. Only by cross-subsidizing the tunnel with revenues from a nearby motorway bridge was it possible to pay for the tunnel.
- The Central Artery/Tunnel project, a megaproject in Boston, USA, that rerouted a highway into a 5.6 kilometre tunnel. Although the CA/T project cost was estimated in 1985 at US$6.0 billion (adjusted for inflation as of 2006), over US$14.6 billion had been spent as of 2006, a 143% cost escalation.

Macro and Micro Levels

As a general comment, something happens on the way between macro and micro, between the macroscopic structure and the microscopic event. From a common sense point of view, the macroscopic structure has emerged from microscopic events and the model designed to cope with the microscopic structure should include parameters from the microscopic event. But as discussed in Figure 2.1, only a limited number of parameters can be included in the model, and there may be parameters decisive for the microscopic event that do not let themselves be translated into macro dimensions.

A model designed for a public transportation system encompasses a number of parameters considered relevant and appropriate for the model, such as analysing frequency of passengers and transport capacity, peak loads, procedures in case of traffic stops, etc. The model can be more or less reliable, depending on how well facts are known and can be predicted. Relevant and adequate facts would be, for example, how individual passengers experience the transport system from their individual perspectives, needs and expectations. If feedback from individuals were to be considered in the model design, the number of model parameters would increase dramatically and would soon reach a level at which the principle of requisite variety applies: The model becomes as complex as reality itself.

CONCLUDING REMARKS

The Polish-British sociologist Zygmunt Bauman maintains that science about man and society only triflingly differs from magic and that the models we use have considerable similarities to what we would call *incantation* in what we have referred to as *primitive cultures*. Even if there is some disagreement with this statement, there is indeed reason to call into question the concept of reality and conviction behind belief in the so-called New Public Management concept. New Public Management is about measuring quality with the help of simple qualitative measures such as economic indicators. Magic is about conjuring up visions and communicating with the help of fragmentary and primitive models that become instruments that justify the political decisions.

Models are based on assumptions about reality. The less one knows about reality the closer the assumptions come to guesswork—or incantations. The primary aspect of New Public Management is the measurement of results, which is therefore the ground for assumptions and design of the models. A term that belongs to the New Public Management vocabulary is *result goal*, a word that is meaningless since present and future times coincide as the future achievement becomes the present goal, rather than the current starting point, the reality. While other goal levels such as *activity goals* and *effect goals* are linked to planned real activities, the result goal is linked to wishful thinking.

The many turnabouts in the global financial system and the many attempts at improving efficiency in government and public systems in recent years by copying models from private business have put the focus on underlying mechanisms and attitudes. Models that were previously of interest mostly to scholars in academic circles have now become of more general interest as people ask what lies behind occurrences that are not easily explained. In these discussions about models, many views have been offered. Sedlacek and Orrell (2013) are of the opinion that currently, society is permeated with the belief that there are models that are not based on assumptions but are completely real, true, absolutely neutral and scientific. This would then lead into something of an anarchistic view, as represented by Feyerabend (1991), who claims that a general methodology cannot exist.

The identification of model parameters is crucial for how well the model can represent a problem. The identification is subject to the observer and the observer's definition of the problem. The observer's understanding and interpretation of the problem and its nature is, however, coloured by manifold factors, including experience, knowledge, skills, cultural background, gender, political views, race, age, etc. The same problem could therefore be interpreted and understood differently by two separate observers. One must therefore assume that a model can never be a perfect representation. The question is, rather, which are the shortcomings of the model in a particular situation?

In the discussion around critical studies, it is inevitable that one will ask if there is a limit to criticism, if there is an elastic boundary around the core of the original theory that can be stretched out infinitely, or if the criticism finally enters into something new. This would then lead into something of an anarchistic view, as represented by Paul Feyerabend, who claims that a general methodology cannot exist. Like Kuhn, he underlines that scientific changes (like a change from traditional organisation and management theories to critical studies) are incommensurable, and each has its own paradigms. If, in addition, the different theories also have their own 'language games' (Wittgenstein) that cannot be compared, then one can never be certain one understands the meaning of what the representative of the other theory says.

REFERENCES

Alvesson, M. (1993) *Cultural perspectives on organisations*. London, Cambridge University Press.

Ashby, R. (1956) *An introduction to cybernetics*. New York, Chapman and Hall.

Bauman, Z. (2006) *Intimations of postmodernity*. London, Routledge.

Baumol, W. and Blinder, A. (1994) *Microeconomics*. Fort Worth, The Dryden Press.

Bergson, H. (1907) *L'évolution créatrice*. Paris, Les Presses Universitaires de France.

Bohm, D. (1980) *Wholeness and the implicate order*. London, Routledge.

Davies, J. (1989) *The challenge to Western management development*. Routledge, London.

Devons, E. (1980) *Essays in economics*. London, Greenwood Press.

Dunleavy, P. (2006) *New Public Management is dead—Long live digital-era governance*. Journal of Public Administration Research and Theory, 16 (3).

Ehrenfeld, D. (1981) *The arrogance of humanism*. London, Oxford University Press.

Einstein, A. (1921) *Geometry and experience*. Berlin, Springer Verlag.

Eklund, K. (1999) *Vår Ekonomi* (in Swedish) (Our Economy). Stockholm, Prisma.

Feyerabend, P. (1991) *Three dialogues on knowledge*. Oxford, Blackwell.

Flyvbjerg, B. (2009) *Survival of the unfittest: why the worst infrastructure gets built—and what we can do about it*. Oxford Review of Economic Policy, 25 (3).

Foucault, M. (1971) L'Ordre du discours. Paris, Gallimard.

Hassard, J. and Parker, M. (1993) *Postmodernism and organisations*. London, Sage Publ.

Hofstadter, D. (1980) *Gödel, Escher, Bach: An eternal golden braid*. New York: Vintage Books.

Jenpanitsub, A. (2011) *Escalating costs in road and rail projects*. Stockholm, Centre for Transport studies, Royal Institute of Technology.

Kraus, E. (1974) *The unpredictable environment*. New Scientist 63.

Krishnamurti, J. (1972) *You are the world*. New York, Harper and Row.

Lind, P. (2012) *Small Business Management in Cross-Cultural Environments*. London, Routledge.

Malinowski, B. (1954) *Magic, science and religion and other essays*. Garden City, NJ, Anchor Books.

McSweeney, B. (2002) *Hofstede's model of national cultural differences and their consequences: A triumph of faith—A failure of analysis*. Human Relations, 55 (1).

Monk, R. (1990) *Ludwig Wittgenstein—The duty of a genius*. London, Jonathan Capr.

Morgan, G. (1986) *Images of organisations*. London, Sage.

Moyo, D. (2009) *Dead aid*. London, Penguin.

Nordin, S. (1996) *Det pessimistiska förnuftet* (in Swedish). Lund, Doxa.

Orrell, D. (2010) *Economyths*. Ontario, John Wiley.

Pagels, H. (1988) *The dreams of reason*. New York, Simon and Schuster.

Pixley, J. (2012) *Emotions in Finance*. Cambridge, Cambridge University Press.

Priemus, H., Flyvbjerg, B. and van Wee, B. (2008) *Decision-Making on Mega-Projects (Cost-Benefit Analysis, Planning and Innovation)*. London, Edward Elgar Publishing.

Prigogine, I. and Stengers, I. (1985) *Order out of chaos*. London, Harper and Collins.

Sedlacek, T. and Orrell, D. (2013) *Bescheidenheit—für eine neue Ökonomie*. München, Carl Hanser Verlag.

Singh, R. (2009) Delays and Cost Overruns in Infrastructure Projects: An Enquiry into Extents, Causes and Remedies. Department of Economics, Delhi School of Economics, Centre for Development Economics. Working Paper No. 181.

Swedish Agency for Economic and Regional Growth (2013) System for the formulation of goals, monitoring and assessment of the regional service programme 2010–2013 (in Swedish). www.tillvaxtverket.se.

Tobaksfakta (2011) Halvering av tobaksbutikerna sedan 2000 (in Swedish) (Halving of tobaconist's shops since 2000). http://tobaksfakta.se/

Wittgenstein, L. (1922) *Tractatus Logico-Philisophicus*. London, Routledge.

von Wright, G. H. (1986) *Vetenskapen och Förnuftet* (in Swedish). Stockholm, Bonniers.

3 Models in Natural and Social Sciences—A Comparison

To what extent can models of natural science be used to develop models in social science? More generally, can the sciences of nature be of relevance to the study of humans and society? From a general point of view, one may claim that the purpose of science is to create understanding, and therefore the models used to illustrate phenomena and cause-effect relations in social contexts could have the same form. The reason, however, to distinguish between the two types of science is that *understanding* has two different connotations. In natural science, *understanding* is closely related to explanation. Explaining a phenomenon or an occurrence means understanding how the underlying mechanisms are related and function together. With this understanding of facts and relations, we may also be able to predict the outcome of a similar situation in the future. The mechanistic view that phenomena can be explained and understood in the same way under identical but different situations is the hallmark of natural science.

Understanding is also the purpose of social science, but with another dimension included. Whereas natural phenomena can (though they do not always) occur repeatedly and therefore be predicted, it is highly uncertain that phenomena involving humans and human behaviour will be repetitive. Although human behaviour can be exceedingly repetitive through traditions and habits, it cannot be taken for granted as it can in a mechanical system. Understanding in social science therefore involves intentionality, the ambition to elucidate the underlying motives and arguments connected with wants and beliefs developed in a social and cultural context.

Understanding and explanation are the roots of models, but understanding has a psychological dimension, which is not the case with explanation. Empathy, in addition to intention, marks a further distinction between natural and social sciences. The risk of using mechanistic models in social contexts is that intention is neglected or omitted. As natural science constituted the original pattern for social science and became the normative model, the mechanistic view came to dominate, which makes accuracy and timing important parameters in the model design. Lewis Mumford, American philosopher of technology, is quoted by Miller (1986) in summarising the period: "In time-keeping, in trading, in fighting, men counted numbers; and finally, as the habit grew, only numbers counted" (332).

AN EVOLUTIONARY PERSPECTIVE ON SCIENCE

For a discussion about science and the development of scientific thought, one may choose to begin in the Renaissance with the pioneering contribution by Newton, Keppler and Galilei, who laid the foundation of modern natural science. Or perhaps a more relevant starting point would be the nineteenth century, when the origin of social science gradually begun to take shape based on natural science. On the other hand, however, the beginning of natural science can be traced back to ancient Greece.

In ancient Greece, one can observe the first traces of what would later become a distinctive feature of natural science—namely, the notion of measuring. The belief in a natural order of things, interpreted from the study of Nature and its guiding laws, was an attempt at making life intelligible without reference to higher authorities found in religion. Life was simple as long as the guidelines from Nature were followed by humans—violating these guidelines by disregarding the laws of Nature was *hubris* that could only be restored by *nemesis*, accepting the laws of Nature.

Measuring had, therefore, a meaning that was different from how we understand the word today. Measure was a key to harmony and the right measure in art and music, like the proper distance between tones, was essential for harmony and beauty. The inner measure showed conformity or lack of conformity with the laws of nature, which were the guiding principles of humankind. Greek tragedies generally portrayed human suffering as a consequence of going beyond the proper measures of things.

In this regard, measure was not looked upon in its modern sense as being the comparison of an object with an external standard or unit. An inheritance from ancient Greece is the notion of the Golden Mean, a measure of harmony that appealed to the human brain and eye. The Golden Mean is a geometrical construction from 2500 years back that turns up in a variety of applications, such as mathematics, architecture and design, biology and animals, and also in ordinary everyday articles. The Golden Mean can be defined and described as the ratio between two sections of a line, as shown in Figure 3.1.

The point B divides the section AC in the Golden Mean if the ratio BC/AB is the same as the ratio AB/AC. The exact position of B is then given by the solution to the corresponding equation as $\frac{1}{2}(\sqrt{5}-1)$, which is approximately equal to 0.62 and corresponds to the ratio BC/AB. The measure can

Figure 3.1   The supply-demand curves

be found in several examples, such as the ratio between breadth and length of a match box, common credit cards, and writing pads of A4 paper size; it is also found in architecture in, for example, the dimensions of doors and windows. A thought that emerges is that the link from the eye to the brain conveys a feeling of harmony and happiness at the sight of the Golden Mean.

The predominant view of Nature in ancient Greece as guiding the behaviour of man was disrupted in the Middle Ages as Nature came to be seen as a threat to man and, therefore, to be mastered. As the Church loosened its grip on souls and as new discoveries about the world and its place in the solar system dawned upon Western society, the collective self-esteem grew and marked the beginning of the Renaissance period from the early sixteenth century. The new approach of controlling Nature created the idea of observing phenomena in Nature and making experiments with the ambition to learn from Nature, thereby becoming able to master and predict the lives of humans.

As science emerged as a discipline during the Renaissance and the idea of making experiments became a key to learning about nature, measurement was the tool by which reality could be grasped. Newton, Galileo and Keppler showed how experimenting with Nature could grow new insight into laws of physics and natural phenomena. As in ancient Greece, the belief that life could be made intelligible emerged again during the Renaissance with the idea that 'the book of nature' could be read and interpreted if scientists could master mathematics—the language of the book. Nature was gradually regarded as a system of intelligible forces instead of being a mere collection of phenomena, a hotchpotch of occult influences or the canvas on which an inscrutable Providence painted its mysterious symbols. God was a mathematician whose calculations, although infinite in their subtle complexity, were accessible to humans' intelligence. What was still unknown could eventually be discovered. In an essay titled *Connecting Human Understanding*, first published in 1690, John Locke, an English philosopher and physician, set out to discover how the formation of human ideas could be controlled, as Newton had discovered the law of gravity (Hampson, 1990). Similar thoughts had been demonstrated by Mme de Stael, a French writer in the eighteenth century, in one of her many quotes (1797):

> The moral powers are decided by the same positive laws as the physical powers. If we had complete knowledge of these we would by means of the cause-effect process be able to foresee all life's events in the same way as Newton measured the movements of the Earth.

The Mechanistic World-View

Ever since the days of Newton, the scientific world-view has been based on the mechanical model, also referred to as the *clock model* because of its predictability. After the discoveries by Keppler leading to the prediction of where to find undiscovered planets, it was not far-fetched to apply similar models in social science based on logic in cause-affect relations. Morgan (1997) uses the machine metaphor to describe how organisations operated like machines in being routinized, efficient, reliable, and predictable. Time and precision, which characterised the mechanical system, became important characteristics also for organisational systems.

The concept of predictability that had been a cornerstone in natural science was, however, challenged in the beginning of the twentieth century as the new physics discovered that prediction is only possible with certain indefiniteness. In a similar way, the English mathematician Alan Turing showed, with the help of his Turing machine, an abstract construction consisting of a tape with numbers and a reading device. The machine prints a series of numbers on the tape; it is of interest to see if the numbers form a pattern whereby a series of numbers eventually begin repeating—i.e., after a succession of numbers forming a sub-series, the same sub-series reappears. If it does, the sub-series, consisting of a finite amount of numbers, is, in fact, a rational number that can be written as a ratio between two integers. If such a pattern cannot be discovered, we might conclude that the seemingly endless row of numbers is indeed endless. But—and this is the famous Halting Problem—if the Turing machine is stopped because we assume the reappearing pattern will not happen, then it could be that had we let the machine continue for one more second, we might have discovered there were indeed a sub-series and hence a pattern. Alternatively, the machine could continue for days and years, but we would still be unable to settle the issue of whether the number series could be a rational number or not. The Turing machine illustrates some of the predictability problem.

With new insight and understanding of the laws of Nature manifested through new disciplines like physics and astronomy, natural science substantiated the view that life is intelligible, which ever since has been the rational foundation of science (von Wright, 1986). This also marks the main divide between natural and social sciences, or, according to the German philosopher Jürgen Habermas, natural science is irrelevant as a model for how we should study human behaviour (Giddens, 1990).

The period of the fifteenth and sixteenth centuries, the early Renaissance, is sometimes referred to as the period of the scientific revolution, with prominent names like Newton, Galileo and Keppler. What follows is a long period of progress in science and technology that culminated in the industrial revolution in Europe and that made way, in turn, for mass production and mass distribution of commodities. Due to mechanisation and new technology, this could be achieved with a significantly higher yield per labour input. The promising development in natural science was in contrast to the philosophical speculations in metaphysics, an epistemological term used by philosophers to describe the essence of life.

A reaction to speculation came in the early twentieth century with the claim that speculating about humanity and Nature did not fill any scientific functions and was therefore of no benefit to mankind. The new idea was rather a unified science for all knowledge, deprived of psychological bias and based on natural science. This positivistic view on science dominated the scientific discourse until the middle of the twentieth century, after which it has had less influence on social science. During the 1950s and through the following decades, a positivistic model of science was in ascendance, and across the social sciences the positivistic hegemony began to be pluralised by varieties of hermeneutic and pragmatic research (Grey and Willmott, 2005).

In a reflection on Critical Management Studies, Fournier & Grey (2000) identified a number of factors that, they suggest, have increased the resonance and appeal of this kind of studies, which also include the crisis of positivism in management research and the development of epistemological and methodological alternatives. More recently, however, social science has begun to adopt measurement in the models created. New Public Management is a token of the new trend of measuring quality in projects within the public sector with relatively simple quantitative methods. New Public Management principles also apply in the academic world through the Bologna Model (Rider, Hasselberg and Waluszewski, 2012).

The Bologna Model starts from the idea that the essential content of an academic subject can be specified and divided into separate courses with specific goals for each course and each module. In this hierarchical structure, teaching is expected to be done in a standardized way that reduces the scope for the traditional academic combination of codified knowledge (course literature) and live teaching based on teachers' individual experience and research. The structure enables a mechanistic control system geared to measuring achievements by predefined measures.

The Bologna Model process tends to cast European universities in the same mould to fit into a bureaucratic administrative system in which teachers and students are all subject to a formal set of rules and regulations. The traditional role of universities as centres for critical thinking is thereby jeopardized. In a world characterised by increasing complexity, the need for critical and reflective knowledge is more important than ever in order to observe and analyse different development scenarios. The Bologna Model is hardly characterised by this understanding and insight.

In the New Public Management concept, output control is one of the central ideas. The strong focus on measuring results implies that model parameters resulting from the cause-effect assumptions translated into a model need to be selected on the basis that they are measurable. This, in turn, ensures that parameters that cannot be measured, such as human behaviour or other non-quantifiable parameters, are not readily included in the model. Morgan (1997) argues that the mechanistic approach to organisations tends to limit, rather than mobilize, the development of human capacities, moulding human beings to fit the requirements of mechanical organisations rather than building the organisation around their strengths and potentials. Both employees and organisations lose from this arrangement.

Criticism by the Frankfurt School

The Frankfurt School dates back to the 1920s, when a group of philosophers associated with the Institute of Social Research in Frankfurt formed it. Its members regarded Marxism as a flexible and critical approach to the study of society, although they argued that capitalism had changed so much since Marx that many of his concepts needed to be discarded or at least radically changed. This is also the view of Jürgen Habermas, the principal representative of the Frankfurt School today. Habermas' criticism of modern society has to a great extent been shared in Critical Management Studies. Habermas has identified two reasons to be critical with respect to the study of human social life as a science on a par with the natural sciences. One is that it produces a mistaken view of what human beings are like as capable, reasoning actors who know a great deal about why they act as they do. The other is that it contributes to a tendency of overestimating the role of science as the only valid form of knowledge that we can have about either the natural or the social world.

BOX 3.1 MINI-ENCYCLOPAEDIA: NEW PUBLIC MANAGEMENT (NPM)

Vigoda (2002), in From Responsiveness to Collaboration: Governance, Citizens, and the Next Generation of Public Administration, *summarizes the research into the most important characteristics of New Public Management:*

What is the essence of NPM and the best way to define it? Hood (1991) identified seven doctrinal components of NPM: 1) "hands on" professional management in the public sector; 2) explicit standards and measures of performance, which were later defined as PIs (Performance Indicators); 3) greater emphasis on output control; 4) a shift to the disaggregation of unit; 5) a shift to greater competition; 6) a stress on private sector styles of management practice; and 7) a stress on greater discipline and parsimony in resource use.

NPM relies heavily on the theory of the marketplace and on a business-like culture in public organizations. Other definitions were suggested in the 1990s and drew on the extensive writing in the field. For example, Hays and Kearney (1994) found that most of the studies on NPM had mentioned five core principles and thus concluded that they represent the most important philosophy of the discipline: 1) downsizing—reducing the size and scope of government; 2) managerialism—using business protocols in government; 3) decentralization—moving decision making closer to the service recipients; 4) de-bureaucratization—restructuring government to emphasize results rather than processes; and 5) privatization—directing the allocation of governmental goods and services to outside firms.

All of these principles have now been applied to public sector institutions. Hence, governments that are far from being simple businesses have been encouraged to manage and run themselves like businesses. An integrative definition for NPM that relies on the previous works would thus argue that NPM represents an approach in public administration that employs knowledge and experiences acquired in business management and other disciplines to improve efficiency, effectiveness, and general performance of public services in modern bureaucracies.

Habermas' criticism of positivism is that it tries to fashion the social upon the natural sciences. But the natural sciences can never become self-reflective; this is a capability of human beings (i.e. to reflect upon our own history, as individuals and as members of larger societies), and by using these reflections it is possible to change the course of history. This criticism of Habermas also applies to Marxism. Natural science is irrelevant as a model for how we should study human behaviour, but there are three different forms of knowledge that correspond to three different aspects of human society.

All societies exist in a material environment, and engage in an interchange with nature, which involves what Habermas calls 'labour'. Such interchanges promote an interest in the prediction and control of events—an interest that is generalised by positivism to all knowledge. All societies also involve 'symbolic interaction'—the communication of individuals with one another. The study of symbolic interaction creates an interest in the understanding of meaning. Finally, every human society involves forms of power or domination—whether it is the domination of nature over human life, or the domination of some individuals or groups over others. The three knowledge types are summarised in Table 3.1.

Habermas' concept of emancipation has been criticised on the grounds that it has been used in political contexts. The Nazi German invasion of Czechoslovakia during World War II took place in the name of the emancipation of the German minorities dominated by the Czech government. Numerous examples bear witness to the many serious incidents that have taken place in the name of emancipation (Nordin, 1996).

Table 3.1 Knowledge-constitutive interests vs. aspects of human society

Aspects of human society	Type of knowledge	Type of study
Labour	Prediction and control	Empirical-analytical sciences
Interaction	Understanding of meaning	Historical-hermeneutic disciplines
Domination	Emancipation	Critical Theory

A SCIENTIFIC HYBRID—FINANCIAL ECONOMICS

The scientific attitude toward financial economics draws on theories and models from both natural and social sciences that sometimes create insurmountable difficulties in connection with model design. Too many parameters of various kinds make the financial system extremely complex, for which sophisticated mathematical models and theories have been developed with sometimes rather limited relevance as pictures of the economic reality. Most of the underlying theories start with highly simplified assumptions, such as the one of economic equilibrium in the supply-and-demand model to determine price.

The assumption behind the supply-and-demand model in a competitive market is that as the price of a product or service goes up, the supply of that good will increase, as it brings more income to the producer (under the assumption that there is a demand for the good!). On the other hand, demand will shrink because of the higher price. The price will therefore vary in accordance with the assumption behind the model until it settles at a point where both the demand (quantity) of customers equals the supply (quantity) of the producers. This is the economic equilibrium for price and quantity, or supply and demand.

The challenge to this and other economic models is the simplified assumption behind the models. Simplification may be necessary to show a possible connection between economic parameters on a high, aggregated level in society. The critical situation occurs if and when the model claims to address the situation on micro levels in the real world. For example, when the price reaches equilibrium, the demand and supply are the same. A not-unusual phenomenon might, however, happen as higher price leads to reduced consumption among certain consumer groups, but has the opposite effect on others who can demonstrate their financial strengths by acquiring the more expensive goods that not everybody can afford.

The model of prices being determined by supply and demand assumes perfect competition. But Alan Kirman, British-French professor in Economics and member of the Institute of New Economic Thinking, concludes that "economists have no adequate model of how individuals and firms adjust prices in a competitive model. If all participants are price-takers by definition, then the actor who adjusts prices to eliminate excess demand is not specified" (Kirman, 1992).

A methodological element often applied in economic theory and modelling is the *ceteris paribus* assumption, which rules out factors that may interfere with examining a specific causal relationship—for example, the demand of a specific product. It goes without saying that the *ceteris paribus* assumption illustrates the weakness and shortcoming of models applied without the necessary consideration of the nature of a situation, the factors to be analysed and the interaction among different factors. In the supply-demand example, the model may therefore intentionally ignore both known and unknown factors (recall the unselected and unknown parameters in Figure 2.1) that may also influence the relationship between price and quantity demanded, and thus to assume *ceteris paribus* is to disregard any interference between factors.

In another comment about the false promise of precision in economic models in connection with the supply-demand curve, Goodwin, Nelson, Ackerman and Weisskopf (2009, 85) claim that

> If we mistakenly confuse precision with accuracy, then we might be misled into thinking that an explanation expressed in precise mathematical or graphical terms is somehow more rigorous or useful than one that takes into account particulars of history, institutions or business strategy. This is not the case. Therefore, it is important not to put too much confidence in the apparent precision of supply and demand graphs. Supply and demand analysis is a useful precisely formulated conceptual tool that clever people have devised to help us gain an abstract understanding of a complex world. It does not—nor should it be expected to—give us in addition an accurate and complete description of any particular real world market.

Numbers tend to have a close to religious effect in the finance sector. Pixley (2012) refers to financial organisations that act, understandably, on past data. But the obsession to extrapolate is like a collective nervous tic, a giant embarrassment writ large in standard operating procedures. Despite extravagant failures, the sector's trust in numbers and repression of uncertainty through redefinition grows. While banks and credit-raters, accountancy and insurance firms, money market actors and forecasters treat risk very differently, the variations in risk show the extreme thinness of speculative models in finance (Pixley, ibid.).

The following reflection illustrates some of the issues and questions that have arisen in the wake of the economic global situation, crisis or not. The situation has clearly proved that the financial economy is not just a mechanism of simple rules that can be translated into models designed with sophisticated mathematic and statistical instruments; rather, it is based on assumptions that underestimate the ambiguity and complexity of the real world where people interact, where often irrational feelings dominate and where any behavioural pattern identified turns out to be either an illusion or wishful thinking. The reflection in Box 3.2 questions whether *the economy* really exists and what it is that the economy really measures, as well as what the proper measure for the economic reality is. It could be jobs created—but that does not seem to be the case. Journalists tend to refer how the stock market shouts in joy when companies lay off workers.

BOX 3.2 MINI-CASE: NO WONDER THEY CAN'T FIX IT: IT DOESN'T EXIST

By Helen Douglas, reprint from the Cape Times, *1 December 2009, in their series on "The Next Economy".*

It's another day in the global financial crisis and I am looking at the front page of the Business Report: "WORSE STILL TO COME, SAYS ECONOMIST". The article offers three expert opinions. One says that the global economy could face a second dip as a result of recent massive injections of liquidity. Another sees a threat in South Africa's reliance on exports. The third is hopeful the current recovery will be sustained.

On SAfm's Market Update, they speak confidently of corrections, profit taking, sideways adjustments and—my favourite—the dead cat bounce.

I recently heard an analyst say that prices had fallen because "traders were nervous". Why were they nervous? "No, it's a herd thing," he laughs. "They'll sell first and make up a reason later." He's equally frank today why the market has rallied. He doesn't know—but he'll "take it".

Such are the specialists who report on the performance of the economy. They have two things in common. First, their analysis is not very reliable. Second, they all work primarily in the financial sector. This is the sector that internationally has caused all the trouble. Can somebody tell me why we're still listening almost exclusively to them? Why share prices are the measure of everything?

Look. See. This emperor is stark naked. His counsellors are blinkered or blind. These economists (and financial journalists) didn't see the crisis coming, and they don't know the way out. The empire's treasury has been stripped by bandits who are laughing all the way to the bailed-out bank.

So the theories get theorised and the numbers get crunched until it all gets so complex that those who dedicate themselves to this work have to tell the rest of us what's going on. And soon these established economists start to think that their beliefs about "self-regulating markets" and such are the actual facts of the matter.

This makes everyone happy, because now all that's needed is disciplined management and technical precision to hold the ever-expanding economy on course. It is just a matter of getting the fundamentals right.

But what happens when it all goes wrong? That's where we are now. We don't know what to believe. The orthodoxy tries to prevail. They are manning the pumps, striving to get the ship of global market capitalism back on keel and on course. Pointing to "green shoots" in the distance, like Noah on his ark. Trying to restore our confidence.

At the same time, a lot of contradictory voices are coming in from the wilderness. Interestingly, we are more likely to find them on the newspaper's general leader page than in the dedicated business pages. If you have always trusted the conventional economic wisdom, then you are used to thinking of these people as cranks, fools and ideologues. But maybe now they are not so easy to dismiss.

Here is the underlying philosophical question. As non-expert members of the general public faced with these conflicting views, what are we to believe?

Should we continue to accept what mainstream economists tell us? How do we gauge the alternatives presented? How do we make up our minds?

I would suggest a return to the fundamentals—that is, to all of us real people trying to make a living, and to how this is understood by conventional economics.

Three related issues come up. First, the range of activities our current economic account includes is rather arbitrary. Not every act of production or trade is counted by the gross domestic product—for instance, unpaid domestic work. Second, inclusion comes without regard to social or environmental costs. A coastal oil spill is good for this economy, and war can be a windfall. Moreover, the objective of "restoring the system" is not a matter of quantitative technical measures. We have to wonder whose cost and whose benefit is considered.

And as the saying goes, not everything that can be counted counts, and not everything that counts can be counted.

Helen Douglas is a philosopher with a counselling practice in Cape Town, South Africa. The essay appeared on her blog, which can be found at her website: www. philosophy-practice.co.za.

Forecasting

Daniel Kahneman (2011), American psychologist and Nobel Prize Laureate in Economics, suggests in *Thinking, Fast and Slow* that the idea that the future is unpredictable is undermined every day by the ease with which the past is explained, and our tendency to construct and believe coherent narratives of the past makes it difficult for us to accept the limits of our forecasting ability. Everything makes sense in hindsight, a fact that financial pundits exploit every evening as they offer convincing accounts of the day's events. And we cannot supress the powerful intuition that that what makes sense in hindsight today was predictable yesterday. The illusion that we understand the past fosters overconfidence in our ability to predict the future (Kahneman, 2011).

Pixley (2012) adopts a similar view and insists that the future is inherently unknowable, an argument that to the politics of global finance is unacceptable. Mathematical chaos theory denies the point of macroeconomic forecasting. A chaotic 'dynamic', being unpredictable, would require an economic model including every seemingly insignificant relationship. None can be known to be relevant, if at all, until after the event.

Paul Krugman, another American economist and Nobel Prize Laureate, is of the opinion that the gloom and doom being preached about the financial crisis is more or less fantasies of scaremongers (Krugman, 2013). Krugman thus asks, "Why should we fear a debt-apocalypse? Surely, you may think, someone in the debt-apocalypse community has offered a clear explanation. But nobody has. So the next time you see some serious-looking man in a suit declaring that we are teetering on the precipice of fiscal doom, don't be afraid. He and his friends have been wrong about everything so far, and they literally have no idea what they are talking about" (3).

An obsession among financial actors and decision makers is to seek inside knowledge about the mechanisms controlling the financial systems and money flows. Mathematical formulas and statistic theory are the rational models and means by which such knowledge is expected to result, with little regard for human nature and its significant role in the financial system. Knowledge without such consideration is merely information. Pagels (1997) suggests in this context that information is just signs and numbers, while knowledge has semantic value. What we want is knowledge, but what we get is information.

CAN MODELS OF NATURAL SCIENCE BECOME MODELS FOR MODELS OF SOCIAL SCIENCE?

The opening question of this chapter was whether models of natural science can be used to develop models in social science, or if the sciences of nature can be of relevance to the study of society and humanity? In the following fictive example of pulling a heavy load up a tilting plane, natural science provides a method based on a model that describes how forces interact. The mechanical model is repetitive and does not depend on the context of the situation in the example. The parameters that have been identified to constitute the model are easily identified and described.

Social science does not provide a ready-made approach for coping with the same example, but we want to test whether a similar approach—formulating and applying a simple formula—can function as an alternative model to determine how many persons would be needed to carry the load up the tilting plane. This would mean applying natural science to address a situation that is, in reality, a social situation involving human beings. The example may seem far-fetched, but has, in fact, logical similarities with models used in organisation, as well as economic models. The obstacle that appears when applying a natural science approach for solving social issues becomes obvious in the New Public Management model, which often measures and assigns numbers to phenomena that are hardly measurable.

The example below illustrates how a problem can be addressed with the use of two very different models. One of the models emanate from natural science, while the other illustrates how social science would address the problem of physically moving a heavy load up an inclined plane. There are two alternative approaches to address the problem: either a solution based on laws of physics or a solution in which individuals carry the load up the plane. The two approaches represent different views of rationality. In ancient Greece, with Nature as the guiding norm, the physical work would have been rational, whereas using a mechanical solution to move the load in an unnatural direction would not. As pointed out by von Wright (1986), the word *mechanics*, with its root in *mechane*, has the original meaning of *trick* or *something artificial*.

For each of the two approaches there are thus two theories, a mechanical system and a social system, respectively. For each theory there is a model or there can be a model constructed based on parameters describing the cause-effect relationship of the problem. The technical (mechanical) model is described by well-defined parameters. The social model that is the response to the same problem (but with a different approach) is less well defined, as it needs to address irrational and human factors that are not easily incorporated in the model.

A Model Based on Natural Science

The model used is well known and proven and belongs to classical mechanics. The effort to slide the heavy load up the plane is accomplished by using a pulling force attached to the load that pulls upward along the plane. At this stage, we do not need to care about how the pulling force is performed. The pulling force must compensate for two other forces acting on the load and working in the opposite direction, thus counteracting the pulling force; the pulling force, consequently, must be stronger than the combined hampering forces in order to move the load in the desired direction—i.e., up the plane.

The relationship between the forces required to move the load upwards is given by the following expression:

$$F_1 > \mu\, F_2 + F_3$$

where F_1 is the force acting in an upwards direction, F_3 is the force that comes from the weight of the load and having a component that tries to pull the load downwards, and $\mu\, F_2$ is a force that hampers all movement of the load due to friction between the two surfaces—the load and the plane. The Greek letter μ denotes a friction coefficient and F_2 is the force acting on the plane due to the weight of the load. Both F_2 and F_3 may be expressed in terms of the gravitation force N acting in the centre of gravity and where α is the angle between the horizontal and the plane. $F_2 = N^* \cos \alpha$ and $F_3 = N^* \sin \alpha$, where cos (or cosines) and sin (sinus) are trigonometric functions. The gravitation force N is directly proportional to the weight (m) of the load through the relation $N = g^* m$, where g is the gravitation coefficient which is an (almost) constant value.

The problem of how to move the load up the inclined plane is thus described with the help of the three parameters N (the gravitation force acting upon the load), α (the angle that measures the slope of the plane) and µ (the friction between the two surfaces).

From the problem's definition, three parameters can thus be identified that describe the problem. Relations between parameters help us construct the model that solves the problem of how to move the load up the plane, which was how the problem was formulated. If the problem had been formulated to find out what effects the sliding on the plane would have on the load itself, different parameters would be needed to create a different model. In this situation, where the moving up or down is not of primary interest, but rather the moving process itself is, involving quite different parameters from the laws of thermodynamics that could be used to analyse heat development as a result of friction. This is a more complex problem requiring other parameters and therefore also a different model.

A Model Based on Social Science

An alternative way of moving the load up the plane would be to rely on human efforts. Industrial and organisational psychology is the scientific study of employees and workplaces that could shed some light on how to create a manageable situation to handle the task. With the specific desire to estimate how many persons will be needed to carry the load, a manager might be tempted to try a method borrowed from natural science and create a model based on what can be considered relevant parameters. At this stage, we would rather talk about a hypothesis than a model, and the number of persons (n) required to move the load is expected to depend on the weight (m) of the load, the individual lifting capacity k_j of Person J, the inclination angle (α) and the slippery factor (μ). The parameters are the same as in Figure 3.2 below. The imagined scenario is shown in the Figure 3.3.

With the help of the tentative parameters, we can set up a fictive model to determine the number of individuals needed to move the load up the plane. Since we do not know how and to what extend the assumed parameters

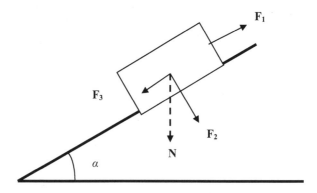

Figure 3.2   Forces acting on a load moving on a leaning plane

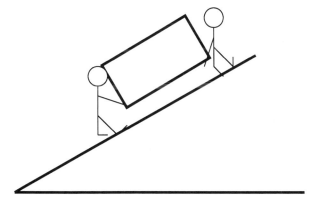

Figure 3.3   Humans moving a load on a leaning plane

would interact, the model should include the parameters, but we can only hypothesise in what way. We may assume that the number of individuals required to carry will be directly proportional to the weight of the load. We can also assume that the steeper the plane, the more people that will be required (until the incline will eventually become so steep that it will not be possible to carry the load no matter how many people are involved).

A further plausible assumption is that a very slippery plane would require more people compared with one that is less slippery. Regarding the lifting capacity, we may assume that more individual lifting capacity (stronger individuals) would reduce the required number of people. The number of persons required is thus dependent on the indicated factors, which may be formulated as $n = f(m, \alpha, \mu, k)$—i.e., a function of the identified parameters. Without knowing anything about this functional relationship between parameters and the number of persons, we can go one step further by copying the methodology of reasoning measurable problems in natural science. We may then arrive at the tentative formula for estimating the required number of people:

$$n = (m^* \, \alpha \, ^* \, \mu) / \sum k.$$

According to this model or hypothesis the heavier the load, the higher the inclination angle, and the more slippery the plane, the more persons we will require, but we might need fewer persons if their joint lifting capacity is high.

This tentative model is basically described by four parameters, but in comparison with the mechanical model, they are significantly more primitive and uncertain. Regarding the relationship between parameters, there is not enough information about the type of impact the inclination α, or the slippery factor μ, or the individual capacity factor k will have in the model. As a matter of fact, the impacts from each of these three factors may require additional models, which have been nestled into the model above. For example, as the inclination α increases walking upwards will gradually change to climbing, and the impact of the inclination will be somewhat different. As each sub-model has an error due to the uncertainty of parameters, the nestling of sub-models leads to an error probability of the final model that grows with the number of nestled sub-models!

The manpower model above is undetermined as additional parameters that have not been considered in the model may have decisive impact on the solution to the problem of moving the load upwards. For example, we do not know the motivation or willingness of the individuals to contribute to the effort due to the weight of the load, or the power of each individual's endurance, etc. A labour union or labour laws may also set limits to the task with respect to insurance policies and rules. If these and similar parameters should be part of the model, its complexity would be considerable.

There is therefore a basic quantitative difference between the two models— it is relatively simple to assess how many parameters are needed in the first example whereas in the second example the number of required parameters is hardly possible to determine as the problem cannot simply be defined as a mechanical problem. But the difference is also qualitative. While the mechanical model used in the first example explains how the interaction between forces can solve the problem, the second model (or hypothesis) involves a wider range of aspects for explanations such as motivation, loyalty, experience and so on. Practically every explanation can be said to further our understanding of things. But *understanding* also has a psychological ring which *explanation* has not (von Wright, 1971).

But it is not only through the psychological twist that understanding may be differentiated from explanation. Understanding is also connected with *intentionality* in a way that explanation is not (von Wright, ibid.). When a mechanical model is applied in the second example, it can help us explain how the identified parameters have effects on the task, and we can understand how they interact to achieve the task. But the model does not help us understand the impact of intention. In a case in which the persons involved have jointly decided to carry the load up the plane, they may be more willing to allocate more effort to the task, even if the load is heavy or the plane is slippery, compared to a situation in which the task has been put on them by an external authority.

Cause-Effect Understanding

While cause-effect understanding about a phenomenon is the genuine aim of scientific research, the question of how to define a problem in social science is not always straightforward. The examples above illustrate that while the model based on natural science is simple and straightforward, the attempt at utilising a natural scientific approach in a social science mode creates serious

Example 1: Car **Example 2: Organisation**

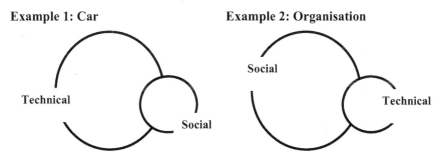

Figure 3.4   Aspects of problem formulation

difficulties. The exact natural sciences set a methodological ideal or standard that does not only measure with a high degree of exactness but also makes measuring possible! Natural science offers a variety of instruments for measurement, such as statistical analysis and mathematical optimisation methods.

Even if the solution to a mechanical problem is not always readily found, at least the formulation of the problem is possible. The same thing is not necessarily true for problems of social science. The problem in the first example in Figure 3.4 refers to a car that does not start; the second problem is an organisation that does not perform to expectation. In both examples, the reasons for malfunction may be mechanical or technical or social (human).

In the first example the problem is likely to be mechanical or technical rather than social. In the second example—a poorly performing organisation—the problem is more likely to be related to the human factor, such as group or individual conflicts or management incapacity. The likelihood of a technical problem, such as a shortage of computers or poor working air conditioning, is less likely. The two scenarios require two very different models to describe the problems.

Embedded Models

In the example illustrated in Figure 3.3, there are various models involved as we try to determine the number of individuals needed to move the heavy load up the plane. Assumptions have been made regarding motivation factors, ways of carrying the load, carrying capacities, and how shoes behave on a slippery plane. The models we create are impaired by varying uncertainties or degrees of exactness, and the uncertainties can be translated into statistical probabilities of failure denoted p_1 through p_4 for the four factors. With the shoe slipping on the inclined plane as an example, we assume investigations of different types of shoes has shown that in eighteen times out of one hundred, a shoe slips, which can be translated into a probability of 0.18 for a shoe slipping when carrying the load up the plane. Similarly, for the other three factors, there are other probabilities. From basic probability theory we know that if the probability of failure is p then the probability of non-failure is 1 − p. In other words, if the probability that all our assumptions about motivation factors, carrying capacities, etc., are correct, then the probability P that the assumptions and, thereby, also the model used to estimate the number of individuals needed to carry the load is (statistically) correct is given by the expression:

$$P = (1 - p_1) * (1 - p_2) * (1 - p_3) * (1 - p_4)$$

If we assume that our assumptions are reasonable and the uncertainty probability p is the same for all four assumptions, say 0.1, rather than 0.18 for the shoe factor (which also means that the probability that all assumptions are correct is 0.9), then the probability that the model is correct is given by:

$$P = (1 - 0.1)^4 \text{ which takes the value } 0.66.$$

This is now significantly lower than the probability for each of the models: 0.9. In other words, when more models are embedded to form a total model, then there is a significant increase in the risk that the model becomes less reliable. In big infrastructure models or even social models with human interaction, there must be several models embedded, each with its own assumptions about relevance and accuracy, that may be based on careful conscious evaluation but sometimes are just imagined or based on guesswork. The probability that very big models fail in explaining cause-effect relations, or fail in predicting future scenarios, is inversely proportional to the number of embedded sub-models.

Embedded models can be formally compared with subsystems of a system, which make the aggregate system vulnerable and potentially unstable, as the model becomes vulnerable due to the embedded sub-models. Prigogine and Stengers (1985) claimed that at times a single fluctuation or a combination of them may become so powerful, as a result of positive feedback, that it shatters the pre-existing organisation. At this moment, it is inherently impossible to determine in advance which direction change will take: whether the system will disintegrate into chaos or leap to a new, more differentiated, higher level of order or organisation.

As a matter of fact, order and organisation can arise spontaneously out of disorder and chaos through a process of 'self-organisation'. Prigogine and Stengers (ibid.) illustrate the importance of making distinctions between systems that are in equilibrium, near equilibrium and far from equilibrium in the following example.

Imagine a primitive tribe. If its birth-rate and death rate are equal, the size of the population remains stable. Assuming adequate food and other resources, the tribe forms part of a local system in ecological equilibrium.

Now increase the birth-rate. A few additional births (without an equivalent number of deaths) might have little effect. The system may move to a near-equilibrial state. Nothing much happens. It takes a big jolt to produce big consequences in systems that are in equilibrial or near-equilibrial states.

But if the birth-rate should suddenly soar, the system is pushed into a far-from-equilibrium condition, and here nonlinear relationships prevail. In this state, systems do strange things. They become inordinately sensitive to external influences. Small inputs yield huge, startling effects. The entire system may reorganize itself in ways that strike us as bizarre (204).

The geopolitical situation since September 11, 2001, when the World Trade Center in New York was bombed, may be used as an example how the geopolitical system was pushed far from equilibrium and was followed by a new kind of reorganised geopolitical system that we may perceive as bizarre because of all the precaution and security measures subsequently introduced.

CONCLUSION

It is possible that natural science takes more pains concerning itself with uncertainty when designing models than is the case in social science, where the probability concept is treated more casually. The quantitative bias of natural science towards measures and classifications makes the use of applied mathematics such as statistics a given instrument to address uncertainty. Social systems, on the other hand, where humans interact both with the system and between themselves create uncertainties that are significantly more complicated and less prone to be addressed by the same type of instruments. When models are designed for social situations, it is therefore not very surprising that the mostly rational assumptions fail to deliver useful results. Keynes (1920) assumed that the lack of understanding or adequate attention to the probability concept most probably contributes to the model problem:

Part of our knowledge we obtain direct; and part by argument. The theory of Probability is concerned with that part which we obtain by argument, and it treats of the different degrees in which the results so obtained are conclusive or inconclusive (3).

The probability that we can correctly judge something that has already happened is reasonably high, with, of course, due caution. The probability that we can judge something that will happen in the future, given that all conditions do not change is, however, significantly smaller. In economics, as well as in scientific experiments, the assumption referred to as *ceteris paribus* is often used to exclude certain parameters in the model so that only the parameter considered most important is isolated from other relevant factors, which are then not considered. The logical mistake in this case is that 'all corresponding conditions' cannot be assumed not to change.

The fundamental question of uncertainty has followed man from the very beginning; in the Book of Genesis, God exclaimed, 'Let us hope it works' as he created the World.

In a society that is obsessed with reducing or eliminating uncertainty, this goal is overly ambitious; life itself bears the impress of uncertainty. The only real certainty is uncertainty.

REFERENCES

Cape Times (2009) "The Next Economy" series, December 1. Cape Town, South Africa.

Douglas, H. (2009) QA 19. (Nov 09) What's fundamental? No wonder they can't fix it: it doesn't exist. Questions Arising: Life and other surprises (blog). www.philosophy-practice.co.za.

Fournier, V. and Grey, C. (2000) *At the critical moment: Conditions and prospects for Critical Management Studies.* Human Relations, 53 (1).

Giddens, A. (1990) Jürgen Habermas in Skinner, Q. (Ed.) *The return of grand theories in the human sciences.* Cambridge, Cambridge University Press.

Goodwin, N., Nelson, J., Ackerman, F. and Weisskopf, T. (2009) *Microeconomics in Context.* Armonk, NY, M.E. Sharpe.

Grey, C. and Willmott, H. (2005) Introduction in Grey, C. and Willmott, H. (Eds.) *Critical Management Studies.* Oxford, Oxford University Press.

Hampson, N. (1990) *The enlightenment. An evaluation of its assumptions, attitudes and values.* London, Penguin Books.

Hays, S. and Kearney, R. (1994) *Public Personnel Administration.* Upper Saddle River, NJ, Pearson Education.

Hood, C. (1991) *A Public Management for All Seasons.* Public Administration, 69 (1).

Kahneman, D. (2011) *Thinking, fast and slow.* New York, Farrar, Straus and Giroux.

Keynes, M. (1920) *A treatise of probability.* London, Macmillan.

Kirman, A. (1992) *Whom or what does the representative individual represent?* Journal of Economic Perspectives, 6 (2).

Krugman, P. (2013) *Addicted to the apocalypse.* International Herald Tribune, October 26.

Miller, L. (1986) *The Lewis Mumford reader.* New York, Pantheon Books.

Morgan, G. (1997) *Images of organisations.* London, Sage Publications.

Nordin, S. (1996) *Det pessimistiska förnuftet.* Stockholm, Nya Doxa.

Pixley, J. (2012) *Emotions in finance. Booms, busts and uncertainty.* Cambridge, Cambridge University Press.

Prigogine, I. and Stengers, I. (1985) *Order out of chaos.* London, Harper and Collins

Rider, S., Hasselberg, Y. and Waluszewski, A. (2012) *Transformations in research, higher education and the academic market: The breakdown of scientific thought.* Berlin, Springer.

Vigoda, E. (2002) *From responsiveness to collaboration: Governance, citizens, and the next generation of public administration.* Public Administration Review, 62 (5).

Von Wright, G. H. (1971) *Explanation and understanding.* Cornell, Cornell University Press.

Von Wright, G. H. (1986) *Vetenskapen och förnuftet* (in Swedish). Stockholm, Bonniers.

4 Are Models Transferable in Time and Space?

Are models transferable or transparent between different contexts? Or, alternatively, are theories transferable? For natural science, the answer is obviously yes—at least in general. A model describing a chemical reaction does not differ between different cultural contexts, whereas a model of organisational behaviour is context dependent. Studies of cultural impact on organisational behaviour have indicated that values, traditions and social patterns are sufficiently different in different parts of the world not to justify the adoption of one uniform organisational theory or model.

A model as a mapping of one particular context or reality may be inappropriate when applied in another context, such as another cultural setting. Since organisation models are formulated in response to problems and norms of rationality identified in particular contexts, their applicability cannot be taken for granted in a cultural setting where other and different types of problems or norms of rationality apply.

Can models be transferred in time while keeping their original mapping power? The French philosopher Jacques Derrida (1982) presented the concept of *representation*, which refers to how the meanings of words changes with time. Since words and concepts are the building blocks used to formulate a model, the question arises of whether earlier theories and models, articulated and developed with respect to specific situations (problem definition, perception of solutions), can have the same explanation value at a later time, when both problems and solutions may have changed meaning. *Culture* is a word that has had different meanings throughout history, from having manners and being educated in the European seventeenth century to a concept in anthropology in the twentieth century. Today *culture* has become a central concept in organisation and management theory through *organisational and management culture*.

Can models be transferred between different cultural and socio-economic contexts without losing their explanation power? The study of facts and phenomena in other cultures requires that activities and concepts are understood and can be accounted for. Language is important not only as a means of communication but also in defining names of subjects and activities. Local names that are deeply culturally rooted cannot always be translated into another language while keeping their original meanings. The following quotation from Lind (2012, 1–2) by P. M. Mutibwa, professor at Makere University in Uganda, shows how distortion of words and meanings can become a complication when theories and models of specific and detailed facts and realities are to be translated.

In religion, for instance the Christian missionaries with the assistance of their few African proselytes translated "God" into all sorts of words. In Acholiland, God was translated as Jok, although, as we have been told, the term Jok does not mean the "High God" which the white missionaries had in mind. The term normally means the God of a particular Acholi chiefdom so that the Jok of an Acholi clan or Chiefdom A is not necessarily the Jok of the Acholi clan or Chiefdom B. For instance, the Jok of the Koch Chiefdom, one of the largest chiefdoms in Acholi, is Lebeja; whereas the Jok of Padibe Chiefdom is Lan'gol. To make it even more complicated, we find that the Payira Chiefdom has seven clans and each of these clans has got its own Jok. The seven Jogi of the Payira people, representing the seven clans of Paiyira are Jok Kalawinya, Jok Kilegaber, Jok Byeyo, Jok ona, Jok Lwamwoci, Jok Ang'weya, and Jok Goma. In other words there is no one Jok for all the Acholi clans; and, consequently Jok cannot be said to represent the Christian High God who is supposed to be the God of all men, including, of course, the Acholi in northern Uganda.

So it is with the African traditional political thought. We are faced with the problem of having to apply European terms to explain concepts which are uniquely African; we have to formulate concepts of African experiences and thought-systems in terms of European languages and philosophy. The result of this is that while we may be able to conceive and appreciate African ideas on politics, economics, religion or culture, we may be unable, because of our inadequacy in the English or French language, to express these ideas articulately and meaningfully. When this happens, we may then conclude that the African ideas are inadequate, poor or even barbarian. On the other hand, while we recognise the problems involved in the use of European languages in explaining African concepts, we cannot all the same avoid using these languages in discussing African political thought because in Africa we do not have one single language in which all Africans can exchange their own ideas and their own experiences in their own language or thought-system. That is why, while a Muganda can sincerely enjoy a joke with an Englishman, he may not be able to enjoy the same joke if it is presented by a Matabele with whom he shares the African continent.

Very detailed levels are, of course, not necessary every time a cultural phenomenon is to be described. The dilemma is, however, that we cannot know how much detailed understanding is necessary to fully grasp a cultural phenomenon. It may be so that cultures are not commensurable and, there-fore, it may not be possible to fully understand a culture unless one is part of that very culture. Clashes between value systems, different perceptions of time and varying approaches to work organisation are just examples where cultural and socio-economic differences have effects on the applicability of models. One example is the ethnocentricity that appears when management or organisation models developed and used in a Western context are applied in a third world country.

The interrelationship between environment and organization has led many scholars to the observation that social models such as organisation practice are in reality culture bound, as can be noticed by Western civiliz-ation and its confrontation with other cultures. Von Wright (1986) and Bärmark (1982) raised the question of whether each culture has its own conception of reasonableness and whether comparison between different forms of rationality is at all possible; they claimed that criteria for rational-ity and knowledge cannot be formulated unless they are tied to the same social and historical context.

WHAT IS THE MEANING OF TRANSFERABILITY?

The transfer of models in social science can be viewed in two ways. A model is transferable if it can be used for the same purpose and with the same explanation value for which it was originally formulated. Alternatively, a model may be perceived as being transferable if it fulfils the formal crite-ria of appropriately addressing a problem. For example, a model originally defined for the monitoring of business performance may be tested in another context for the same purpose. The new context may, however, require other parameters because the model was originally designed in another cultural or socio-economic context or even designed at another time. In this case, it must be questioned whether the model is really transferable.

The advent of computers in organisations and their use to improve organ-isational performance and efficiency has led to a variety of highly rational assumptions translated into models like those of management information systems (MIS). Management information systems were in great vogue in the middle of the previous century and coincided with the management para-digm that we refer to as Systems Rationality. There was a broad interest in applying this approach in firms and organisations, and MIS software pack-ages were promoted and transferred by the major computer companies at the time. But the models were not transferable, not because they were less applicable in certain contexts, but because they turned out not to be appli-cable in any context! They were simply too rational in a less rational world.

Knowledge-based management information systems were meant to arrive at intelligent solutions by using rules developed for the system's knowledge base (Thierauf, 1987). The knowledge base was developed from mathematical rules and formulae of the "if-then" type. Knowledge was submitted by "knowledge engineers" who obtained their data from so-called "domain experts". The role of the knowledge engineer was vital for the MIS, and a number of crucial issues were asked about this role—questions, for example, about the terminology used by the knowledge engineer and the domain expert, or how much the domain expert could be able to understand problems that had not yet been articulated. In hindsight, it appears extremely strange that knowledge and knowing could be embraced with such uncritical interest!

TRANSFERABILITY AND RATIONALITY

In the 1970s, a Swedish economist with influence on the political debate about the role of the State with regard to economic development was of the opinion that politicians created problems by not letting facts be measured and judged objectively. He criticised politicians for starting by valuing rather than by considering consequences of political decisions, claiming that it is important to distinguish between a judgement and a valuation. The professor's view from the 1970s has gradually been shared by policy makers and politicians and has resulted in New Public Management, with its focus on measurable consequences.

Rationality is a contextually related concept, and in the study of organizations in different cultures (i.e., different from the observer's) needs arise to identify what characterizes rationality and rational behaviour within a particular culture. This motivates the treatment of culture as an independent environmental variable that influences the appropriateness of different organization forms.

The examples of rational thinking that we have observed in the computer models of this study—for example, in the assumptions about authority and predictability—belong to a Western rationality, as discussed earlier. The applicability of these models in a non-Western society can therefore not be accepted a priori unless the same rationality is at hand. With reference to von Wright (ibid.) and Bärmark (ibid.) above, different cultures have different sets of rationality. Applicability of computer models or degree of fit between model and reality can therefore be assessed only through analysis on the level and in the place where the model is to be applied.

Morgan (1997) addresses the attitude to rationality in organisations:

> Modern organisations are sustained by belief systems that emphasise the importance of rationality, and their legitimacy in the public eye usually depends on their ability to demonstrate rationality and objectivity in action. It is for this reason that anthropologists often refer to rationality as the myth of modern society, for, like primitive myth, it provides us with a comprehensive frame of reference, or structure of

belief, through which we can negotiate day-to-day experience and help to make it intelligible. The myth of rationality helps us see certain patterns of action as legitimate, credible and normal. It helps us avoid the wrangling and debate that would arise if we were to recognise the basic uncertainty and ambiguity underlying many of our values and the situations with which we have to deal (146).

As rationality is gradually losing its grip on our way of thinking and perceiving, it is interesting to observe how the awareness about limits of rationality have emerged and been treated at greater length in natural science, whereas the opposite can be noticed in social science. Prigogine and Stengers (1985) thus observed that we are now entering a time where the natural sciences have rid themselves of a conception of objective reality that implied that novelty and diversity had to be denied in the name of immutable universal laws. They have rid themselves of a fascination with a rationality taken as closed and a knowledge seen as nearly achieved. They are now open to the unexpected, which they no longer define as the result of imperfect knowledge or insufficient control.

In social science there is a compact resistance to accept non-rational arguments when explanations are sought for failures or shortcomings. Pixley (2012) illustrates from the finance sector:

> Behavioural finance assumes crashes are not from banking but people's 'faulty estimates' of probability. That is relevant to gambling, but uncertainty cannot be 'estimated'; no one knows it. To orthodoxy, emotions are impulsive and unpredictable, and 'greed' or 'irrational exuberance' creates crashes. It asserts there is a 'predictable normality', perfect if greed had not intervened, and so rationalises the 'excuses' for predictive failures. The rational economic man assumes certainty and only emotions ruin it (38).

BOX 4.1 MINI-ENCYCLOPAEDIA: MANAGEMENT INFORMATION SYSTEMS—EXAMPLE OF RATIONALITY

The concept of a management information system can be used as an example of how the highly rational model of knowledge-based information systems was thought to make organisations more efficient. A typical characteristic of knowledge-based management information systems was a focus on the future. Forward-looking systems emphasised the integration of future and current operations as the base for management decisions. The view that the future is predictable was a characteristic of the management information system.

To make errorless conclusions from what we know is difficult not only in practice but even in theory. In those situations where humans interfere with the socio-economic system—for example, in economics and business—linear systems hardly exist. Mathematics does not provide us with any general tools to solve non-linear problems, and in most cases we can only have approximate qualitative solutions. Chaos theory has shown that even a simple growth process can turn chaotic. A system exhibiting chaotic dynamics may evolve in a deterministic way, but measurements of the system do not allow the prediction of the state of the system even moderately far into the future.

The concept of knowledge-based information systems must therefore be seen as conveying a world-view that has predominated in Western thought for the last three hundred years. This view is now being challenged in the wake of a new awareness about fundamental limitations in technical systems that point at the fact that human and mechanical information processing do not involve the same elementary processes. All knowledge cannot be formalised, and whatever can be understood cannot be expressed in terms of logical relations. Vital facts cannot be abstracted, stored and used independently of their original contexts.

While the concept of knowledge-based management information systems has contributed value by providing a broader focus on management information needs, it has also demonstrated that managers need more than formal knowledge that can be articulated and stored in a database. Experience, insight, and intuition are other elements besides formal knowledge that are equally important in managerial work. The crucial question is then: How can a computer-based system be designed to assist managers in their daily work, taking into account, and utilising, the experience and skill of the individual manager himself? The starting point must be the manager and his competence level. A knowledge-based management information system does not comprise the knowledge, experience and skill of individual managers. Instead, the domain expert enters data. Human knowledge may, to some extent, be accumulated in knowledge databases, whereas individual experience and skill do not let themselves be mapped into general algorithms.

ARE MODELS TRANSFERABLE IN TIME?

Are models vulnerable to 'fatigue', and should they, therefore, have a best-before date? Figure 4.1 illustrates as an example the differences between how conflicts in organisations were understood and the assumptions about how conflicts should be treated in two different time periods. The assumptions about conflicts, why they happened and their impact on the organisation are denoted by "Conflicts A" in the figure. As the views about conflicts have shifted based on research and increased interest in the interaction between individuals and the organisational structure, a somewhat different approach has developed about the grounds for conflicts, their impact on the organisation and—not least important—how much conflict can be accepted. The later situation is denoted by "Conflicts B" in the figure.

Traditionally (in a previous model) it was assumed that conflicts can be avoided, conflicts are caused by trouble-makers and boat rockers,

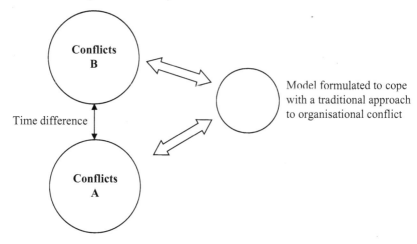

Figure 4.1   Transfer of models in time

authoritative management sticks to the rules and establishes reporting channels to avoid conflicts, and blaming and finding scapegoats is a management task. A more recent approach to organisational conflicts suggests that conflicts in the organisation are inevitable; conflicts are determined by structural factors, by the design of hierarchy and career and by class systems in society. Conflicts are furthermore integrated into organisational change and a certain level of conflict is optimal.

Figure 4.1 illustrates how traditional studies (A) of organisational conflicts resulted in a model based on traditional assumptions about causes, effects and solutions to organisational conflicts. As a result of more recent studies and research (B) growing knowledge and understanding about conflicts and their impact on organisational behaviour and performance has gradually developed. The new assumptions about conflicts do, however, not comply with earlier assumptions and hence not with explanations provided by the earlier model. The time difference has made the original model more or less obsolete!

BOX 4.2 MINI-ENCYCLOPAEDIA: CHANGING MODELS OF MANAGING CONFLICTS

The traditional approach to coping with organisational conflicts contained some vital assumptions, such as:

- Conflicts in organisations can be avoided.
- Conflicts are caused by trouble-makers and boat-rockers in the organisation.

- Authoritative management sticks to the rules and establishes reporting channels from which they can observe and identify symptoms that may lead to conflicts and thus avoids conflicts.
- Blaming and finding scapegoats is inevitable.

Later views have been unified under the concept of Interaction Management, which is characterised by aspects such as:

- Conflicts in organisations are inevitable.
- Conflicts are primarily determined by structural factors, by the design of hierarchy and career and influenced by the class system in society.
- Conflicts are an inevitable and integrated part of organisational change.
- Avoiding conflicts in organisations is not advisable, but a certain level of conflict is optimal.

In the 1970s, there was a major shift from the traditional and rational and mechanical approaches to business management towards paying increasing attention to people, processes and customers. This shift broke from the previous attitude of measuring business performance by means of accounting data to adopting a broader set of measures like product and service quality. An illustration of the changed view has been spelled out as follows:

> If companies are to compete effectively, they must remove accounting information from their operational control systems and relieve their accounting departments of responsibility for providing information to control business operations. The chief problem with using accounting information to control operations is the tendency for businesses to lose sight of the processes by which people and customers make a company competitive and profitable. (Johnson, 1992, 30)

The new business models, developed from the new approach, became closely interlinked with the paradigm that is referred to as Organisational Culture.

ARE MODELS TRANSFERABLE IN SPACE?

Transferring and applying a model developed in a particular context into other cultural or socio-economic settings where the formulations of problems and solutions are subject to different value systems and norms of rationality makes its usefulness unreliable. The more context dependent a model is, the more unlikely it is that it will retain its purposefulness in a different context.

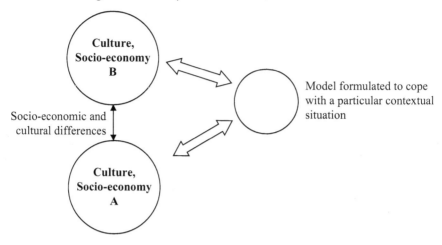

Figure 4.2   Transfer of models in space

In a study of an Egyptian factory, Lind (1991) showed that a Western model of production failed to give the desired efficiency results because of an organisational authority structure that did not comply with the assumptions in the model; it was developed in another context where other norms and constraints prevailed. Figure 4.2 illustrates how a model that describes a process or a situation defined in a particular socio-economic and cultural context, A, is transferred to another context, B, that is characterised by partly different cultural and socio-economic conditions.

The cultural and socio-economic conditions in context A that are the basis for the model is, for example, a Western industry with unconstrained access to material and spare parts and timely deliveries, with delegated organisational responsibilities, and with reliable infrastructure systems that make transport lead-times predictable. In a different context, B, the same characteristics may be missing or different, which makes the applicability of the model more uncertain. The transfer of production models is described at a more detailed level below.

Models of Production

Major industries in middle and low income countries have an organisational form that very closely follows a traditional Western pattern of organising and managing industrial production. In this Western view lie assumptions about production problems and how planning and control can reduce or eliminate these problems. The assumptions have been further elaborated and ideas have been formalised into computer programs for production management.

The formal resemblance between an industry in a developing country and the traditional Western production models has therefore brought about an illusionary expectation that the computer systems should be particularly applicable in those industries. But as production is linked to the outside world through the flow of materials, a good deal of organisational behaviour can be understood only by knowing something about the environment the organization is in and the problem it creates in obtaining resources. In a non-Western environment that is characterized by constraints and contingencies partly not found in the West, we must therefore ask what is the guarantee that a Western model of production, and hence also the computer programs, will fit?

This question goes back to the organisation research of the 1950s and 1960s and a number of studies showing how different organisations may exhibit very different characteristics. An important finding in these studies was that an organisational structure or a planning system or a particular management style that works well in one organization may be inappropriate in another. The reason is that the organization cannot be regarded as isolated from its environment. Different environments with different characteristics therefore lead to different organizational behaviour.

With this insight, organisation theory abandoned its former ambition to create a general model for the study of organisations. Instead it has been accepted that it is only by studying an organisation in its environment that its behaviour can be understood; this is referred to as the 'contingency theory'.

In 1956, James Thompson called on readers of *Administrative Science Quarterly* to contribute to the building of an applied administrative science applicable not only to Western societies but also in other parts of the world (Thompson, 1956). Thompson's motivation for this step was dissatisfaction with existing administrative theories and models, which he found appropriate to one type of cultural setting only.

In a paper published after his death, Thompson (1974) returned to this theme by drawing on his earlier concept about organizations as open systems; terms like *uncertainty*, *interdependence* and *rational behaviour* constitute cornerstones of the concept. The conception of rationality as used by Thompson, but also by Katz and Kahn (1966) and by March and Simon (1958), broke with a traditional view of organisational behaviour (e.g., the simplified rationality of 'the economic man') and accepted the 'cognitive limits of rationality' or 'bounded rationality' (Thompson) in which choice is always exercised with respect to a limited, approximate, simplified 'model' of the real situation, the chooser's definition of the situation.

But rationality is a contextually related concept, and assumptions characterised by rationality are facilitated if the attempts to reduce uncertainty can rely on abundant resources such as money, skills, materials and the like. As this form of abundance is not a privilege in many low and middle income countries, production models with origins in the West are not readily transferred.

BOX 4.3 MINI-ENCYCLOPAEDIA: THE CONTINGENCY THEORY

The contingency theory can be traced back to the 1960s and the pioneering research of scholars like Burns and Stalker, Lawrence and Lorsch, and Thompson and Woodward, who concluded in their applied organisational research that organisation structures tend to not only be based on the tasks assigned to the organisation but also on other factors, such as environmental conditions, technology and culture patterns. The core concept of the theory is openness; in other words, that organisations must be conceived as open systems and that it is external uncertainty that constitutes this openness.

Thompson found that this openness, as opposed to an earlier dominating conception of organisations as closed systems, becomes apparent once the organisation is regarded together with its environment. With this approach, Thompson suggested that organisations respond to external and internal uncertainty with different forms of rational behaviour, adjusted to cope with different forms of constraints and contingency.

Industrial production can be described in different ways, depending on what is to be highlighted. In a study of production in an Egyptian industry with the focus on material and how material needs were planned and coordinated, it was fruitful to conceive of production as a flow of raw materials and components transformed into products (Lind, 1991). As material is used in the different production steps along the line, information is collected and disseminated as appropriate to suppliers for subsequent material supply. The material information flow can be regarded as a flow of energy, used in a broad sense, to include both material and other relevant information elements.

In a production model, the availability of spare parts for machines is essential for an efficient production system, and timely availability of adequate spare parts when needed is seldom a problem in industrialised countries. Raw material supply typically operates in similar circumstances and with acceptable lead-times, with most models of production systems developed from operating environments specific to dependable spare parts and raw material sources.

Computer Models

The step from a model to a computer program is a further simplification, like the step from reality to model, wherein simplification is deliberate as the model is to be a manageable yet trustworthy image of reality. In the second step, however, the transformation becomes a simplification because the computer technology sets limits. This simplification is therefore not deliberate because the computer program itself is designed in accordance with a pre-defined logical structure to fit with the technological constraints. Ambiguity in the model, implicit or unavoidable if the model is to reflect a social system with human integration, is not allowed in the computer program, simply because the computer program cannot by itself judge whether a conclusion arrived at in the program is reasonable or not. Every situation of reality must therefore be a priori foreseen in the model to be reflected in the program; otherwise it will not be recognised at all. It is thus a simplification, and also a limitation in the usability of the model, that all forms of ambiguity must be avoided in the computer program.

Models help us to understand the world around us and to communicate this understanding to others via textbooks, discussions, articles, etc. This communication is based on language, albeit the language is sometimes inadequate to express specific phenomena and subtle meanings. As long as the communication takes place in a cultural domain with a common frame of reference for abstract reasoning and metaphors, these difficulties can be more or less manageable. But as soon as this common reference frame can no longer be assumed as a basis (for example in communication between different cultural domains with different value patterns and intellectual traditions), communication may become distorted and meanings become defective or misleading.

In this respect, computer language can be regarded as an expression of a specific culture in which the language is based on formal logic and deprived of inexactness and ambiguities. In this culture, exact wording in the formal language and semantic accuracy are cornerstones. It is therefore possible that the computer language is too straightforward to serve as an interpreter of the conceptual thinking behind many models.

Models can be regarded as a kind of intellectual tool that helps to understand the world around us. One and the same reality can be interpreted by different models, each model having its perspective and highlighting particular phenomena. But one and the same reality can also be interpreted differently by different interpreters and thus produce different models. Such models often represent different schools of thought and show thereby the inexactness and uncertainty in our attempts to describe reality. General models are therefore no more general than the underlying world-view of their originators. In other words, no model can claim absolute credibility.

However, when a model is transformed into a computer program, it has a tendency to become a generalization. There are primarily two reasons behind this. First, a computer program is regarded by many as the result of a consensus decision in which the most appropriate model has been selected to be transformed into a computer program. The second reason is that those suppliers who invest in producing this particular computer program promote their product as being as generally applicable as possible in order to maximize the volume of sales.

As long as the model can be traced back to the originator, validation of the model can be done by evaluating the arguments of its originator. In the computer program, the bridges back to the underlying model and its originator are, in general, blurred. The transfer from model to computer programs is therefore also a step of 'impersonalisation'. The view of a computer program as an expression of formalised logic has contributed to the conception of a higher veracity.

BOX 4.4 MINI-ENCYCLOPAEDIA: CHALLENGES TO WESTERN MANAGEMENT PRINCIPLES

The predominant management, organisation and economic principles and models are characterised by views, norms and values having deep roots in Western culture. Adopted into other cultural settings but without being integrated into their cultural contexts, the models remain alien and do not contribute to the development of indigenous and more appropriate management concepts and theories. Although there is a growing awareness and understanding of management theory and techniques as being deeply culture-bound, management education on the academic level in developing countries is treated as largely context-free. Indigenously developed models and theories are largely non-existent, whereas Western theories are readily accepted.

The challenges to Western management models are central to the current debate on management and culture in which two opposite standpoints define the spectrum of discourse. One standpoint claims that the non-cultural factors (which act in the same direction upon management in all cultures) are getting stronger; the other standpoint has it that, while some features of particular 'recipes' may be readily transferred between contexts, others require substantial modifications or translations. Cultural differences have a major impact on how organisations function. Since national cultures change slowly, transfer of technology, knowledge and skills will always be reinterpreted by the receiving culture, and this will set firm limits on the tendencies to managerial convergence. Any conclusion on this issue must necessarily be a tentative one. (Lind, 2012)

This is much in line with Thompson's view (1974) that our Western culture does not contain concepts for simultaneous thinking about rationality and indeterminateness. The interrelation between society and organisation, a central theme in this study, has as a matter of fact led many researchers to the observation that administrative practice is in reality culture bound (e.g., Fleming, 1966; Luckham, 1971).

Lind (1991) found in a study of applying a Western computer model in an Egyptian factory that:

- the computer model was designed and developed within the framework of a given (Western) cultural conception, which includes norms of rationality that determine the model design.

- in another cultural setting (Egypt), where different norms of rationality apply and influence the behaviour of an organization, the applicability of the model can only be determined in direct confrontation with its actual application in the organization.
- in another cultural setting, where different norms of rationality apply, an organization may be looked upon as a closed system. If the boundary between the environment and this closed system is suitably chosen, similar norms of rationality as in the model can be expected.
- in the case of the Egyptian factory where the open-system approach has been used to study the organization's interaction with its environment, the conditions and the problems facing the company's production management exhibit significant discrepancies in comparison with those of the model.
- it can therefore be concluded that there are not the technical characteristics of the computer model that in the first place determine its applicability. Of primary importance is the problem-solving design of the model and the implicit assumptions of the model regarding rational behaviour and practices.

Models are images of reality in such a way that facts of reality are interpreted, through the language, into a structure of words that must have something in common with the structure of the facts. This latter structure must obviously be known a priori in order to structure the words into a meaningful model. This structuring, we argued, was culturally affected in the sense that words of the model, explanations, symbols, etc. must allude to something that belongs to the cultural environment in order to be intelligible and to make sense. The question is, then: What meaning has the model in another cultural context? How can such a model help to create understanding of, for example, causes and effects in a particular situation in a different context with a different cause-effect structure?

The explanation value of many models has been questioned also in the West, in particular as simple and lawful relations in economic, technical and social systems—where individuals interact with technology—which can easily lead to complex, hazardous and even completely unpredictable situations. In systems with three or more parameters, which is not at all unusual even for simple systems, the combination of parameters may, under certain conditions, lead to chaotic situations. Instead of accepting that a model is not completely reliable unless it equals reality in complexity, and hence is of no use as a model, the desire to make reality intelligible and to predict the future leads to over-simplification in our attempts to interpret reality.

The deterministic and mechanical world view that has dominated Western thinking and which has been so important for the development of computer models has emerged within the scientific (and philosophical) framework that spans from Newton to Einstein. However, a new awareness seems to have emerged that questions many of the existing rationality concepts and that accepts that interpretation of reality is more complex than has been assumed. The fact that most processes of dynamic, economic, technical, social and biological systems are non-linear creates a need for partly new thinking in models.

As this need for new thinking also applies to developing countries with low utilization of computers and uncertainty about their contribution to the development process, the discussion should focus on alternative models rather than just concentrate on new techniques. In many developing countries, however, the misfit between models and reality is not only because reality is wrongly interpreted but also, as we have seen, because other meanings of rationality apply. For example, better utilization of capital was a driving force for computerization in Western industries in the last half of the 1970s and 1980s. In many developing industries, however, protection of industry makes domestic production monopolistic, or at least nearly monopolistic, which introduces inefficiency, both directly because monopolists exploit their market strength by producing less and charging more, and indirectly because lack of competition reduces the incentive to keep costs low. Even if protection fails to increase monopoly power, sheltered domestic producers will have less incentive to pay attention to quality control and innovations. Under these conditions there is no real incentive to invest in computers for improved quality control or better cost efficiency.

Other conditions thus lead to another organizational behaviour and to different rationality concepts. The way to more effective computer usage must start here, with the development of models that reflect local needs and conditions. This development must be based on reality rather than on foreign models as long as the foreign models do not correspond with the actual reality and, in particular, as reality tends to be set aside as soon as a formal theory is adopted.

THE *AS IF* SYNDROME

The cultural, social, technological and economic contexts into which a model is transferred can differ in various ways from the original context where the model was first formulated and applied in response to problems having been identified in that context. The greatest challenge for applicability in another context occurs where the difference is significant in all four aspects above. This may happen in low income countries where economic planning based on economic models has high priority. A number of challenges meet the planners as they strive to adopt the available models in non-Western contexts.

The first challenge is when the model is tested in the new environment with data that is often unreliable. Lind (2012) observed that the need for reliable data creates challenges for statistical offices in many countries around the world, many of which are already weak and lacking capacity. Reliable and accurate statistical data are therefore almost non-existent. The lack of uniform principles to define, collect and aggregate data makes comparison between countries hazardous. The majority of statistical data available on many countries in Africa, Asia and Latin America is therefore not suitable for comparative analysis. The systems of data gathering do not comply with the same standards (methodology, definition and mode of calculation of indicators or of economic aggregates). Wrong statistical data used for economic analyses and private sector development runs the risk of leading to wrong policy recommendations or strategies.

A second challenge arises in such environments where uncertainty is of the most serious kind—i.e., genuine uncertainty in which the future cannot be predicted at all and no cause-effect understanding can be established. Uncertainty is always an essential component of planning and ranges from least to genuine uncertainty, the latter being totally outside of forecasting possibility. In many countries at the lower end of income levels, genuine uncertainty applies because of instable political systems, lack of infrastructure reliability, changes in the decision hierarchies due to obscure leaderships inside the political cadres and establishments. Genuine uncertainty makes the design and formulation of models for planning hazardous because no cause-effect understanding can be established.

A third challenge has to do with the absence of economic models particularly researched and developed for non-Western contexts characterised by shortages in venture capital, skills, independent institutions and stable political systems, most of which are taken for granted in a Western context. This also implies that models for economic development are almost entirely from the West, where they have been developed in response to problems and solutions as they occurred during the economic development process in the West. A majority of economic experts working on development in low and middle income countries come with Western models, theories and pre-understandings when addressing economic development issues in those countries. Lack of economic development models adapted to socio-economic and cultural conditions of less developed countries can be attributed to many poor outcomes or results that have failed to appear in economic development projects (Streeten, 1973, Ghatak, 2003, Moyo, 2009).

Due to a variety of factors—missing reliable data to be fed into the models, models having been developed in response to specific Western problems and conditions, and economic experts implementing the models without asking fundamental questions about their applicability—the *as if* syndrome becomes a critical reality. The *as if* syndrome occurs when models are applied not because they have been carefully evaluated and considered relevant and appropriate in a specific situation but mostly because no other alternative models have been developed. They are therefore implemented and used *as if* they were appropriate.

CONCLUSION

Do models have 'best-before' dates? A model is, and cannot be otherwise than, rooted in the present, reflecting knowledge and experience that has been accumulated up until the present time. The German historian Rein hard Koselleck (1989) is of the opinion that modern time is characterised by a basic asymmetry between experience space and the expectation horizon, where the future all the time withdraws from our collective experiences (Koselleck, 1989). The *experience space* does not provide knowledge of what is going to happen, whereas the *expectation horizon* is part of a process which all the time makes anything possible to happen (Koselleck, ibid). The sociologist Daniel Bell (1976) wondered how it is that all our collected experience, accumulated through generations, does not build a collective experience platform for people to draw from and thereby become wiser and more knowledgeable in every new generation. Any future scenario would then have reduced uncertainties and made prognostication safer. But this is not so because each new generation tends to go through the same process of making mistakes and learning, without recognising the essentials of what has been learnt. And what is perhaps the most important—the future is too uncertain to draw conclusions about a current model and its imaginable application in a future scenario. A conclusion is, therefore, that models do have 'best-before' dates.

REFERENCES

Bärmark, J. (1982) *Om vetenskap, pseudovetenskap och motvetenskap* (in Swedish). Göteborg, Institutionen för Vetenskapsteori. Report 134.

Bell, D. (1976) The cultural contradictions of capitalism. New York, Basic Books.

Derrida, J. (1982) *Position*. Chicago, University of Chicago Press.

Fleming, W. (1966) *Authority, efficiency and role stress: Problems in the development of East-African bureaucracies*. Administrative Science Quarterly, 11 (3).

Ghatak, S. (2003) *Introduction to development economics*. Routledge, London.

Johnson, T. (1992) *Relevance regained. From top-down control to bottom-up empowerment*. New York, The Free Press.

Katz, D. and Kahn, R. (1966) *The social psychology of organisations*. New York, John Wiley & Sons.

Koselleck, R. (1989) *Vergangene Zukunft. Zur Semantik geschichtlicher Zeiten*. Frankfurt am Main, Suhrkamp Verlag.

Lind, P. (1991) *Computerisation in developing countries: Model and reality*. London, Routledge.

Lind, P. (2012) *Small business management in cross-cultural environments*. London, Routledge.

Luckham, A. (1971) *Institutional transfer and breakdown in a new nation: The Nigerian military*. Administrative Science Quarterly, 16 (4).

March, J. and Simon, H. (1958) *Organisations*. New York, John Wiley & Sons.

Morgan, G. (1997) *Images of organisations*. London, Sage.

Moyo, D. (2009) *Dead aid*. London, Penguin Books.

Pixley, J. (2012) *Emotions in Finance*. Cambridge, Cambridge University Press.

Prigogine, I. and Stengers, I. (1985) *Order out of chaos*. London, Harper and Collins.
Streeten, P. (1973) *Trade strategies for development*. London, Macmillan.
Thierauf, R. (1987) *Effective management information systems*. Columbus, Ohio, Merrill.
Thompson, J. (1956) *Organisations in action*. New York, McGraw-Hill.
Thompson, J. (1974) *Technology, polity and social development*. Administrative Science Quarterly, 19 (1).
von Wright, G. H. (1986) *Vetenskapen och förnuftet* (in Swedish). Stockholm, Bonniers.

5   Models as Reflections of Knowledge and Ideas

Two main traditions can be distinguished in the history of ideas, differing as to the conditions an explanation has to satisfy in order to be scientifically respectable. One tradition is sometimes called Aristotelian, the other Galilean. The names suggest that that the first has very ancient roots in the intellectual history of man, while the second is of relatively recent origin. The two traditions represent two different views about the aim of science—the Galilean, with its efforts to explain and predict, and the Aristotelian, aiming at understanding from a teleological perspective. Ideas and the question of how new ideas emerge and develop are closely connected to a historic view of research, and through this research knowledge develops from ideas (von Wright, 1971)

The Galilean tradition was permeated with the ambition that science is capable of addressing problems globally and discovering global truths. This approach to science dominated scientific thinking for many centuries and also came to impregnate social sciences, including organisation studies, with its search for generic models applicable in global contexts. The mechanical world-view gave rise to organisation models that were strictly logical in a mechanical sense. In contrast to this was the Aristotelian view that knowledge starts with the perception of the whole rather than individual parts that are added to the whole. The Aristotelian view of understanding is today part of the hermeneutic scientific tradition, with its focus on interpretation of meaning in the contexts of human interaction.

THE CONCEPT OF KNOWLEDGE

For disciplines in social sciences such as organisation and management studies, the appropriate knowledge must correspond with the type of study that is needed in a particular development phase of society, according to the German philosopher Jürgen Habermas, who suggests that all societies exist in a material environment and engage in interchange with nature (Habermas, 1971). Labour may here be the dominant aspect, requiring an understanding about prediction and control achieved through empirical and analytical studies. However, all societies are also involved in communication among groups and individuals as well as between authorities and people. Such communication may be of low or high context type and involve symbolic interaction, creating a need for understanding of meaning. Finally, every human society involves forms of power or domination—whether it is the domination of nature over human life, or the domination of some individuals or groups over others. Knowledge about different forms of domination and how emancipation will ultimately free man from dogmatic persuasion is framed within the concept of critical theory.

There is no single mould into which all knowledge can be compressed. Habermas' view of domination and emancipation has been criticised on the grounds that many political cruelties have happened in the name of emancipation; people have been 'emancipated' by another nation without having asked to become 'liberated'. Different types of knowledge thus dominate in different scenarios, which leads to the question: Is knowledge not relative? For example, what do we actually know about the economic reality or organisation realities? *How* do we know about them?

Ontology and Epistemology

The fundamental question raised above about *how* we can know and *what is it* that we know is the focus of the philosophical concepts of ontology and epistemology.

Ontology is an explicit specification of something we try to make a picture of—i.e., a conceptualization. Ontology is also interested in categorising the things that can perhaps be pictured. The basic ontological question is: How is reality shaped?

We distinguish between realistic and constructive ontology. From the basic question about how reality is shaped, we can formulate the two ontological approaches:

- Realistic ontology: Reality is there, regardless of whether we observe it or not, independent of the observer.
- Constructive ontology: We perceive reality based on what and how we think about it, and how we communicate with each other about it.

Epistemology poses the question: How can we acquire knowledge about reality? Two epistemological approaches can be formulated:

- Explaining epistemology: Reality can be studied and explained in a neutral and objective way.
- Understanding epistemology: Reality is interpreted by the observer, and all knowledge about reality is therefore subjective.

From an ontological and epistemological point of view, knowledge can thus be characterised differently depending on how we perceive that reality is based and how we can deal with reality. Grounded in the two ontological and two epistemological approaches, we can define different types of knowledge, as shown in Figure 5.1.

- If we assume that reality exists, regardless of whether we or anybody else has been able to observe it, and if we assume that reality can be studied and explained in a neutral and objective way, we will know how it is shaped. We refer to this type of knowledge as *positivism*.
- If, on the other hand, we assume that reality is a construction that does not exist *per se* but is a fiction created by our filtered perception, then interpretation of reality is subjective and, hence, so is our knowledge of reality. We refer to this type of knowledge, based on interpretation, as *hermeneutics*.

Studies and assumptions about reality are conceptualised in models reflecting the underlying type of knowledge. Models based on a positivistic approach are characterised by strong confidence in natural science that only accepts real facts and observable phenomena and that discovers relations and finds patterns and regularities that help facilitate prediction of future events. Positivistic knowledge also claims that as nature can be explained from the laws of physics, so can social phenomena be explained by laws in analogy with natural science!

The hermeneutic approach does not make the same rational assumptions about reality. Patterns and regularities cannot be taken for granted, and the path from now to a future state is by no means obvious. The field of hermeneutics is social sciences dealing with humans and human relations. Exactness and prediction are here of secondary importance compared to depth and understanding through interpretation.

Knowledge must be seen as a model concept because it develops from ideas, and what is considered to be knowledge is therefore dependent upon the prevalent understanding that applies within a given discipline at a given time. Knowledge does not *exist per se* but emerges as a consequence of what we assume to be important and thereby define as knowledge. The British philosopher Roy Bhaskar argues that knowledge does not lie exposed on the face of the world, prone to the gaze of the casual observer. Rather, it is, for the most part, hidden and encrusted in things, needing to be excavated

EPISTEMOLOGY

		Positivism	
ONTOLOGY	Realistic	Positivism	
	Constructive		Hermeneutics

Figure 5.1 Epistemology and ontology

in the theoretical and practical labours of the most arduous kind (Bhaskar, 1986). Quentin Skinner (1985), in addition, reminds us of Wittgenstein's insistence that all our attempts to understand what we call *facts* will always be relative to the framework of a particular form of life.

The development of knowledge is not a linear phenomenon: During periods which Thomas Kuhn (1962)[1] calls normal science, a continuous development of knowledge takes place that is at times interrupted by revolutionary science. Kuhn's contribution to deepening our understanding of scientific history and how periods of science succeed and partly supersede each other was considered by many a breakthrough in the history of science. It is, however, important to know that Kuhn's perspective is a rather narrow one—it deals only with the physical world-view, and, in addition, it is focused on what happens when one world-view is substituted for another and not on the long periods of 'normal science'. The popularisation of Kuhn's views and, in particular, the use of his term *paradigm* gave raise to several interpretations and applications in social sciences, including organisation and management studies, that were sometimes more confusing than enlightening.

ONTOLOGY, EPISTEMOLOGY AND MODEL DESIGN

The discussion in previous chapters about models and model design can be elucidated from Figure 5.1. Reality is there regardless of whether we observe it or not, independent of the observer: This is the standpoint of realistic ontology. But from that we cannot take for granted that reality can be studied and explained in a neutral and objective way in contexts where human beings interact. Rather, each observer studies and explains phenomena in a personal and subjective way. This makes the positivistic attitude less adequate for model design in social contexts.

"Making to ourselves pictures of facts" is how models are created, according to Wittgenstein, which is in line with the epistemological understanding perspective and also how reality is perceived based on what and how we think about it, the ontological aspect. In social science, the hermeneutic scientific approach has dominated research in the recent past.

OVERVIEW OF THE HISTORY OF IDEAS

Western thinking can be traced back to two great traditions of ideas: that of Ancient Greece and that of Judaism, based on the understanding of a natural order versus the authority of the word.

Judaism

Judaism stood under the strong influence of the Babylonian culture (for example, resulting from the study of the stars, the idea arose of a hidden connection in nature, governed by given rules that developed into rules of law to govern people's dealings with one another). Within Judaism, these rules of law developed into a moral/religious rule of order, based on the authority of the word as interpreted in the Old Testament.

For Judaism's two great offshoots, Islam and Christianity, the leading concept in both cases applies *The Book* as the guiding rule that man must follow. Thus the authority of the word came to be attached to the Bible and the Koran, through which God's word was conveyed to man. (Characteristics of the Babylonian rule of order can be found here in the form of the Ten Commandments; the so-called Law of Moses was seen as the valid law in most European countries up until the seventeenth century, especially where crimes or morality were concerned.) The word's orthodoxy is absolute and cannot be questioned. However, different interpretations arise competing with one another, as can be illustrated through the fundamentalist movements in part of the Muslim society today.

Ancient Greece

The Ancient Greeks had no uniform interpretation of rules of law or moral rules by which to govern people's behaviour. Instead, different interpretations emerged to compete against one another, an expression of the classical disposition towards speculation and discussion. The rational Greek thinking can be described as a natural philosophy, with the universe as a cosmos of law-bound order. This order of nature even became decisive for man: If health is the natural condition for man, then a harmonious relationship between man and the cosmos becomes the ideal state. Only by living in harmony with nature can man live a positive life: to set oneself above nature leads to *hubris*.

Ancient Greece was less intent on developing knowledge than conveying wisdom. We can perhaps obtain a certain insight into this theory of wisdom by studying the equivalent thought found in the Chinese culture, in Yin and Yang, the universe's primal forces, which in unceasing variation succeed one another. Yin is seen as the Earth, female, dark, passive and receptive. Yang is the heavens, male, light and active. There are no undertones of good and bad in the division. Yin and Yang are opposites, but the universe is alive, not static, and is subject to constant change. Harmony is seen as the ideal state and only if Yin and Yang are in balance can the universe function. There is, however, an 'innocence' in Greek, as in Eastern philosophy, which can no longer be recaptured in us because it can no longer be understood in those comprehensible terms that have become ours.

Two Traditions

The two traditions, Judaism and the Ancient Greek (nowadays the Greek-Roman), have partly stood in opposition to one another (however, both are centred around mankind, in contrast to many other great religions—for example, Buddhism) and came to constitute that which clearly characterises the Western culture: duality between the worldly and the religious/moral. This duality is expressed in many ways throughout history—for example, in the conflict between the Church and the State during the Middle Ages. The tension in this dualism has probably lain behind much of what we see as creative in the development of the Western world. In the same way, the falling behind in, for example, technical development in large parts of the present Islamic culture can be explained: The Church and the State as a single unit do not create a field of tension where creativity can flourish, but become an institution, which due to lack of internal criticism, does not need to change itself.

The question of man's attitude toward nature, which constitutes an important part of the legacy from Ancient Greece, has created perhaps the most important ground for our search for knowledge and can be said to be the basis of the development that we usually refer to as the Renaissance. The Jewish legacy has, on the other hand, meant that with the authority of the word, a limit has been set for man's search for knowledge because increased knowledge can lead to God's authority being questioned. (Even during antiquity, the search for the wrong knowledge was seen as something negative, hubris.)

Our double-edged relationship with increased knowing can thus be traced a long way back: On the one hand, increased knowledge creates better possibilities to overcome those natural dangers that threaten; on the other hand, a life in balance with nature, "on nature's terms", is a condition for a harmonious life. That these questions even today influence our minds can be seen from the three myths that run through Western civilisation: first, the myth about Prometheus, who stole fire (a symbol of technique) from the Gods and gave it to humans, who now were in possession of the technique themselves and were, therefore, punished by the Gods; second, the myth of creation from the Old Testament in which Adam and Eve ate a fruit that gave them the knowledge to distinguish between good and evil, knowledge until then reserved for God only; third, the myth about Faust, who enters into an agreement with the Devil to teach him about humans in exchange for eternal life. It is obvious that these three myths, which play an important role in literature and art throughout history, circle around the question of rationality in relation to human happiness.

Feudalism

From the ruins of the Roman Empire, the Church stood out as the only lasting, functioning organisation. The feudal system, which followed the Roman administration and which thus represented worldly power, soon started to crumble from within and never came to be a lasting and functioning alternative. When the feudal system led to social disorder, the Church changed its previously dismissive attitude toward the world and made efforts to create peace and order. The dream of a Roman Empire and its stability once again arose, and 300 years after the fall of Rome, Charles the Great was crowned Emperor of Rome in the year of 800. It wasn't long, however, before conflict between the Pope and the Emperor arose, and a large part of the history of the Middle Ages concerns the struggle between them.

This struggle between the Pope and the Emperor, between ecclesiastical and worldly power, went on for nearly 600 years and resulted in defeat for the Catholic Church's claim to worldly power. The power of the Pope stood at its peak at around the year 1000, when Pope Gregory VII was able to exile Emperor Henry IV, who was forced to suffer the humiliation of walking to the Pope's residence in Canossa in order to be released. However, three hundred years later, the power of the pope had almost ceased to exist, and the Church's standing had, to a great extent, been wiped out. Towards the end of the papal era, there were no less than three popes; all exiled each other! In an attempt to restore the importance of the Church and its potential to influence society, what would today be called a reorganisation was carried out: the so-called Reformation.

Here, we can once again notice how the development of ideas influences what is considered to be knowledge: As divine questions came to the fore, questions that (deliberately) went beyond reason, it became less interesting to acquire knowledge about life through the study of nature. Thus, during this time, nature lost its positive standing (from ancient times) and to a large extent the ancient culture sank into oblivion during the first half of the Middle Ages. The dominant view of the world was characterised by the Scholars: God's laws governed that which was physics and science.

Renewed Interest in Ancient Times

During the eleventh century, a cultural upswing appears that is at first characterised by the rediscovery of ancient ideology, mainly thanks to the Arabs and later even to the Crusaders, who brought about contacts between eastern Rome and Spain, Italy and Malta. The distinctive feature of the rediscovered (and colourful) antiquity is magic. Arabic magic, which even included the phenomena of astrology and numerology, came to play an important role in Europe for a long time and even influenced the view of knowledge.

The principal advocate for ancient culture, as it was rediscovered in Europe, came to be Aristotle. In his posthumous works, one finds an attempt at a logical description and explanation of the natural world. But how was one to react to the fact that Aristotle was not a Christian? The solution was that human reason is sufficient up to a certain level; thereafter, faith takes over. Aristotle's thoughts were to gain extraordinary influence on the formulation of the great philosophical questions and, thus, even on the development of knowledge for a long time to come. Thus, when order was restored in the Church and papal rule reinstated in Rome (in the fifteenth century), the new flood of ideas had already begun.

The Renaissance

The Renaissance as an expression for the rebirth of Ancient Greece is correct, in the sense that questions about man's relationship to nature were reawakened, though with a new overtone: The concern was no longer how man should live in balance with nature but how man should conquer nature and gain control (nature was cruel and constituted a threat). Here, natural science would come to offer methods for exploiting nature and its resources in the service of man.

The change from the Middle Ages to modern thinking was, however, a drawn-out process in which two humanistic traditions lived side by side for a long time. The latter was characterised by the notion that knowledge of the causes of events is fundamental and can be investigated by means of experiment with models of reality. This method of working with a simplified and unrealistic picture would have been totally foreign to the Ancient Greeks, but it has come to be characteristic of the Western ideal of knowledge.

Questions about humans and their relationship to nature also created the question about humans' position in nature. According to Pico della Mirandolla, Man, as the highest, had no given place but chose his place and his role himself. Kepler, however, was of the opinion that a human's life was governed entirely according to the planets and thus had a predestined place in a greater system. From here we can anticipate a development towards humanistic and natural scientific disciplines.

The struggle towards a better knowledge of humanity and deeper discussion about humans' position in existence became topical again after the French Revolution, when a new set of values was being sought. Humans must be educated and tamed in order to achieve great worth. "Bildung und Erziehung" became the concept that was to dominate the attitudes of an epoch that is usually referred to as the Age of Enlightenment. During this period of enlightenment, increased insight into and understanding of humans' place and role in existence was achieved (e.g., through Darwinism and studies of the behaviour of humans and organisations in other cultures). Universities, as suppliers and innovators of knowledge since the sixteenth century, were now reinstated primarily as learning institutions. The newly established university in Berlin, by Alexander von Humbold, became a model for the new ideal of university. (During the seventeenth and eighteenth centuries, the role of the universities as scientific pioneers had, to a great extent, been taken over by the academies established by the courts, with the Royal Academy of Science in London as prototype.)

The greatest thinkers during the Age of Enlightenment, Rousseau, Kant and Hegel, have had a great influence on the development of ideas. Kant's criticism of, in order, pure reason, practical sense and the ability to form an opinion, deals with the possibilities for independent thought within the central areas of knowledge, morality and the arts. In the spirit of enlightenment, Kant (1788) speaks of "man's development from his self-imposed innocence". It is thus necessary to free knowledge from the authority of the word, morality from the imposed obedience to the Church, and art from the constraint of honouring the holders of power (God).

This process of emancipation had been taking place since the late Middle Ages as a consequence of the broken power of the united Church and the emerging thoughts of an exact natural science. This liberation of the European culture and lifestyle from the Christian faith (secularisation) has been called "breaking the spell" and marks that particular European attitude known as "philosophy of progress" or "myth of progress".

THE NINETEENTH CENTURY

During the nineteenth century, the polarisation between humanism and naturalism increases as the concept of progress comes to be grounded on the natural scientific (Newton/Kepler) model as a general norm to apply even in the exploration of the laws of human life.

These and similar thoughts were kindled and further developed in England by, amongst others, Mill and Spencer and in France primarily by Auguste Comte, whose ideas of progress gave rise to the movement known as *positivism*. Comte saw the social sciences as the last stage in a chain of development, where *thought* was liberated bit by bit, first from religion, then from metaphysics and its speculative and unscientific attitude. Comte believed that mathematics and astronomy had already been liberated in ancient times, physics during the Renaissance, and biology and chemistry during the period of enlightenment; these fields were thus found to be in a positivist condition.

Comte saw ahead a unified science, a joint theoretic base for all science. This struggle towards a unified science would come to occupy science well into the twentieth century. Comte's motto for science: to know, to foresee, to be able (in French: *savoir pour prevoir pour pouvoir*) constitutes a direct continuation from Francis Bacon ("knowledge is power"). Science, according to Comte, constituted the ground to predict future events. Progress is built from Science, and Science will help us to build the perfect society. The scientific tradition based on positivism maintains that there exists a *real* understanding from which different scientific disciplines can be constructed. When all misinterpretations, preconceived ideas, superstition, etc. have been removed, what remains is the real knowledge that we acquire through our senses and with the help of our logical reasoning power.

The reaction against positivism, the New Humanism, which came into being at the end of the nineteenth century, was short-lived. Soon positivism returned, with the help of the new mathematics and the new symbolic logic, in the form of logical positivism.

THE TWENTIETH CENTURY

Logical Positivism

Logical positivism (or logical empiricism) grew out of the self-searching that physicists devoted themselves to at the end of the nineteenth century and was a reaction to philosophical speculation in the form of metaphysics. (The word *logic* should be seen in contrast to psychology—i.e., solving problems by logical definition rather than with empirical psychology.) The idea of a singular science constituted a central concept within logical positivism. In contrast to Kant, whose basic philosophical point of view was that it is not intelligence that complies with nature but nature that complies with intelligence, logical positivism denied that there is such a thing as synthetic (a priori) knowledge, but that the only acceptable knowledge is empirical. Knowledge shall thus be reliable, for only then is it final and able to become an established principle.

Logical positivism originated in Vienna at the turn of the century, at that time a melting-pot where the Habsburg era was coming to an end and signs of a new era were beginning to take form: a society disintegrating and calling for renewal. Vienna is once again an example of how creativity originates in the field of tension between contrasts in two different systems, in the gap between old and new, between that which was considered bourgeois dishonesty in the Habsburg monarchy and the health and freedom that the new era's ideas brought. Amongst the names connected with the new Viennese epoch, which were to become of great importance for knowledge and art, are Freud, Jung, Carnap, Wittgenstein (psychology, philosophy), Schiele, Klimt, Kokoschka, Musil (literature and art), Loos (architecture), and Schönberg (music).

Physics, Mathematics

Some of the questions that physics and mathematics were faced with towards the end of the nineteenth century, such as the question as to whether the nature of light was a particle or wave movement, and the paradoxes in mathematics, were to appear to have far-reaching consequences for the continued acquisition of knowledge. Logical positivism, for which the main task was to contribute to the solution of problems of physics, would amongst other things appear insufficient as a scientific method because of its inability to encompass human/irrational behaviour in its scientific model.

Of greatest importance for the continued development was once again the discovery of the particle nature of light (Einstein) and the concept of numeration (Cantor). (Newton had already claimed that light was comprised of particles, something that was contradicted by Huygen's proof that light was a wave movement.) The insight that light had both particles as well as wave characteristics resulted in quantum physics, in which determinism and the predictability of the physical system, one of the cornerstones of

Newtonian physics, came to be replaced by a non-determinist point of view. Cantor's discovery encouraged Hilbert, chief mathematics architect of the 1920s, to try to complete his monumental construction, meta-mathematics, with whose help all mathematics could be proven, something which was to be seen to be impossible (Gödel).

These events/discoveries during the first half of the twentieth century have successively affected the growth of ideas far outside the areas of physics and mathematics. For example, the so-called Heisenberg relations of uncertainty ("one cannot measure the position and speed of an electron at the same time") came to be heralded as a sign of the uncertainty of almost everything! Criticism of the too-free usage of analogies, taken from quantum physics and applied to non-physical phenomena, has not ceased, and even criticism within the field of physics has occurred: Einstein considered that if only one could discover the "hidden variable" in physics—i.e., the variable that ties quantum mechanics together with classical physics—then the deterministic nature of physics would be restored.

The picture of knowledge today has been strongly influenced by discoveries and insights made during the twentieth century within natural science. The historical view spread by the French School of Anales (Braudel), which shows how history has developed in an undetermined way, often affected by unforeseen events in day-to-day life, has also been of importance. Much point to the fact that the development of knowledge that has taken place since the fifteenth century has partly changed direction, influenced by new attitudes and ideas developed during the twentieth century.

The understanding that the Renaissance era is going/has gone towards its end has been strengthened. (A certain care should however be recommended concerning the retroactive division of history into periods: Definitions in time are seldom clear-cut and content in the various periods is often greatly simplified.) There is a generally widespread belief that physics has gone through a paradigmatic shift (Kuhn, 1962) as discoveries in quantum physics cannot be explained with models from classical physics. Whether one can speak of a paradigmatic shift in a wider perspective (e.g., within the behavioural sciences) seems more uncertain. Meanwhile, Thomas Kuhn's scientific theoretic model of normal science and revolutionary science is important as an instrument in understanding when new ideas have resulted in new knowledge.

BOX 5.1 MINI-ENCYCLOPAEDIA: PARADIGM

A paradigm is a scientific concept that has given rise to a scientific tradition, of which the most famous example is Newton's *Principia*, the model for classical physics. A paradigm is therefore not a general philosophical principle, but a well-defined set of thoughts that may lead to certain general principles. Being part of such a paradigmatic tradition implies being deterministic in one's thinking.

A reason for the paradigms being imperative can be found in the scientific education. Academic and research training has the objective of providing the research student with a specific set of models and theories that leads to a dogmatic approach to the subject. Alternative theories and views are seldom conveyed to the students—even less conveyed is the history of the subject, including historic mistakes or doubtful assumptions that accrue to the paradigm.

The human view imbedded in the paradigm is deterministic, and every new generation of researchers is lead into this network of readymade ideas and perceptions. When critical views related to these readymade ideas become too intense and strong, the reaction, in the form of a scientific revolution (Kuhn, 1962), can be the consequence.

At the same time, there are signs indicating that a new paradigm of science is emerging as new ideas take form according to the concept of the world of the Renaissance. Even the new picture will centre on the main question of man's relationship to nature, possibly with a closer association with the point of view of ancient times that harmony is achieved in the balance between humans and nature. Ideologically, the discussion is already well established—e.g., that occurrences in our surroundings can neither be described by the models of Newtonian physics nor from the perspective of the science of positivism. The reason often quoted is the newfound complexity in our existence (unpredictability as a result of non-linearization), which in part can only be "understood" by the help of intuition and an attempt at an overall view. From these ideas, we also now see how knowledge is established to cope with new insight (perhaps the so-called chaos research is an expression of this).

The concept of chaos is perhaps, in its current form, more an expression for the popularising of applied mathematics (above all the theories of non-linear systems) than it is a new theory. However, as an example of ideas that already partly contribute to the development of new knowledge are those phenomena which are usually illustrated by the so-called Verhulst formula: In an apparently simple expression for non-linear growth, growth can occur, by means of a suitable choice of parameters and initial values, which is deterministic (i.e., strives towards a limit), oscillating (i.e., swinging around a mean value) or chaotic (i.e., a future condition cannot be separated from a random number). Studies of these phenomena have, amongst other things, given rise to speculation as to in what degree of ordered system (social, biological, economic) a state can suddenly enter whereby the continued development is unpredictable (so-called bifurcation). The representatives for these ideas consider that they have numerous illustrations of such a course of events. It is very likely that scientific work in, e.g., the economy during the next few years, will test projections based on these models.

The belief that increased knowledge is synonymous with or leads to development (scientific, moral) and success is relatively new in man's history. This concept of linear development is not to be found in the two great traditions of ideas, Judaism and the Greek-Roman. Instead, man saw existence as cyclical, with changes in nature as natural stages of development. (In certain tribes of Indians, e.g., Hopi Indians, the same idea of time is still to be found.)

Both Judaism and Ancient Greece held in common the belief that the best times had passed and that man was heading for ruin. Waiting for the world's destruction was almost a constant state during the Middle Ages. The Renaissance altered this dreary mood, as we have seen, in a noticeable way, and we have perhaps never before had such a long and conscious belief in the future as during the last five hundred years.

Francis Bacon, one of the main figures of the Renaissance, claimed that Knowledge is Power—i.e., the power to bring about that which is wanted and to prevent the unwanted by influencing the causal mechanisms that govern natural processes. Today certain scepticism is spreading as to whether we will increase knowledge at the rate needed to solve the problems that increased knowledge has brought. A new concept has been coined to encompass the new views and ideas that have taken form: Postmodernity.

POSTMODERNITY

How can we understand all the different visions, views and ideas that circulate around us in today's society, and how can we manage to create a structure where it is possible to see the red line that ties different views together into a coherent context? Postmodernity is such an attempt.

Postmodernity is a multifarious concept that aims at attracting our attention to a number of significant social and cultural changes taking place towards the end of the twentieth century in the most advanced and 'modern' societies. These changes have been related to rapid technological change, not least within the areas of information and communication technology; to increasing political commitment; to the emergence of social movements, with particular focus on discrimination between the sexes; on environmental issues and on ethnicity and race issues. But there are even greater issues at stake: Is the whole idea of modernity, which originates in the period we commonly refer to as the Enlightenment in the eighteenth century, about to break up? And is there a new type of society emerging, a society structured around consumers and consumption rather than workers and production? The need for a concept where these and similar issues can be discussed and debated has resulted in the term Postmodernity.[2]

Very much simplified, Postmodernity can be conceived as a distrust of the Modern Tale, which begins with the Enlightenment (see above) in which Science for the first time in the history of humanity is regarded as a bearer of liberation. The Modern Tale is about modern society, which has been built on modern scientific knowledge, and prepared to serve humans, providing wealth for everybody and liberation of the masses. A considerable part of the criticism of the Modern Tale is that Science has lost its objectivity. Science has become an instrument in the hands of those with power and has, according to the critics, lead to increased repression. Others point at achievements in medicine, transports and communication and other areas where humans have been able to benefit from Science.

The historic background of Postmodernity should be seen in the light of the three major ideas that have been prevalent and succeeded each other in Western development (Lyon, 1994): Providence, Progress and Nihilism. Providence alludes to the way God cares for humans and for the world after Creation. After Providence arises the idea of Progress, in which trust in God's care gradually is taken over by trust in humanity's own ability to create a rich and strong society, released from traditional dogmas. Today, finally, we can see how the idea of Progress is gradually passing over into Nihilism, a state in which everything becomes relative: Morality is a falsehood, truth merely a fiction. Friedrich Nietzsche became famous as he announced 'God is dead', with the symbolic meaning that humans have lost their reference system in life.

Because 'Postmodernity' seeks to describe a state of things that comes after ('post') Modernity, we need to know what kind of concept 'Modernity' is. In the fifth century, the Latin term *modernus* was used to distinguish between the official Christian present and the heathen Roman past. During the Enlightenment, when a new type of society started to take shape, Modernity was the term to describe this new type of society, characterised by a strong dynamic power, by global consequences and by its marginalisation of traditions. Reason and Rationality have been the words that best describe Modernity.

The combination of rationality and progress is both the strength and weakness of Modernity. The strength is the almost limitless ability of adaptation to new circumstances, the weakness that values have become relative and partly reduced to articles that can be bought and exchanged for a price. Truth and justice have likewise become relative concepts. Life has, for many, become consumption, reality is fragmented into pieces that are randomly selected and magnified in television shows that, for many, constitute the real reality.

Modernity is held accountable for its double-dealing—promising what it was not able to deliver: happiness for everybody on earth. When the problem of freedom is reduced to the freedom to consume, then Modernity has obviously failed.

In the wake of the consumption society that may ultimately lead to ecological imbalance, waste of vital resources and a hazardous social and economic development, growing focus has been placed on the concept of sustainability. Development of a sustainable society requires that the utilisation of resources does not exceed the renewing of the same resources, and that utilisation does not create negative effects for present and future generations. A model that tries to formulate the sustainability problem refers to the need of reconciliation of environmental, social equity and economic demands—the "three pillars" of sustainability (Edwards, 2005; Hawken, 1994).

SUSTAINABILITY AND CONSUMERISM

Consumerism can be regarded from a historic perspective. The three institutions Church, Factory and Shopping Mall, used here as metaphors for religion, industry and consumerism, have played a significant role in the development of the consumption society (Blomkvist and Lind, 2011).

Church, Factory, Shopping Mall—An Unholy Alliance

In an effort to trace what may have led up to today's society becoming characterised by plentiful production of items that have hardly reached the market and been consumed before the next set of items are waiting to reach the market to be consumed, three institutions seem to be in focus. The three identified institutions taken as metaphors are the Church, the Factory and the Shopping Mall, which together seem to have had, and have, a paradigmatic influence and importance for the development of society—in the first place, in the Western world, and nowadays, probably also in most other areas of the world.

The Church metaphor applies to the spiritual sphere in which man seeks and finds comfort in existential matters. The Factory metaphor alludes to the growing ambitions that emerged with the discoveries of the world and the scientific and technical innovations, enabling the production of goods at a scale hitherto unseen. The Shopping Mall, finally, is the metaphor for consumerism, where man seeks and finds comfort in worldly matters. To claim that these three metaphors have a paradigmatic influence on society requires that they have not only dominated thinking and thought for long periods, but also defined the development of knowledge and ideas. The question to what extent this is a plausible, explanatory model will be discussed below.

The three suggested paradigmatic institutions each represents a time period in which the actual paradigm was a bearer of an ideology that dominated human thought. The ideology linked to the Church declared God as creator of the world and the Book as the guiding principle for man's life on earth. The time period we select, not quite arbitrarily, is from the year 1100 through 1450. A distinctive change in man's attitude towards Nature and to the Power of Authorities happened as the New Time broke in around 1450 in the wake of the Black Death, new world discoveries and the growing self-confidence of humanity. Emancipation and freedom from authorities led to an unprecedented and unrestrained period of human innovation, spurred by scientific development and technological advancements. The different streams coming from science, technology and innovative thinking ultimately merged into the industrial society, symbolised by the Factory. In the middle of the twentieth century, around 1950, the beginning of a sceptical and critical view emerged in the most advanced countries from critics of humanity's negative influence on the ecological balance in Nature, who explained how technological innovations created ecological and also social problems at a rate that could not be compensated for by new technological innovations. As materialism spread in the most advanced countries, alienation and mistrust about unlimited progress identified ever-growing and seemingly unlimited consumerism as a symptom of something profoundly wrong in the modern society. The Shopping Mall became the metaphor for the consumption society.

The three metaphors, each bearer of an ideology, appear in chronological order, and it is therefore of interest to analyse the transition from one ideology into the next.

The Church

During the fifteenth century, opposition grew against the global outlook of the Middle Ages, encouraged by the great geographical discoveries that widened the horizon and showed that the European culture of the Middle Ages was only embraced by a small part of the Earth's population. Of even greater importance for new ideas was Copernicus' picture of the universe in which the Earth was no longer in the centre. The art of printing books contributed to new ideas being spread quickly, and thus new knowledge hurried the demolition of the Church's authority. Feudalism disappeared as the knights' castles did not withstand gunpowder, and nationalistic states grew up at the cost of the Empire's sovereignty. In the same way, the reformation contributed to the creation of national churches at the cost of an all-embracing Church with its seat in Rome. Thus the dominant hierarchical double powers of the Middle Ages—the Church and the State—were finally dissolved. In the national states, which now grew up in Europe, the Church and the State would, from then on, come to represent two separate spheres of interest.

The Factory

At an early stage in the history of Europe, pre-industrial production was widely spread. The use of water mills in the mining industry was known in Europe before the twentieth century, and cottage industries existed for the production of a variety of products, ranging from pins to ploughs. Weapon factories were established already in the seventeenth century—for example, in Nuremberg—although it was not until the eighteenth century that factories in today's meaning were set up. With the steam engine it was possible to benefit from scale production. The technical development and the advent of new production facilities went hand-in-hand with new forms of organising work. Large-scale introduction of factories changed societies as the so-called industrial revolution accelerated.

The ideological similarity that evolves through the three institutions does not mean that the institutions *per se* are identical. The factory is not an equivalent to the church, although they both produce and transform in a regular and procedural pattern. They both use symbols of power, such as the church tower and the factory chimney, to dominate the landscape and remind the population of their presence. They also both use hierarchical organization structures that effectively introduce an authoritative leadership style. But it is not until the factory becomes linked to the shopping mall through the flow of goods that spiritual similarities become apparent; the combination of factory and shopping mall develops into a materialistic correspondence to the church.

The Shopping Mall

The shopping mall becomes a temple with its own liturgy of background music, latest fashions and beauty of consumption. Neither in the shopping mall nor in the church has the concept of 'consumer sovereignty' has ever applied, but consumer tastes are moulded in the factories by production decisions and in the shopping malls by advertising campaigns. In analogue with the two institutions, church consumers bought letters of indulgence, the credibility of which they could neither assess nor judge.

BOX 5.2 MINI-CASE: AMERICA'S ADDICTION TO CHINESE EXPORT

Chen Hsien, an employee of Fenguha Ningbo Plastic Works Ltd., a plastic factory that manufactures lightweight household items for Western markets, expressed his disbelief over the "sheer amount of [garbage] Americans will buy. Often, when we are assigned a new order for, say, 'salad shooters' I will say to myself 'there is no way that anyone will ever buy these . . . One month later, we will receive an order for the same product, but three times the quantity. How can anyone have a need for such useless [garbage]? I hear that Americans can buy anything they want, and I believe it, judging from the things I have made for them," Chen said. "And I also hear that, when they no longer want an item, they simply throw it away. So wasteful and contemptible" (Friedman, 2009).

The three institutions would hardly have survived for long periods had it not been for their close integration with economic growth. The 'discovery' of the New World, through missions supported and partly funded by the Church to save the pagans, brought considerable fortunes back into Europe, which promoted trade and technological development but also enriched the Church. Technological innovations and their applications in turn increased industrial productivity many times over and spurred industrialists towards producing more. As factories gradually generated higher profits, they also became attractive as investment objects for the early capitalists. The same development applied to the shopping malls, and both types of institutions developed into self-generating profit systems—nowadays to extremes in the form of multinational corporations.

Increasing consumerism is a precondition for economic growth, which has also become a mantra in political life and among policy makers generally. Recently, however, the economic growth focus tends to come in conflict with the idea of sustainable growth, as a sustainable society requires that the utilisation of resources does not exceed the renewal rate of the same resources. The present development does not meet these requirements because of the very high consumption of commodities, driven by and driving the economic growth process.

CONCLUSION

During the last fifty years, no real theories have been developed with impact outside of their individual research domains. Quantum theory and DNA are both examples of groundbreaking new theories that led to dramatic changes in scientific thinking. The last fifty years have seen new concepts emerge and smart terminology like *Postmodernity* and *paradigm* develop; these have partly helped structure scientific thinking but have not created new knowledge and theories.

These new labels do not say very much, and their contents have not provided any genuine new knowledge; they adapt to what Kuhn described as 'normal science'. In a critical approach to current research attitudes, Alvesson and Sandberg (2011) claim that established ways of generating research questions rarely express more ambitious and systematic attempts to challenge the assumptions underlying existing theories. Instead, they mainly try to identify and make use of gaps in existing research literature that seem necessary to fill. *Gap-spotting* thus tends to "remain within the box" rather than challenging existing models and theories or venturing out of the box to address problems from new and less orthodox angles.

Critical approaches towards modern society are by no means unique and are characteristic of the modern and democratic society itself, and the question of whether technological and economic progress in reality leads to a better society has been debated parallel to technological development.

Jürgen Habermas of the Frankfurt School questions the intelligibility of the modem society through its complex and non-transparent structures. Zygmunt Bauman (2004) raised a number of questions about whether modern society will survive in its present form, and Robert Putnam (2000) sees lack of human interaction as a sign of isolation and alienation ('Bowling Alone'). Weber early on questioned the strong influence from economic theory and economic models on political and societal development, and more recently the current organisation and management paradigms have been criticised by (among others) Garret Morgan (1997) and Mats Alvesson (1993).

There is a tendency today to regard economy, economic development and economic theory in a broader context in which history, social contexts, experiments and more realistic assumptions about society and human behaviour should replace abstract, unhistorical and unrealistic theories. The renewed interest in institutional theory and economic history is a hallmark of the new trend. The criticism does not, however, only affect the pure economists but also management and leadership theories. The late John Kenneth Galbraith, one of the more prominent critics of contemporary political and economic leadership, emphasised the role of mental insufficiency as an explanation factor for our inabilities ('for some strange reason much resistance has been mobilised to avoid regarding stupidity a decisive role in history') (1967).

Economic theory has been exposed to critical views ever since it first appeared as an academic discipline, resulting in major theory changes from the classical economy to the neoclassical school that now is under attack by contemporary economists who criticised many of the highly rational assumptions on which the neo-classicists based their theories and models—e.g., the perfect balance between demand and supply, the rational assumptions of the consumer (the economic man) and the self-inflicted (by economists) isolation of economic theory from the rest of society and other disciplines.

In the Western history of ideas, the concept of progress and the idea that development leads to progress is deeply rooted in contrast to earlier historic periods where life went on in regular cycles. The notion that progress is a linear development towards a better society is unique for the Western world and none of the two civilisations from which we have descended, the Jewish and the Greek-Roman ever had the thought of a linear, uninhibited progress.

As man's self-confidence was restored during the Renaissance, the power and influence of God gradually decreased as man put himself in the centre of things, manifested through his demand for the right of self-determination. Kant formulated this demand as "man's development from his self-imposed innocence", to free knowledge from the authority of the word, morality from the imposed obedience to the Church, and art from the constraint of honouring the holder of power (God). It was accepted not only that man had needs, but also that man himself was in the possession of the means to fill the needs.

NOTES

1. Thomas Kuhn became famous in the 1960s with his book *On the Structure of Scientific Revolutions* for using the word *paradigm* to mean a set of perceptions, values, methods, etc. held in common within a research community.
2. The term *Postmodernity* was introduced in 1979 by Jean-Francois Lyotard in his book *La Condition Postmoderne.*

REFERENCES

Alvesson, M. (1993) *Cultural Perspectives on Organisations.* London, Cambridge University Press.

Alvesson, M. and Sandberg, J. (2011) *Generating research questions through problematization.* Academy of Managements Review, 36 (2).

Bauman, Z. (2004) *Wasted Lives.* Cambridge, Blackwell Publishing.

Bhaskar, R. (1986) *Scientific realism and human emancipation.* London, Verso.

Blomkvist, N. and Lind, P. (2011) *The idea of progress and the needs of man.* Visby, Gotland University.

Edwards, A. (2005) *The sustainability revolution: Portrait of a paradigm shift.* Canada, New Society Publishers.

Friedman, T. (2009) *The great disruption.* International Herald Tribune, March 9.

Galbraith, J. (1967) *The New Industrial State.* Boston: Houghton Mifflin.

Habermas, J. (1971) *Knowledge and human interests.* Boston, Beacon Press.

Hawken, P. (1994) *The ecology of commerce: A declaration of sustainability.* New York, Harper Collins.

Kant, I. (1788/2003) *Kritik der Praktischen Vernunft* (Critique of Pure Reason). Horst D. Brandt und Heiner F. Klemme. Hamburg, Felix Meiner Verlag.

Kuhn, T. (1962) *The structure of scientific revolutions.* Chicago, The University of Chicago Press.

Lyon, D. (1994) *Postmodernity.* Buckingham, Open University Press.

Lyotard, J.-F. (1979) *La condition postmoderne.* Paris, Les Editions de Minuit.

Morgan, G. (1997) *Images of Organisation.* London, Sage.

Putnam, R. (2000) *Bowling Alone: The Collapse and Revival of American Community.* New York, Simon & Schuster.

Skinner, Q. (1985) Introduction: The return to grand theory in Skinner, Q. (Ed.) *The return of grand theories in the human sciences.* Cambridge, Cambridge University Press.

Von Wright, G.H. (1971) *Explanation and understanding.* Cornell, Cornell University Press.

Part II

Methods and Tools

In the 1970s, there was a growing focus on the individual in organisations as a reaction to the predominantly rational view that had reigned since the early 1950s. Scholars found ideas for alternative organisation studies in the field of anthropology with cultural values, symbols, rituals, and traditions, as well as stories being nurtured about heroes and historic events. Knowledge and understanding about different cultures was well documented in anthropological research, which had, however, not attracted any particular interest in organisation studies until the 1960s. With the decline of the hitherto dominant management paradigm referred to as Systems Rationality, the Human in the organisation came into focus. Consultants and researchers found relevant evidence in the new ideas from studies of firms and organisations and the culture metaphor established itself within a short time. Organisations that had developed a strong internal state of commitment and business effectiveness were said to have developed a strong organisation culture.

The cultural metaphor continued to attract interest in the 1970s and 80s in organisational studies, not least as Japanese management practice received increasing attention for its approach to individual responsibilities in the workplace and for its impact on quality in service and products. Focus on the individual in organisations had been a central theme in earlier research and had also characterised earlier organisation and management paradigms. But as models from anthropology were adopted and merged with organisational theory, the result was an organisational paradigm or model referred to as organisational culture in which the strong emphasis on individuals and human aspects broadened the definition of organisation and business performance.

An example of this broadening is the focus on customer and customer satisfaction as a theory for how to improve business and become competitive. From the theory, methods were developed to handle customer relations and to make customer requirements part of the business strategy. Regular customer contacts developed into feedback to measure service and quality levels from customer perspectives. Measuring tools such as the customer service index were developed (see Chapter 7).

In Chapter 6, we return to business performance and make a distinction between monitoring and assessment. The difference affects the models used, and examples of models such as benchmarking and SWOT are discussed and analysed.

Chapter 7 is dedicated to indicators used for performance monitoring. A brief history of indicators and several examples of indicators in business are presented. Criteria for the use of indicators for performance analysis are discussed.

Chapter 8 focuses on methods and tools for business development. Business development can have different objectives, such as growth and competiveness, and the methods vary depending on objective.

Chapter 9 deals with information technology and systems as important tools for business monitoring. Computer models are the result of two steps of simplification, from reality to a descriptive model of a phenomenon and from this descriptive model to a computer model characterised by restrictions in the computer software.

The conclusion of Part 2 resides with Chapter 10 in a discussion from a critical perspective of business models and their application in public sector organisations. Problems arise when a business model designed for private firms (with their short-term and well defined commitments to customers and clients) is adopted by public organisations (charged with very different obligations of long-term and varying commitments).

6 Models for Assessing Business Performance

When creating a model for performance assessment, it is of crucial importance to have as good an understanding as possible about those factors having the most significant impact on performance. In certain situations, assessment depends on and is subject to contextual rules and regulations, standards, references, principles and legal conditions that influence and sometimes determine whether performance is satisfactory or not. In other situations, where such endorsed references cannot be applied but assessment is rather based on perceptions, such as in the case of assessing work performance of individual employees, other types of models are needed. Such models are based on observations and assumptions about factors leading to poor or satisfactory performance. When rules, regulations and standards can be used as references, assessment is facilitated because actual performance is compared with established reference values. Actual cost or revenue results are satisfactory if they tally with specified reference estimates. Various models like those based on indicators (see Chapter 7) have been developed to facilitate this kind of assessment.

When endorsed references cannot be used to determine performance, there is need for specific understanding and awareness guiding subjective assumptions and interpretations for determination of satisfactory performance. With reference to the discussion about ontology and epistemology in Chapter 5, it is clear that different forms of knowledge are required, depending on the context. The ontological and epistemological questions concerning what is performance and how can we understand performance are the starting points as we endeavour to describe relevant models for assessing business performance. From an ontological perspective, performance does not exist per se, but we construct the concept of performance based on implicit assumptions, such as the completion of an activity or task. While *accomplish* refers to meeting a target or not, *performance* can vary on a scale from poor to excellent. When formal accounting routines were still the prevailing tools for performance assessment there were well defined models to measure liquidity, solidity and other accounting concepts. Nowadays, other parameters have become vital for assessing performance—not only one, but many different models have been formulated for assessing business performance.

The epistemological approach is central to our ability to comprehend performance—not only how we know but also who is to judge whether performance is acceptable or not. The models, having been developed for this purpose, tend to take either an external or internal perspective, or both. Taking both perspectives implies that the organisation must be seen both in its external and internal environment, defined by customers and clients, products and services, employees, management styles, history and readiness to change and adapt to changes in the environment. All these aspects are necessary to consider, and together they provide an impression of the organisation based on its internal culture, the managers' vision of the company, and the customers and client's impressions. Identifying how these three aspects correspond is important to obtain a complete picture about how the different organisational elements harmonize.

ALIGNING ESSENTIAL ORGANISATION ELEMENTS

A variety of organisation models exist where essential elements have been identified as being particularly important, both for performance in general as well as for branding. Such a model of three elements for a coherent organisation with clear objectives is based on vision, image and culture (Hatch and Schultz, 2001). Vision is the top management's aspirations for the strategy of the organisation. Culture is defined as the organisation's values, behaviour, history, and attitudes—the way the employees all through the ranks feel about the organisation they are working for. The third element is the Image, the outside world's overall impression of the company—customers, shareholders and owners, the media, the general public.

It is suggested that if the three elements are not properly aligned, there are alignment gaps. There may be a Vision and Culture *Gap,* an Image and Culture *Gap* or an Image and Vision *Gap.* Each of these gaps leads to poorer performance.

The Vision–Culture Gap

This misalignment develops when management moves the organisation in a strategic direction that employees don't understand or support. The gap usually emerges when management establishes a vision that is too ambitious for the organisation to implement. The main symptom: a breach between rhetoric and reality. Disappointed managers often blame employees for resisting change; frustrated employees react with suspicion. Such scapegoating is extremely dangerous for companies. To uncover possible gaps between corporate vision and culture, managers must determine if the organisation really practices the values it promotes and whether the vision and culture of the company is sufficiently different from those of its competitors.

The Image–Culture Gap

Misalignment between a company's image and organisational culture leads to confusion among customers and clients about what the company stands for. This usually means that the company does not practice what it preaches. To identify image–culture gaps, the company needs to compare what the employees are saying with what the customers and clients as well as other stakeholders are saying. For example, do employees care what stakeholders think of the company? And what images do stakeholders associate with the company?

The Image–Vision Gap

The third misalignment is the conflict between outsiders' images and management's strategic visions. Companies cannot afford to ignore their stakeholders: Indeed, the most carefully crafted strategic visions will fail if they are not aligned with what customers want from the company. Having sounded out employees and stakeholders, managers need to find out whether they are out of sync themselves. Important issues for resolution in this context include establishing a clear identification of company stakeholders and whether the company is effectively communicating its vision to these same stakeholders.

INTERNAL ASSESSMENT MODELS

Performance assessment is meant to provide an objective picture of the business, and a variety of methods have been developed with objectivity as the guiding principle. Since traditional methods of setting business targets (e.g., Standard Cost Analysis) have failed many companies, and blindsided their managers to competition in the process, a more general approach of assessing business and organisational strengths and opportunities has developed.

Two methods addressing this general approach are briefly discussed below viz. Benchmarking and the Balanced Scorecard.

BENCHMARKING

Two ancient truths illustrate the essence of benchmarking. More than two thousand years ago, a Chinese general (Sun Tzu) wrote, "If you know your enemy and know yourself, you need not fear the result of a hundred battles". More recently practitioners have observed the formal analogies between military and business strategies, between surviving on the battlefield and surviving in the marketplace. The other truth is a simple Japanese rule, viz. to be the best of the best. Both spell out the very essence of benchmarking (Lind, 2012).

Benchmarking is therefore a process with the ambition to change operations in a structured fashion to achieve superior (i.e., compared with competitors) performance. The suggested benefits of using benchmarking in a business context are that organisation functions are forced to investigate external industry best practices and incorporate those practices into their operations. The four steps of the benchmarking process are:

- Know your operation by assessing internal weakness and strengths. Your competitors will know your weaknesses. By knowing your strengths, you can defend yourself.
- Know the business leaders and the competitors so that you can differentiate your capabilities in the marketplace.
- Incorporate the best. Learn from business leaders and competitors. Why are they best in their competitive areas?
- Gain superiority by investigating, understanding, and implementing best practice.

Each step in the benchmarking process can be quite comprehensive, requiring both time and effort contributions to the process. In the first step the SWOT method (see below) can be a useful tool to further improve competitive profile information about the strong and weak aspects and parts of the organisation—for example, the way it is organised, the way it operates on the market and the way it manages its resources. Strengths and weaknesses may be influenced, and it is an important part of a manager's job to reinforce the strengths and to diminish the weaknesses. Too often, however, all the critical strengths and weaknesses that may apply to an organisation have not been properly identified.

The underlying benchmarking model suggests that certain parameters are identified both in the user organisation and in the compared organisation. This takes us back to the same basic problem of modelling: What are the criteria for choosing precisely the selected parameters? And in particular, is the understanding of the comparison organisation deep enough to justify a proper parameter choice?

Assessing the Model

By studying and analysing best practice among competitors and other types of seemingly successful organisations and firms, one must have identified and selected certain criteria for comparison. Such criteria originate within paradigms and from other models and are based on assumptions and convictions of what should be considered good performance. Like most generic models, they have managed to create pictures of facts and relationships that may hold sufficiently less detailed levels. The gap between macro and micro levels (of models) leads to inconsistency between models—actual behaviour and circumstances on micro level are not always possible to discern on a macro level and consequently not included in models on macro levels.

Benchmarking is a process and each step in the process spells out what is to be done in a generic manner. The second of the four steps described above—i.e., know the business leaders and the competitors so that you can differentiate your capabilities in the marketplace—can be described as a model in itself. Assumptions are made about the process to identify the business leaders (criteria, sustainability) and how the identified characteristics, features and functions of the specific culture of the 'best practice' company should be learnt and implemented into the specific culture of the 'follower'.

From what is known from innovation theory and practice about the three steps described as product innovation, process innovation and proprietary capability that comes from knowledge distinctive to the firm (Forbes and Wield, 2002), the learning process of the follower is a lengthy procedure and not only about 'differentiating your capabilities in the marketplace'. After this lengthy learning process has been carried out and is completed, it cannot be taken for granted that the 'best practice' company is still market leader and worthy of being imitated any longer. In their (at the time) highly influential and persuasive bestseller *In Search of Excellence* (Peters and Waterman, 1985) a number of 'best practice' companies were identified and analysed. Already in 1984 it was obvious that some of the 'best practice' firms were not exhibiting best practices anymore rather, they were in poor business condition. The whole idea of imitating 'best practice' as a highly vulnerable effort was noted by Chapman (2006) in his book *In Search of Stupidity: Over Twenty Years of High Tech Marketing Disasters*, which was published as a parody of *In Search of Excellence*.

When applying a generic model in a specific situation (a specific firm or organisation), we cannot know to what extent the 'best practice' example is best practice from a sustainability perspective, taking into account the effortful learning process. Benchmarking is a simplified model that provides a useful way of understanding important steps to improve business performance. To what extent it is also a useful model for a specific firm with a specific culture is another question.

BALANCED SCORECARD

"The balanced scorecard is defined as a strategic planning and management system to be used in business and industry as well as in government and non-profit organisations to align business activities to the vision and strategy of the organisation, improve internal and external communications, and monitor organization performance against strategic goals" (Kaplan and Norton, 1996). The balanced scorecard suggests that we view the organization from four perspectives, and to develop metrics, collect data and analyse it relative to each of these perspectives.

The balanced scorecard is a performance management approach that starts from a set of identified performance indicators with focus on learning and growth, the business process, customers' views of the organisation and the financial performance. The organisation's strategic goals are set after indicator values have been measured and results have been analysed. The complexity of the method and the time required to have all modules in place and evaluated suggests that the balanced scorecard method requires considerable time and staff resources. As with the benchmarking method, the crucial question is how parameters are selected and to what extent the selected parameters measure what really matters. A common approach behind the four selected perspectives is to investigate how others assess and value the company—for example, "How do we look to customers" and "How do we look to shareholders", with a bias toward financial stakeholders over others. Kaplan and Norton (ibid., 7) have commented upon the latter aspect:

> The balanced scorecard retains traditional financial measures. But financial measures tell the story of past events, an adequate story for industrial age companies for which investments in long-term capabilities and customer relationships were not critical for success. These financial measures are inadequate, however, for guiding and evaluating the journey that information age companies must make to create future value through investment in customers, suppliers, employees, processes, technology, and innovation.

Assessing the Model

A great variety of definitions can be found in response to the frequently asked question, 'What is a balanced scorecard model?' In combination with the difficulties noting a clear link between using the model and improvements in financial performance or more efficient decision making, another weakness is the scarcity of evidence about impacts on business performance. Lack of references to relevant research has also been noted (e.g., Norreklit, 2000).

The balanced scorecard is one of the most applied models for business performance, although the same or similar methods of business monitoring have been applied for a long time. Referring to the balanced scorecard as a revolution in management, therefore, seems slightly exaggerated. As with most generic models, it is embraced by supporters and criticised by others. Benchmarking and balanced scorecard are both such generic models that though they have many merits as concepts, they may turn out to be difficult to adapt for individual organisations trying to measure parameters that are stipulated by the model but not applicable to their own situations. If the information provided by the model cannot be traced back to a recognizable situation in the organisation, then the information, but also the measuring principles, are meaningless.

Increased awareness and understanding of the four areas that constitute the core of the balance scorecard model is essential to assess and improve performance. During the implementation process, the model will contribute to internal communication and learning, which may well be one of the real benefits. However, since the implementation of the balanced scorecard is a drawn-out and resource-demanding process, its focus may obscure consideration of other relevant and necessary performance indicators. The balanced scorecard hardly solves all performance shortcomings and should, therefore, be part of a bigger strategy that has been carefully found to be relevant and optimal for the specific organisation and firm.

> Balanced Scorecard can often paint with such a broad brush so many of a company's managers and employees will scoff at it, because they are being asked to measure objectives that have no bearing on them. This approach often fails to focus on how certain departments contribute to the overall direction of the business. When this occurs, logic is compromised and commitment to the approach wanes. Balanced Scorecard does not encourage open analysis and exploration of a company's strategy, and that may be its biggest fault (The Business Report, 2012).

EXTERNAL/INTERNAL ASSESSMENT MODELS—SWOT

Strengths, Weaknesses, Opportunities, Threats—SWOT

The SWOT analysis is well-known and widely used as a method to address the question of strategy formation from two perspectives: the *external perspective*, taking into account threats and opportunities in an organisation's environment, and the *internal perspective*, where strengths and weaknesses of the organisation come into focus. The two perspectives exhibit different degrees of control by the organisation.

Internal factors are important for achieving operational goals, but they are not unique in terms of influence, and while internal factors can be influenced by the organisation itself, this is normally not the case for *external factors* that originate outside of the organisation. External factors may be referred to as Opportunities and Threats in that they may create both opportunities as well as threats to the organisation and its prospects for reaching operational goals.

Taken together, Strengths and Opportunities constitute *driving* forces in the sense that they together facilitate achieving operational goals. Threats and Weaknesses are *hampering forces*, impairing achieving operational goals. In a collective context, driving and hampering forces are the critical success factors of the organisation. Identifying these factors and responding to them proactively is therefore a high priority management task.

The aim of the SWOT analysis is to identify possible appropriate actions that may have positive impact on the strategic and operational situation. Traditionally this analysis resulted in a large number of factors being identified through the SWOT exercise, leading to a cumbersome process of prioritising among those factors.

A revised version of the SWOT method enables a step-wise reduction of the numbers of factors until a handful of so-called Critical Success Factors remains as the final result of the SWOT exercise.

Factors Affecting Organisational Change

Assessing business performance may ultimately lead to a change process. The organisational culture tends, however, to develop its own mechanisms for preserving values and views, which may lead to a balance between the desire for internal stability and the need for adaptation to external change. Changing the culture of an organisation is one of the most difficult tasks facing all its constituent individuals (Rosenfeld and Wilson, 1999). This balance pattern was identified by Kurt Lewin (1951), an organisational psychologist who argued that changing this balance required an *unfreezing* of status quo in order to initiate a change process within the organisation, and later a *refreezing* to consolidate the new organisational status. The SWOT method is useful for observing and identifying factors leading to unfreezing.

Brief Description of the SWOT Method

The SWOT method was originally developed as a business analysis tool in the management literature where the analysis had a clearly identifiable strategic goal to shed light on *outside* opportunities and threats that could affect the future of a business. The analysis of a company's *internal* strengths and weaknesses, in turn, was intended to highlight certain strategies that the company could exploit, in particular, drawing attention to certain practices that the company needed to correct. Since exploitation and correction imply a change process, the related activities should be seen as a change project, and in analogy to using the SWOT method for strategy planning purposes, organisations also found the method useful to identify driving and hampering factors when implementing change projects. During the 1980s, public administration embraced this classical model of strategic planning, adopting the basic managerial model across such areas as regional development and municipal planning (Bryson and Roaring, 1987).

The SWOT method has thus found two application levels—on the organisational level, to identify driving and hampering factors of importance for business strategy decisions, and on the project level, to identify driving and hampering factors of importance for successful project implementation.

A SWOT analysis of the organisation will result in a number of critical success factors, each factor of particular importance and significance for the organisation to achieve its objectives. Once a critical success factor has been identified, a project may be formulated to carry out what is revealed by the factor. The project may in turn be analysed through a further SWOT analysis.

The four elements of an organisational SWOT analysis are:

- Strength—a resource or capacity of the organisation that can be used effectively to achieve its objectives;
- Weakness—a limitation, fault or defect in the organisation that will keep it from achieving its objectives;
- Opportunity—any favourable situation in the organisation's environment;
- Threat—any unfavourable situation in the organisation's environment that is potentially damaging to its strategy.

The actions to be undertaken that can be deduced from these four elements are to build on strengths, eliminate weaknesses, exploit opportunities and mitigate the effect of threats. The SWOT instrument is intended to highlight those dominant and determining factors, both within and outside of the organisation, that are likely to influence the success of the organisation, as well as to produce relevant strategic guidelines by linking the project to its environment. Simply put, the aim of the strategy is to increase both the level and relevance of information and thus reduce uncertainty.

The issue of context-sensitivity is seldom over-emphasised and may need further attention within strategic planning. The management literature itself acknowledges that SWOT analyses (and similar strategic planning exercises) should not be detached cerebral/academic exercises, but rather should be empirical exercises instructed by context-sensitive testing. Yet strategic planning has not been particularly sensitive to either action or context, instead portraying strategy formation as a systematic, highly rational, conscious, top-down process. Once strategies have been formed, they become a matter of pure implementation and action.

Even though the strategy formation stage (e.g., the assessment of strengths, weaknesses, opportunities and threats) is often depicted as thought independent of action, and strategy making as a process of conception rather than one of learning, it is necessary for all of these elements to be present in the strategic planning process. Concentrating on whether or not planners, civil servants or academics can effectively model a SWOT analysis matrix, which will form the basis of their actual development strategies, seems to neglect the fact that all of the elements of such an analysis are necessarily situational: internal capability can be assessed only with respect to an external context comprised of markets, political and social forces, competitors and their actions.

The above-mentioned problem can also be stated in terms of planning/ strategy formation and strategy implementation on different administrative levels. Regional SWOT analysis concentrates on the *region* in question, not on the *organisation* undertaking the SWOT, as was originally intended in the management sphere. Thus the risk exists that the strengths or weaknesses of the organisation implementing the strategy in a particular regional context will be overlooked. One could therefore argue that, difficult as it may be, organisational analysis of the *implementing* organisation should be an integral part of any SWOT analysis.

SWOT as a Learning Tool

The SWOT analysis is widely utilised and has an important role in balancing the external and internal elements influencing the implementation of a change project and allowing for project introspection as well as implementation planning that is sensitive to the external environment. As such, it can be seen as part of the *learning process* by which organisational change is filtered into the organisational development process. In current economic circumstances, enhancing organisational competitiveness is increasingly tied to the unique resources available within the organisation, and the notion of social capital as a resource has become all the more central. This, however, needs to be much more clearly acknowledged in the strategic planning process in order for organisational specificity to emerge as a strategic advantage.

In addition to the basic functional characteristics of SWOT analysis, the development of a SWOT exercise is almost by definition a *consensual* process. This is largely explained by the nature of change projects as well as by the fact that the issues included in the analysis seldom lend themselves to strictly objective or simply quantifiable indicators. The fact that the SWOT analysis is by definition a subjective process is further exacerbated by the dimension of internal analysis involved: The strengths and weaknesses outlined in the analysis should be based on the characteristics of the change project itself, and hence not *a priori* provable.

Assessing the SWOT Method

The SWOT method is assessed following the view that models are developed from assumptions leading to theories and methods. The underlying assumption that also makes the SWOT method different from other methods is the understanding that external as well as internal factors are of relevance and importance to review for performance. Based on this, the model identifies four parameters called strengths, weaknesses, opportunities and threats. This is, of course, a limitation since also other parameters might have been selected as model parameters. For example, organisations have acquired various degrees and forms of experience during their lifetimes that have settled as sediments that are decisive for how the organisation further develops. Such sediments are organisation culture, ownership ambitions, product ranges and the like. By considering such parameters, the static view in simply analysing the present situation can be enhanced to make the SWOT analysis a dynamic one in time. This would improve the logical consistency within the analysis and ensure correspondence to prevailing circumstances in the external environment.

The balance between external and internal analysis is a weak point in the method. Internal factors are more open to be discovered than external ones and the relevance of external factors may be difficult to grade on an importance and relevance scale. Attention should be paid to the degree of control. While internal factors may be easier to observe and influence, external factors, although important, may not be easily influenced or may be only marginally possible to influence. Also, identified factors can be perceived as catch phrases rather than relevant factors difficult to operationalize. Government rules and regulations, such as tax levels and import restrictions, may be seen as hampering the business but cannot be controlled on firm levels.

The SWOT analysis or exercise is the operational part of the method and performed as a group work with members of the analysed organisation. The result of the exercise is therefore subject to the members' capacity and understanding of the organisation. The exercise itself, in which views and opinions are exchanged, may be the most important result of the SWOT exercise and lead to essential discussions about problems and solutions from new and untried angles. The SWOT method does not, by itself, solve organisational problems, but it assesses critical success factors and is therefore a vital method for performance management!

CREATING AN ASSESSMENT MODEL FOR SMALL BUSINESS MANAGEMENT—EXAMPLE

In this example, a performance assessment model was created in which managers subjectively assessed general management attitudes within a region with regard to dynamism, problem orientation and opportunity orientation. Opinions are collected through questionnaires in which managers are asked to what extent they agree with a set of statements related to the three attitudes above. The model is not restricted to small firms but was developed with the focus on small and medium enterprises (SMEs).

Finding and analysing the subjective views of managers would be an important first step to describe managerial professional traits within a region. Data from the responders will show the statistical deviation and hence to what extent there is consensus or discrepancy between responders. In culturally homogenous regions, managers share views, to a large extent, with respect to the three aspects (Lind, 2009). As many programmes aiming at management capacity building start from a generic view about what type of managerial skills managers should have, the alternative approach suggested by the model is that managers themselves assess the type of competence, awareness and skills they would need in their professional activities. The model focus is on three identified generic aspects of management requirements—namely, dynamism, problem orientation and opportunity orientation.

Model Assumptions

Cultural aspects of organisational and management behaviour were hardly of any general interest until pioneering research in the early 1970s first linked the concept of culture with the study of organisations (Smircich, 1983). In the following years, the area expanded through extensive research and publications by Trompenaars (1993), Hofstede (1984), Schwarz (1992), Galtey, Lessem and Altman (1996), just to mention a few of the more influential scholars. Comparison of business attitudes in different regions has been presented by Bjerke (1999), as well as by Hickson and Pugh (1995), the latter in a somewhat anecdotal but still relevant account on managers in different cultures. Detailed studies of management in different European countries were conducted by Lawrence and Spybey (1986). Focus on the different research projects differs slightly among different scholars, even if the relations between humans and society and between individuals constitute the common focus.

The model suggested here may lend itself to identifying cultural influences on managers' attitudes and business behaviour. Although this is by now an established research area, it is not without controversy, as spelled out in the various critical approaches to the Hofstede studies (e.g., McSweeney, 2002). Rather than being too broad, the model focuses on three management attitudes—only and to what extent they may be related to cultural traits. For example, managers may be more or less prone to take business risks, or they may see the world as full of opportunities or problems. The three attitudes in focus here are dynamism (the manager being dynamic), the manager being problem oriented, and the manager being open to opportunities. In an attempt to correlate the three management attitudes with cultural characteristics, two of the cultural dimensions suggested by Hofstede (Power Distance and Uncertainty Avoidance) have been considered relevant (Lind, ibid.).

The model starts from the assumption that perceptions about problems (or threats) and opportunities can be used to characterise managers' attitudes to external events. The third variable is dynamism—a driving force of the manager that comes close to an individual desire for goal attainment. Although it is not obvious that these three dimensions should be typical for small business managers only, they are often referred to directly or indirectly in entrepreneurial research and literature (e.g., Schumpeter, 1934).

The Model

How can one identify a very few but still representative characteristics of management attitudes to constitute the basis for a questionnaire? Since the firm is part of its environment, the manager's behaviour is a response to perceptions about events, external as well as internal to the firm. Perception is a process through which the individual organises and interprets external information. Perceptions are therefore influenced by context but also by personality, experience, motivation and needs (Kaufmann and Kaufmann, 1996).

The individual perception process is strongly selective and predetermined in the sense that the mental and intellectual reference framework has already been established. Interpretation of events seeks support from the reference framework and is the basis for decisions and actions. Managers' perceptions of the environment seem to be influenced by such predetermined interpretation about *threats* and *opportunities* (Jackson and Dutton, 1988). Threats imply that events are seen as negative and difficult to control, whereas opportunities are easier to control, are positive and are associated with profit.

In order to identify each of the three characteristics through the questionnaire, four statements were defined accordingly, and managers were requested to decide what attitude was to be taken to each of the twelve statements according to a Lickert scale (Fully Agree, Partly Agree, etc.). A high degree of agreement with the statements in the opportunity group indicated predominantly opportunity-oriented mangers. A typical statement in this group is, for example, 'SME managers are aware that concern about environment issues is an important business asset'.

Table 6.1 presents the statements used in the model. The grouping into opportunity, problem and dynamism was not shown to the managers; the statements were randomly presented in the questionnaire in order not to become leading.

The model suggests that the three selected aspects of management traits can be linked to cultural differences. The current critical discussion about Western management theories and models and their applicability or lack of applicability in non-Western contexts has been on the agenda for the last twenty years (Davies et al 1989; Alvesson and Willmott 1992) and has painted rather broad pictures without going much into details. Culture and cultural aspects of management behaviour have been in focus in management training both on academic and professional levels. As many of the attempts to explain weak organisational and management performance are of a general nature, the model has the capability to relate dynamism, opportunity orientation and problem orientation with different cultural attributes , such as the distribution of power in organisations or uncertainty and lack of trust.

Assessing the Model

The arbitrary grouping of management characteristics into opportunity and problem orientation together with dynamism is one out of many alternative selections, and there is limited substantial support from theory and not enough evidence that the selection should be of particular relevance and importance. On the other hand, with reference to earlier discussion in Chapter 2 about the discrepancy between models and hypotheses, we must accept that models are mostly more akin to hypotheses than to certainty. And a hypothesis is justified until its antithesis has not been proved.

The vast literature on cultural impact on management behaviour is predominantly a discussion on a high aggregate level with efforts to characterise

Table 6.1   Statements used in the model

Characteristics	Statements
Opportunity oriented (sensitive and open to current trends in business and society)	• There is a general awareness among SME managers that concern about environment issues is becoming a true business asset • Women are encouraged to actively participate in the business process as entrepreneurs and managers • SMEs in general consider employees as their most important resources • SMEs are innovative in exploiting new product and service niches
Problem oriented (a feeling of being exposed to and threatened by external uncontrollable factors)	• Uncertainty about the future is a hampering factor for SME business • SME development is primarily constrained by lack of capital • SME development is hampered by a general lack of technology • SMEs compete primarily with the help of price
Dynamic (proactive and eager to take initiatives)	• SMEs in general have close customer contacts and are keen to meet customer needs • It happens quite often that SMEs co-operate in networks to win customer orders • SMEs are in general very quality minded in the products and services they provide • It is acceptable for an employee to argue with the manager

countries according to different scales and dimensions. With these studies as starting points it is not, however, obvious if the same dimensions, scales and characteristics can be used for the vertical comparison between regions or individual firms. By letting individual managers give witness to what their concerns are in doing business, the cultural aspects may come out as explanation factors.

PERFORMANCE MANAGEMENT

Performance Management refers to a term coined by Aubrey Daniels in the late 1970s to describe an application method for managing behaviour and results, the two critical elements of what is known as performance.

Performance Management followed as a further extension to the total quality management concept with a more systematic focus on overall performance that can be improved by improving the performance of individuals within a team framework.

A variety of definitions and characteristic features of Performance Management break with earlier and traditional measures of performance, which were almost entirely based on the accounting systems. Johnson (1992) was an early critic of using traditional accounting information to measure business performance. He thus insisted that if companies were to compete effectively, they would need to remove accounting information from their operational control systems and relieve their accounting departments of responsibility for providing information to control business operations. Accounting systems provide almost no information about customers other than revenue data. And revenue data simply tell what customers paid for items received. They say nothing about whether customers wanted or liked what they received (Johnson, ibid.).

Performance Management programmes are based on assumptions about what customers appreciate and demand in terms of attitudes and service. A number of activities are recommended and promoted in the Performance Management literature, such as communicating and clarifying job responsibilities, adding value by encouraging skills development and defining performance standards. Performance Management is also said to promote superior performance by communicating expectations and establishing achievable benchmarks.

From such brief characterisations, it is not easy to see what makes the Performance Management concept differ significantly from other concepts promoting effective organisations. Theories about business performance are not isolated from theories about organisational performance, even if all organisations are not business oriented. The difference lies in the measure—business performance should be assessed by the customer, while other types of non-business organisation may have other ways of measuring goal achievements. As discussed briefly in the first chapter, organisational performance is a nuanced concept that means different things depending on perspective.

The Concept

A key feature of Performance Management is that managers and employees together drive the organisation in a direction where performance targets consistent with the organisation's capacity and capability are developed. This implicitly assumes, however, that the earlier discussed organisation elements of Vision, Culture and Image are sufficiently well aligned and that gaps between them have been adequately eliminated. Benefits alleged to be achieved through Performance Management range from direct financial gains to a motivated workforce and improved management control.

A literature review indicates that financial gains come from *inter alia* growth in sales and cost reduction; a motivated workforce results from *inter alia* optimisation of incentive plans to specific goals for overachievement and high confidence in bonus programmes; improved management control is facilitated by simplified communication of strategic goals. Performance is thought of as actual results versus desired results. Any discrepancy where actual is less than desired could constitute the performance improvement zone. The simplicity of this criterion as well as the generic list of perceived benefits does not take the Performance Management concept beyond other very basic performance concepts.

Practically all activities in an organisation are geared at providing value for somebody who is prepared to pay for it. A simple and also very basic question is therefore recipient satisfaction with what he receives. Numerous parts of the current Performance Management mumbo jumbo can be scrapped and replaced with serious efforts to establish a customer dialogue for performance feedback. In a review of Performance Management published in *Forbes* in 2012, Effron and Ort (2010) claim that

> "Everybody hates it—employees and managers alike";
> "Nobody does it well—it's a skill that seemingly fails to be acquired despite exhaustive training efforts";
> "It fails the test of construct validity—it doesn't do what it was designed to do, i.e. increase performance".

The performance management process gets subjected to its own methods of setting criteria and rating performance against them—and fails.

Performance studies presuppose a set of assumptions about cause-effect relations that conceptualize *performance* as a model. The model recognises various factors with impact on the company's performance, albeit in a hierarchical order: All factors should be subject to meeting customer satisfaction, as illustrated in the Sandcone model below.

The Sandcone Performance Model

This model was introduced in the 1990s by Ferdows and de Meyer (1990). It suggests that a lasting gain in performance develops only if service attitudes to the customers are implemented in a logical sequence, layer-on-layer—hence the analogy of building a sandcone. For stability, the base of the Sandcone must be both wide enough and sound enough to support additional 'layers' (i.e., the further performance improvements).

The Sandcone model (Figure 6.1) has four layers: quality, dependency or reliability, speed and costs. The foundation is quality. There is enough evidence today that a basic requirement of business is quality in products and services. The model therefore underlines that reducing production or delivery times to customers has limited value unless quality is satisfactory.

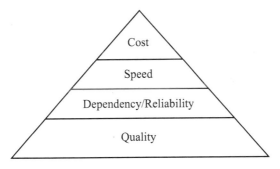

Figure 6.1   The Sandcone model (Ferdows and de Meyer, 1990)

Even more unsuccessful is any attempt at reducing costs in the company if quality cannot be guaranteed.

In summary, the Sandcone model indicates that costs should not be reduced without first considering quality improvements, reliability and speed, in that order. Therefore, the creation of value requires that quality improvements be made prior to the hunt for speed, reliability or cost reductions. The base of the cone is built with quality. Without the base, the sand cone cannot achieve the next step of reliability because the interior cone, quality, is missing. By the same token, the development of speed in an organization cannot take place without the supporting cones of quality and reliability, and once speed is accomplished, the final step, cost reductions, is made possible.

Morgan (1997) recounts many companies that have shown that it is impossible to truly know one's customers and potential customers at a distance. One has to join them. One has to share their experience. One has to understand the relevance and benefits from products and services from *their* point of view. Lind (2012) claims there is a general lack of a dialogue between supplier and customer. It is of utmost importance for a supplier to research what the expected or perceived benefits to the client are. Such information can only be obtained through dialogue, and through the creation of sufficient trust between the two parties.

The Customer's Customer Concept

The aim of the supplier-customer dialogue should therefore be to understand how the supplier's products and services can contribute to improving the customer's business with its own customers. The Customer's Customer Concept (Figure 6.2) is a simple way of highlighting the importance of a creative and explorative supplier-customer dialogue in which not only selling but also listening to customer requirements is of importance.

Traditionally, contact between supplier and customer is aimed at maximising sales of the supplier's products and services. As such, the supplier has

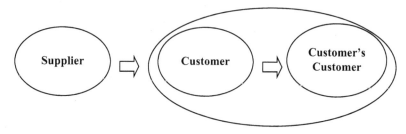

Figure 6.2   The Customer's Customer Concept (Lind, 2012)

little knowledge about the customer's market situation and no real incentives to learn. By finding out more about the customer, and in particular about the customer's customer(s), the supplier can learn how its products and services contribute to the customer's business, leading ultimately to increased trust on the part of the customer and dependence on the supplier. Customer encounters are seen as opportunities to learn and inform, not just as opportunities to present and sell. When trust has been created, such encounters will increase over time as customer and supplier learn more about each other's wants and opportunities and become more mutually dependent.

Measuring a company's performance must be based on how performance is perceived by an outsider rather than by reference to a variety of internally developed procedures and rules irrespective of their perceived relevance and importance. Essentially, performance can only be assessed by the receiver of a service. Performance Management is only a thin shield without any real substance unless it is based on a thorough dialogue and created trust between supplier and receiver of business activities.

PERFORMANCE MANAGEMENT AND ORGANISATIONAL CULTURE

Performance Management was hardly a coherent concept before the 1950s, when accounting-based management information was designed to meet performance targets set through the management accounting system! The prevailing organisation paradigm of that time is mostly referred to as systems rationality. This paradigm was essentially characterised by a strong focus on technology and systematisation. The organisation was regarded as a system of bolts and wheels and machines—and humans. By defining the organisation as a set of components, it was possible to define problems and solutions in the language of natural science, where mathematics and formal approaches could be applied.

As Organisation Culture gradually became a more attractive perspective for organisation studies around the end of the 1970s and early 1980s, the focus also shifted to the role and importance of the individual in the organisation, and in this way Organisation Culture marked a difference from the previous Systems Rationality. While earlier measures of performance were based on accounting data, individuals within as well as outside of the organisation now became the key.

BOX 6.1 MINI-ENCYCLOPAEDIA: SYSTEMS RATIONALITY AND ORGANISATIONAL CULTURE

A. Systems Rationality
This management and organisational paradigm may be approximately dated to the period 1950–1980 and was to a great extent a consequence of the Cold War and tension between the West (particularly the USA) and the Soviet Union. The launching of the Sputnik satellite in 1957 marked a significant Soviet advantage over the USA in development in science—in particular, in the application of computers for scientific purposes. The immediate reaction in the USA was more emphasis on technology and natural science in teaching and research. A similar development was seen in the social sciences, with a growing focus on and application of systems theory, encouraged by views expressed in *General Systems Theory* published in 1968 by the biologist van Bertalanffy. In organisations, both machines and people can be regarded as systems components, according to the systems theory. New disciplines emerged, like Operational Analysis and Cybernetics, both convinced that scientific methods borrowed from mathematics, physics and statistics were superior in addressing and resolving organisational issues. Systems Rationality was obviously a highly rational approach to organisation theory.

B. Organisational Culture
The decline of the Systems Rationality period began with a notion that had gradually developed that suggested that people cannot simply be regarded as systems components. In addition, systems are grave simplifications when it comes to describing organisations, in particular as the human interaction with organisation structures creates non-linearity; for example, doubling input does not necessarily lead to double the output. Chaos theory, when applied to organisations, showed that under specific conditions organisations can behave completely unexpectedly. Organisations involving people cannot be predicted based on the past.

An alternative to traditional studies of organisations has come from anthropology and the notion that organisations tend to develop their own cultures. Large companies like IBM were identified as examples of how a strong internal culture image with emphasis on customers, suppliers and employees creates business assets. Lately, however, recent events from the corporate sphere history tell us that organisational cultures can be manipulated. Attempts at broadening the view about what organisations really are have been successful though the introduction of metaphors that, in addition to cultures, also can compare the organisation with machines, political systems, prisons, etc. Using culture as the platform for research on organisational behaviour has created new insights into the contextual importance for understanding organisational behaviour. Too much popularisation of some of the research that has been conducted on organisation and country levels (e.g. Hofstede, 1984) has, however, simplified reality and measured often-immeasurable parameters, such as degrees of masculinity or femininity, which cannot be assumed to be evenly distributed within an organisation, even less on a national level.

In the new paradigm, in which the metaphor of organisational culture has been quickly absorbed by consultants and academics as a catchy concept, it has been readily adopted for many purposes—for example, as Performance Management. Figure 6.3 illustrates how a concept like Performance Management develops as a consequence of the prevailing paradigm.

MANAGEMENT PERFORMANCE BY FEEDBACK

Organisational performance can be measured on different levels in the organisation. Utilisation of financial as well as physical resources is determined by comparing actual consumption of energy, or actual costs for material, with respective estimated targets. Productivity as a ratio between created output and required input can be a performance measure, depending on which variables are selected. Added value as the difference between income from sales and costs for purchased material is a relevant performance measure.

Regardless of whether the performance measure focus is on internal resource utilisation or productivity, like added value, the very basic aspect of performance is to what extent the customers are satisfied with what they get! Figure 6.3 is a schematic illustrating how Performance Management has been developed within the framework of the current organisation paradigm.

Organisations are continuously being studied and observed by those who have this as their interest—researchers, consultants and others. Sharing and exchanging views and tentative conclusions from such observation will ultimately lead to a shared view about anomalies that cannot be accepted as a basis for organisational studies and which therefore have to be modified or abandoned, as with the Systems Rationality view. As the new understanding developed about organisations and humans in organisations, the emerging shared view justified new questions to be formulated and to be asked. Other and maybe hitherto new and unexplored areas were identified where opportunities were created for new concepts like Performance Management.

The new concept is now introduced to managers through training and consulting service as a practice to become adopted and integrated in the organisation's strategic approach. Like many other concepts being introduced and adopted by firms for improvement purposes, the 'one size fits all' approach is a handicap that negatively affects most of them. Even if a generic codification of management practice may have been integrated into the concept at the design phase, it is highly unlikely that it can be generalised to all organisations. Since we define performance as a model

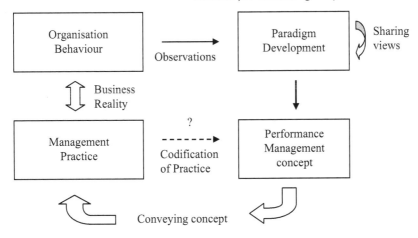

Figure 6.3   Performance Management by feedback

concept where cause-effect relations are assumed, the performance model has the same limitations as other models. We can therefore refer back to Chapter 4 and its question of whether the performance model is transferable in space.

IS PERFORMANCE MANAGEMENT A FAD?

By a *fad*, we mean a characterisation, in a pejorative sense, of a new business concept with an attractive message that is not necessarily called for by the business community but for various reasons has become popular. After a period, the fad is replaced by a newer popular idea that also is not required. Adrian Furnham, a British organisational psychologist, identified twelve business concepts that he identified as business fads. They all appeared in the period from the 1950s through the 1990s and are listed below in chronological order (Furnham, 2004):

- Management by objectives
- Matrix management
- Theory Z
- One-minute management
- Management by wandering around
- Total quality management
- Business process reengineering
- Delayering
- Empowerment
- 360-degree feedback
- Re-engineering
- Teamwork

Performance Management should not be considered a fad because monitoring performance is a vital management task in any organisation. But the current conception of Performance Management and its suggested implementation meets the criteria of a fad. It is a simple concept and easy to understand and framed with buzzwords like 'direct financial gains through sales growth', 'cost reductions', 'no project overruns', and so on. A few key sentences convey fundamental messages like, 'There is a clear and immediate correlation between using performance management programmes or software and improved business and organisation results'. Such an assertion qualifies well for the fad label!

Performance Management is prescriptive and tells managers to implement the concept without any detailed knowledge about the context of the firm, its capacity and competence levels and its market situation. As with other fads in the list above, it prescribes the recipes that managers must follow in order to achieve the benefits. But recipes can be misinterpreted or misunderstood and the concept be inadequately applied. Fads promise outcomes such as greater effectiveness, more motivated and productive employees, and deeply satisfied customers. But reality shows that most fads are good at raising hopes—not as good at delivering results.

A pretentious characteristic of a fad is its 'one size fits all' approach and the absence of any self-critical views. An article on leadership in *Forbes* business magazine (Vorhauser-Smith, 2012) acknowledges the failure of Performance Management to achieve what it set out to achieve, and the author assures that "there are three reasons almost all current performance management systems are broken". The three reasons mentioned (without any references) are that people have changed, technology has changed and people's relationship with their technology has changed. The author claims, however, that there is light at the end of the tunnel.

> Performance Management will change in 2013 as the "big data and analytics movement" has now really raised the bar—not just in terms of what data can be gathered, aggregated and analysed but also how it is filtered and presented to audiences to provide immediate management insights. And also there will be a shift in focus from process to outcomes—burn the forms!

It seems that Performance Management will continue being a fad.

CONCLUSION

While strategic tools assist the manager in strategic thinking and formulating strategic plans, operational tools assist the manager in dealing with problems in real time. Measuring and comparing is the same as managing operational performance to meet expectations, such as controlling costs within budget frames or maintaining customer service at high levels.

To assess operational performance, one needs to measure those output parameters that give the most adequate picture of the firm or organisation from a performance point of view. Such parameters typically include production, finance, and customer-market relations. Performance assessment must be of highest quality and be taken seriously within the organisation. Ready-made models can be useful but must comply with the contextual conditions that apply in each individual case.

The Performance Management concept as discussed in this chapter has attracted much interest but has also been met with scepticism and complaints that promises have not been fulfilled. Generic concepts that are sometimes referred to as business fads fail because they simplify reality too much, they are too rational in their views about humans and the roles they play in organisations, and they mostly underestimate the time and effort it takes to implement new organisational procedures.

Because fads are by their very nature suited for a simple world, they have limited utility in the real one.

Few management approaches are universally applicable, and attempts to implement a mismatched approach can do more harm than good.

REFERENCES

Alvesson, M. and Willmott, H. (1992) *Making sense of management: A critical introduction.* London, Sage.

Bjerke, B. (1999): *Business leadership and culture.* London, Edward Elgar.

Bryson, J. and Roaring, W. (1987) *Applying private sector strategic planning in the public sector.* Journal of the American Planning Association, 53 (1).

Chapman, R. (2006) *In search of stupidity: Over twenty years of high tech marketing disasters.* New York, Apress.

Davies, J. (Ed.) (1989) *The challenge to Western management development.* London, Routledge.

Effron, M. and Ort, M. (2010)*One page talent management: Eliminating complexity, adding value.* Harvard, Harvard Business School Press.

Ferdows, K. and de Meyer, A. (1990) *Lasting improvements in manufacturing performance: In search of a new theory.* Journal of Operations Management, 9 (2).

Forbes, N. and Wield, D. (2002) *From leaders to followers—Managing technology and innovation.* London, Routledge.

Furnham, A. (2004) *Management and myths: Challenging business fads, fallacies and fashions.* Basingstoke, Palgrave Macmillan.

Galtey, S., Lessem, R. and Altman, Y. (1996) *Comparative management—A transcultural odyssey.* London, McGraw-Hill.

Hatch, M. and Schultz, M. (2001) *Are the strategic stars aligned for your corporate brand. Boston,* Harvard Business Review (February).

Hickson, D. and Pugh, D. (1995): *Management worldwide: The impact of societal culture on organisations around the globe.* London, Penguin Books.

Hofstede, G. (1984): *Culture's consequences.* Beverly Hills, CA, Sage.

Jackson, S. and Dutton, J. (1988) *Discerning threats and opportunities.* Administrative Science Quarterly, 33 (3).

Johnson, T. (1992) *Relevance regained. From top-down control to bottom-up empowerment.* New York, The Free Press.

Kaplan, R. and Norton, D. (1996) *The balanced scorecard.* Boston, Harvard University Press.

Kaufmann, G. and Kaufmann, A. (1996) *Psykologi i organisation och ledning* (in Swedish). Studentlitteratur, Lund.

Lawrence, P. and Spybey, T. (1986) *Management and society in Sweden.* London, Routledge.

Lewin, K. (1951) *Field theory in social science.* New York, Harper.

Lind, P. (2009) *SME managers' views on SME Management—a comparative study.* The 4th International Conference on Management Theory and Practice. Tartu University, Estonia. April.

Lind, P. (2012) *Small business management in cross-cultural environments.* London, Routledge.

McSweeney, B. (2002) *Hofstede's model of national cultural differences and their consequences: A triumph of faith—a failure of analysis.* Human Relations, 55 (1).

Morgan, G. (1997) *Images of organisations.* Thousand Oaks, CA, Sage.

Norreklit, H. (2000) *The balance on the Balanced Scorecard—A critical analysis of some of its assumptions.* Management Accounting Research, 11 (1).

Peters, T. and Waterman, R. (1985) *In search of excellence.* New York, Grand Central Publishing.

Rosenfeld, R. and Wilson, D. (1999) *Managing organizations.* Berkshire, McGraw-Hill.

Schumpeter, J. (1934) *The theory of economic development.* Cambridge, MA., Harvard University Press.

Schwarz, S. (1992) *Universals in the content and structure of values: Theoretical advances and empirical tests in 20 countries.* Advances in Experimental Social Psychology, 25.

Smircich, L. (1983) *Concepts of culture and organisational analysis.* Administrative Science Quarterly, 28 (3).

The Business Report. (2012) Is the Balanced Scorecard 'strategic approach' revolutionary or fallacy? December 14. http://brandyourbiz.blogspot.com/2012_12_01_archive.html

Trompenaars, F. (1993) *Riding the waves of culture.* London, The Economist Books.

van Bertalanffy, L. (1968) *General system theory: Foundations, development, applications.* New York, Braziller Publisher.

Vorhauser-Smith, S. (2012) Three Reasons Performance Management will Change in 2013. Forbes. December 16. http://www.forbes.com/sites/sylviavorhausersmith/2012/12/16/the-new-face-of-performance-management-trading-annual-reviews-for-agile-management/

7 Performance Indicators

An indicator is a simple key to access information about an activity, a process, or situation development. One of the simplest indicators is a ratio between numbers such as a part compared with the whole—for example, the number of people in a region out of work as a share of all people of the region. This indicator enables the comparison between regions and provides more information than just the absolute comparison of jobless in one region with the number of jobless in another region. By calculating the ratio between jobless and total population, the percentage of jobless in one region can easily be compared with the percentage in another. The percentage is thus one type of an indicator. The French historian Fernand Braudel created simple ratios between data series over long periods in Europe to discover occurrences of significant impact on the economic and social development of Europe. Data series of harvests of wheat in a region for a period of years was compared with another series showing the population growth for the same region and the same time period. By calculating the ratio between tons of wheat and growth of people, he could detect a break in the trend that might indicate the beginning of a period of hunger and famine (Braudel, 1979).

Performance can be measured and determined at a specific point in time or during a time period. In the first case, the measure can be a well-defined unit, such as the number of jobless people at a certain point in time or change during a period. The measure can also be in the form of an indicator designed as a ratio between actual jobless and the number of jobless that had been expected in predictions made a year before. Measure can be a product of price and volume to obtain the total revenue, as a difference between business revenues in two markets, or simply a categorical statement like *function* and *does not function*. Performance measured during a time period can be based on a series of indicators. Indicators are thus used as relative measures for comparison and also for creation of time series as trends extrapolated into the future for forecasting.

A most common use of indicators in business is for financial purposes to measure the financial condition of the firm or organisation. Such indicators illustrate the strength of the percentage share of equity, also referred to as the solvency ratio, one of many ratios used to measure a company's ability to meet long-term obligations. Liquidity is another financial measure of the extent to which an organization has cash to meet immediate and short-term obligations, or assets that can be quickly converted to do this. Other common measures are return on capital employed and the profitability ratio, defined as earnings compared to expenses and other relevant costs incurred during a specific time period. The annual financial report that is compulsory for registered firms and organisations uses indicators as a neat way to get quick insight into the financial condition of each organisation.

PERFORMANCE INDICATORS

Non-financial indicators for industry purposes were developed in the 1890s and later for automatic ship steering by the Russian-American engineer Nicholas Minorsky, who designed an automatic steering system for the US Navy (Bennet, 1984). Minorsky observed the behaviour of a helmsman controlling the ship's movements by means of the helm connected to the rudder. The helmsman controlled the ship not only based on the current difference between set and actual course error, but also on past error and current rate of change. The task of the helmsman is to keep the ship on a stable course, which means that proportional control should provide stability against small disturbances. That was, however, not enough for dealing with a steady disturbance like rough weather, which required managing an accumulated deviation from course. Finally, based on the accumulated deviation, future expected deviations from the course must be managed.

The thus-introduced algorithm for automatic control involves three indicators referred to as the PID algorithm, an acronym for Proportional, Integral and Derivative. These values can be interpreted in terms of time: *P* depends on the *present* error (i.e., deviation from a planned value), *I* on the accumulation of *past* errors, and *D* is a prediction of *future* errors (trend), based on current rate of change. P-type indicators are often in the form of ratios for which the reference value can be a number. Typical P-type indicators are of the expression (All–Some)/All, which should be as close to 1 as possible. An example is production efficiency, where *All* is all produced and *Some* is the number of defective products produced.

Another P-type indicator has the form Actual/Estimated, which should be less than 1 or greater than 1, depending on the situation. An example is actual revenue compared to forecasted revenue, which should preferably be greater than 1. The P-type indicator can also have the form (Actual X)/(Actual Y), which should be greater than 1 or less than 1. An example is total enterprise performance, where Actual X is sales and Actual Y is cost, which should always be greater than 1.

For these indicators, it may also be of interest to monitor the trend (D-type) to assess how performance is developing over time. This comparison is often more useful than comparing one and the same parameter with another enterprise, since the underlying conditions in different enterprises can often be very different. Financial reporting is mostly of I-type—for example, accu mulated sales. The parameter is here integrated with time, which means that more significant information leading to a follow-up activity requires that sufficient time has elapsed.

Indicator Example—Customer Service Index (CSX)

The following indicator measures one aspect of customer relations—serviceability. The Customer Service Index (CSX) measures the accumulated ratio between good and bad shipment per period and is thus of I-type. The indicator is constructed in the following way:

CSX = (Number of total shipments – Defective shipments)/(Number of total shipments)

The idea of the CSX is that customers who order products to be delivered are anxious to receive the shipment on time, in the right quantity and according to specifications (size, colour, etc.). The number of total shipments is counted per period (e.g., per month) and it is volume of shipments rather than value that is of interest. CSX can never be greater than 1.0 (number of faulty shipments can never be greater than total shipments!) but should ideally come as close to 1.0 as possible, where 1.0 is the ultimate goal for good customer service. The CSX may vary with time, as shown in Figure 7.1.

The reference value in the diagram above is set as a quality goal—for example, a value of 0.85 means that at least 85 per cent of all shipments in a month should be according to specifications (on time, in right quantity, etc.). In the diagram, this happens for the first time at point T. Now the service level should be further improved, and the next step is to set the reference value at 0.88, then at 0.90, etc. The ultimate goal is, of course, 1.0.

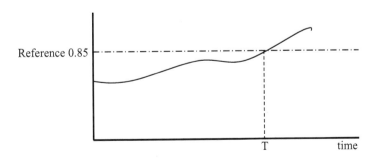

Figure 7.1   Customer service index (CSX)

This indicator serves both as a quality measure and an incentive tool: Those employees responsible for shipments may have extra benefits when the CSX value for the first time reaches the reference line!

It can be argued that the CSX indicator is too simple a tool to be used as a proper service quality measure. However, most small and medium enterprises rarely use any particularly sophisticated methods for quality follow-up of shipments, yet it is one of the more important aspects of customer service. As a matter of fact, most SMEs do not even know if they have a good or a bad record when it comes to customer shipments! Initiating a system to record shipments is the very important first step towards better quality in customer service.

The Customer Service Index is one of a family of indicators with similar function. For example, a Production Quality Index (PQX) in which defective produced parts are compared with total produced parts is constructed in the same way as the CSX.

KPI—KEY PERFORMANCE INDICATORS

Key performance indicators or key success indicators are based on the assumption that successful business management requires continuous monitoring of the business process in order to assess the performance of the firm. Improved performance can only be achieved when managers are properly informed about current performance. Key Performance Indicators are supposed to be the key to business success by providing the decision maker with instant information about activities as they happen compared with what was estimated or expected. Changes in organisations may benefit by applying key performance indicators to monitor the change process. Each indicator is responsible for a specific aspect of the monitoring and there should not be too many of them in order to make them manageable.

The balanced scorecard method discussed in Chapter 6 is also about identifying relevant indicators as monitoring tools to judge performance. Indicators are highly instrumental as they provide a quick glance of the situation, and they are also well suited for showing trends. But indicators are defined through a selection process in which seemingly important parameters are selected to make the indicator. The dilemma is the same that has been discussed about models elsewhere in this book—how do we know that the selected parameters are the most important and significant and what about those parameters may we be aware of but cannot quantify, let alone measure. Examples of such parameters are individual creativity, working atmosphere in the firm, and managers' ability to create motivated employees.

DJS Research Ltd is a UK-based market research company with views about key performance indicators and their usefulness. With our ambition to critically scrutinize this and other models used for business monitoring purposes, the statements about KPIs below are reviewed from this perspective.

DJS Research Ltd (n.d.) states:

> Motivated people are good for business. The relationship between strong motivation and strong performance is well recognised. Not only are well motivated people usually more productive but they also present a more positive image to outsiders (including clients). To this end it is important to identify key performance indicators (KPIs) that will enable management to monitor progress. There are three areas of activity within a professional firm that are critical to commercial and professional success and KPIs need to be established in each: 1) Measures relating to financial performance and business development; 2) Views of clients about the range, provision and delivery of the professional service firm's services; 3) Views of personnel about all aspects of their relationship with the professional service firm.

Assessment: Key performance indicators are supposed to help managers monitor progress, which comes naturally from motivated employees; this is a core assumption behind the model wherein strongly motivated employees are more productive and also present a more positive image to outsiders, including clients. This is an assumption that may be justified, but is also suggested without any proof. There are two critical approaches to this assumption. First, with reference to earlier discussion (in Chapter 6) about aligning essential organisation elements and the gaps between image and vision as well as between image and internal culture, there are various means to motivate employees (salaries, benefits, rewards), but the image to outsiders can still be weak or even bad because of wide image-vision or image-culture gaps.

Second, strong motivation and strong performance are not necessarily correlated, according to Hirschman (1970), who groups the employees into four categories with respect to two dimensions—degree of creativity and attitudes towards the company. Figure 7.2 describes the typology:

The four categories can be described as follows. The *engaged* employee is creative, positive toward the company and its employer, and motivated. The *critical* employee can be described as the *devil's advocate*—creative, competent and well performing but critical about the state of affairs, dominated by a negative attitude toward the firm and, hence, not very motivated. The *loyal* employee may have worked in the firm for a long time and due to age or reduced capacity has lost creativity and ambition. The *exit* refers to an employee who is uncomfortable in the company for a variety of reasons, which makes him or her less creative and not positive toward the company. It can therefore not be taken for granted that "motivated people are good for business", but probably that a high performance business has motivated people. That is, however, a different model.

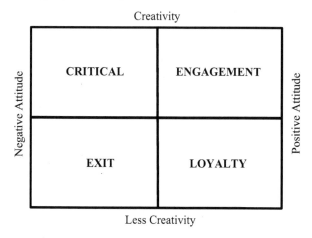

Figure 7.2   Hirschman's typology (1970)

DJS Research Ltd (n.d.) further states:

> A successful professional firm will typically start by identifying and
> agreeing specific KPIs and considering how best to measure them.
> Armed with the desired measures the next step will be to establish target
> performance levels for all the chosen KPIs using as guides information
> gained from benchmarking exercises, past performance or experience.

Assessment: The same as in the assessment of the benchmarking model in
Chapter 6.

The most critical aspect of the discussion above is the naivety and vague
suppositions by which the model is designed and applied. This is particularly obvious when the model deals with cause-effect relations and setting
targets for performance. In the discussion below about the applicability of
indicators in general, certain criteria have been identified, such as the possibility of measuring results.

INDICATORS FOR FORECASTING

Pindaros, the Greek poet who lived 518–442 B.C., said about the future:

> *Blind are the thoughts that we cast to the future. Against all the odds,*
> *innumerable things will happen.*

This sententious phrase captures the essence of the forecasting dilemma—we
do not know what will happen from now on, we must assume unpredictable

or unknown things will happen and hence we can only with varying degrees of probability make assumptions about future situations. By using indicators to monitor trends as in the example above about customer service (Figure 7.1) or in the following section about early warning, we implicitly assume that previous trends will continue, so that coming events can therefore be predicted and trends be forecasted. The concept of continuality plays an important role, similar to mathematics where continuous functions are fundamental and trends of functions must not take abrupt turns ('the derivate must be continuous') for the trend to be predictable.

But human logic does not follow the mathematical or formal logic that was a guiding principle in the neoclassical model. Kahneman and Tversky (1974) found a number of results that directly question the neoclassical assumption that we make decisions rationally such as, for example, that man seems to be biased by recent events and therefore believes the trend to continue, underestimating the likelihood of extreme events. Kahneman and Tversky (ibid.) claim that groups, on the other hand, tend to be more extreme than individuals. Groups also tend to be more optimistic, supress doubts, and exhibit group-think. In larger informal groups such as markets, this can translate into herd behaviour in which investors all rush into the market, or out of it, at the same time (Orrell, 2010).

The tendency to question the rational approach to human behaviour in the neoclassical economic theory, not least in economic thinking, has created concepts like behavioural finance and opened up for uncertainty and unpredictability with examples from chaos theory. Chaos theory applied in social sciences such as economic development uses the notion of bifurcation points. A bifurcation means that a continuous trend suddenly deviates and goes in a direction that was impossible to foresee. The September 11, 2001, attack in New York is a bifurcation point example—i.e., it was unforeseen and led to completely changed conditions for politics and business worldwide. The severe tsunami in 2004 in Asia as well as the collapse of the Soviet Union in 1991 are both examples of bifurcation points on the time axis with significant impact on regional and international politics and business.

A rigorous discussion about models in financial systems has been carried out by Pixley (2012), who claims that forecasts take a run of numbers or static preferences; a model explains only what can be derived from the chosen assumptions. Extrapolating that past trends *will* continue is our vapid 'history tells us' assumption. This approach is sometimes combined with the *ceteris paribus* assumption as an attempt at qualifying (sic!) a prediction by identifying one parameter assumed to be of particular significance and hence ruling out others. By not acknowledging the possibility of all parameters being significant and important as well, we make the model simpler but achieve a poorer picture of reality. The *ceteris paribus* exemplifies the model problem discussed earlier: elimination of parameters in the mapping that cannot be accounted for or that are not well enough known.

Heinz Pagels, late executive director of the New York Academy of Science, asked:

> What are the chances that we will ever understand economic systems? They are clearly examples of extremely complex systems, but there is lots of quantitative data to check one's ideas out on. Professional economists who bother to concern themselves with practical matters don't have an especially good batting average when it comes to predicting the future of the economy. They are smart, but they just don't have the right intellectual tools in their hands. (Pagels, 1988, 145)

With the introduction of computers and new forecasting models based on statistical and mathematical theory and methods, a new step was taken in the development of strategic tools for business such as indicators for trend spotting. The 1970s saw the advent of many knowledge-based systems that fostered the development of applications for business operations and strategic planning. A typical characteristic of knowledge-based management information systems is a focus on the future. The forward-looking systems emphasised the integration of future and current operations that constituted the base for management decisions. This was fundamental not only as a characterisation of knowledge-based Management Information Systems (MIS), but it also revealed their weakness: the presumption that the future is predictable!

Forecasting is an important management task in business and applies to functions such as product development, market development and budgeting. Different analysis frameworks have been suggested and developed to identify a firm's position in the market with its current range of products. By comparing different alternatives, the manager makes strategic decisions about which alternative to choose—for example, to promote one type of product for a growing market sector. Another type of forecasting framework helps the manager to analyse the different strategic steps the firm should take to grow. One such analytical framework is Ansoff's Growth Matrix, presented by Igor Ansoff (1965) in his book *Corporate Strategy* as a tool to assist in choosing a product and market growth strategy. The assumption was that firms can grow by identifying the optimal match between new or existing products and new or existing market sectors.

The product-mission matrix as presented in Figure 7.3 is a model that describes a strategy for business growth by improving the present situation of existing products and existing markets *(market penetration)*. When the company tries to sell its current products in a new market, Ansoff refers to *market development;* when new products are developed and introduced to an existing market the efforts may be higher and also more costly because additional skills and innovation capacity may be required. The most advanced and also the most risky business strategy, *diversification,* is to develop and introduce new products into new markets.

Penetrating an existing market includes inter alia efforts to expand market share, promote products and services by reinforcing selling and advertising

	Present product	New product
Present mission	Market Penetration	Product Development
New mission	Market Development	Diversification

Figure 7.3 Ansoff's product/mission matrix

and focus on priority customers. Developing new markets requires knowledge and understanding about what customers demand now and in the future.

The Ansoff growth matrix is one of several models and tools developed for use in strategic business planning. It may seem attractive to managers, but its tangible ability to contribute as a decision tool is undermined by the fact that problems we encounter in the real world are very seldom precisely specified because information is incomplete or data accuracy cannot be taken for granted. A new product may be new to the producer but not necessarily to the market because market information about competitors and what they have in their product pipe lines is incomplete. Perception of future customer demand is also inadequate, and any ambition to develop new markets based on such understanding can only be considered uncertain. Henry Ford, the founder of the Ford Motor Company, is supposed to have said: 'If I ask the customer what he wants he will most probably say—a faster horse'. A customer cannot be expected to formulate demand for a product or service he cannot visualize.

EARLY WARNING ANALYSIS

By early warning, we mean the capacity to recognize unfavourable or threatening events that may seriously jeopardise or even render impossible the current process to achieve a predefined and specific goal. By *early warning analysis* we thus refer to the systematic activity of identifying beforehand events or situations that would have a negative impact on the organisation and its operations. Creating methods to capture early warning signals and designing early warning analysis for business survival and growth is a challenge to organisations and firms, bringing reasons and opportunities to *recognise, acknowledge, and react* as keys to improve performance and competitiveness.

The crucial idea of an early warning is to have enough reaction time between "warning" and impending "disaster" to react to the warning and thereby avert the disaster. "Disaster" is not taken literally but denotes an event that will have a negative effect if it cannot be avoided. The early warning concept can be illustrated as in Figure 7.4.

Intuitively, we can assume that the 'value' of the early warning is somehow related to the length of the reaction time and the importance or seriousness of the disaster. The more serious the potential disaster, the longer reaction time is desirable. In practice, however, this is not always possible and quite often the opposite applies. Signals about inadequate customer service are always a serious threat to a firm's business. It should be a top priority issue among managers to identify the most serious real and potential 'disasters' that can happen.

Table 7.1 presents some examples of 'disasters', their origin (external or internal) and whether the time to react is long or short.

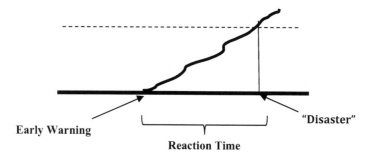

Figure 7.4   Early warning concept

Table 7.1   Examples of events in early warning analysis

Event	External/Internal	Long/Short
Unhappy customer	external	short
New competition	external	long
Change in government policy	external	long
Machine break-down	internal	short
Material missing	internal	short
Increase in oil price	external	long
Power cut	external / internal	short
Increase in admin. costs	internal	long
Productivity drop	internal	long
Quality drop	internal	long
Discontented employees	internal	long
Wrong strategy	internal	long

Tools that can be developed to pick up signals about future 'disasters' are of course subject to a stipulation that the future is predictable to some degree. This is not always possible since a basic feature of uncertainty is the blurring of cause and effect. Even if one knows that a certain event is going to happen, the range of possible consequences creates uncertainty. If the future is relatively clear, there is basically only one likely future scenario, and hence just one possible outcome. But if the future is likely to be one of several alternatives, statistical methods may be required to determine the most likely scenario.

The success of information systems in coping with uncertainty would increase if the future were predictable. Conversely, the greater the uncertainty the more difficult it is to link the variables of the description model by causes and effects, limiting the usefulness of information technology. In organisations exposed to genuine uncertainty (as in less developed countries, but occasionally also in more developed countries), the use of information systems is mostly unsuccessful because of the inability to predict future events. In such situations, uncertainty can only be dealt with in an *ad hoc* manner—i.e., no particular rules apply, and situations have to be dealt with on a case-by-case basis.

Depending on the type of 'disaster', different types of measures and tools can be used to pick up the early warning signals. These indicators include ratios between actual and expected costs, and ratios between total produced goods and scrapped parts. Such ratios are easily plotted in diagrams that can be extrapolated into the future. Similarly, an organisation's cash flow can be monitored to avoid a sudden lack of liquid capital.

Formal information through the media and other channels can provide useful and important early warning signals, but formal methods are not the only ones used in early warning analysis. Informal methods are also important—for example, experienced managers' intuition and gossip and small talk among colleagues often contain useful signals that can be further analysed and used to assess important situations.

Early Warning Tools

Three groups of tools that can be used to pick up warnings about future situations and events are:

- Indicators for the monitoring of trends
- Cash Flow Analysis for the specific monitoring of floating assets
- Strategy development methods

By monitoring trends it is possible to extrapolate the current trend into the future and predict (with an ample degree of uncertainty) when an unfavourable situation might happen. Cash Flow Analysis and other kinds of economic and accounting indicators have turned out to be useful for quick assessment of trends and possible financial shortages. However, the use

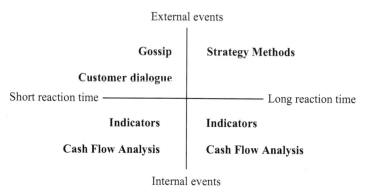

Figure 7.5   Categorisation of events

of indicators to measure non-financial trends assumes that results can be measured, and that there is sufficient knowledge about operations (production, marketing, etc.). Limited knowledge about operations implies limited knowledge about the resulting effects of an unfavourable event ('disaster'). And if operational goals have not been explicitly formulated and used as reference parameters for planning, results cannot be adequately measured because of lack of reference values. Common planning tools, such as work scheduling, maintenance schemes and budgeting, all require that operational goals have been articulated and specified. Figure 7.5 summarises the discussion so far.

Probably one of the most important early warning methods is direct communication with clients, suppliers and other important stakeholders. Having an open dialogue with customers is an efficient way of learning what is happening in the market. Changes in customer buying habits are key indicators that something is happening that needs to be looked into. Whatever that *something* is, it will be reflected in future business when it may be too late for corrective actions! Ordinary business knows about the various forms of supplier-customer contacts and relations, ranging from inviting customers for lunch, visiting their places of business, undertaking plant tours, trying to understand their business and concerns and staying plugged into their thoughts and perceptions. All this provides the most important early warning information under the condition that negative information is also heard. Every manager should force him- or herself to find out why people are not buying their products or services. This is the most valuable information!

WHEN ARE INDICATORS APPLICABLE?

If there were a means of measuring performance with total accuracy, there would be no need for indicators or other tools. Uncertainty is caused by the fact that we can never be fully confident that the parameters selected for measuring will be the most significant or relevant. Handling uncertainty has always been a management task, regardless of whether it relates to long-term strategy or short-term uncertainties of daily operations. Managing uncertainty in this context refers to finding the most proper tool for a reliable performance measure. The early warning analysis discussed above is a systematic approach that attempts to identify beforehand all events or situations that could have a negative impact on the organisation's ability to achieve its goals.

Monitoring performance of daily operations is another kind of uncertainty that depends on the extent to which the cause-effect relationship for performance is comprehensible. In a model presented by Ouchi and Maguire (1975), it is suggested that a distinction needs to be drawn between two modes of monitoring and control: behaviour control (based on personal surveillance) and output control (based on the measurement of outputs). Ouchi (1979) later suggested that when there is sufficient knowledge about a process, rules can be developed and applied as tools in behavioural control. Such rules are in reality a codification of organisational and management behaviour. However, it was also noted that such rules may mostly be too general and too static to be applicable in more dynamic situations.

A pre-condition for *output control* is the identification of measures that correspond adequately with the actual processes of the enterprise. Such after-the-fact measures make business control possible only if the factors measured are sufficiently well known and capable of being influenced. If the underlying mechanisms influencing these factors have been identified, it is possible to construct indicators or other simple measures that may be well suited to monitor trends.

To summarise, *output control* measures effects, *behaviour control* uses rules, and the choice of which to apply depends on knowledge of the process and the extent to which the effects and performance of the process can be measured. If there is insufficient knowledge or no relevant measures can be identified, then the scope for controlling the business process is limited. In such situations, the enterprise has to resort to rituals and ceremonies. The different control alternatives are illustrated in Figure 7.6.

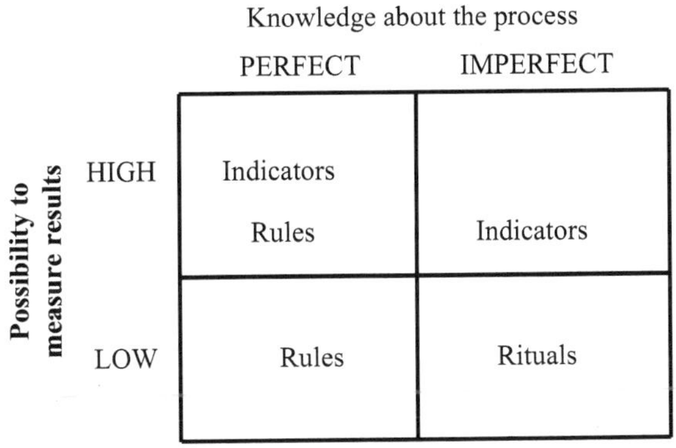

Knowledge about the process

		PERFECT	IMPERFECT
Possibility to measure results	HIGH	Indicators Rules	Indicators
	LOW	Rules	Rituals

Figure 7.6 Two modes of control (Ouchi, 1979)

EXAMPLES OF INDICATORS

Numerous generic indicators have been suggested in management literature in which different models, methods and tools are presented, such as key performance indicators and balanced scorecards. The question of whether a general indicator is applicable or not in a specific situation is not easily determined. Tailor-made indicators for particular use in a specific context are more likely to be appropriate and useful because they have been developed based on experience and clear goals.

The following examples of indicators are generic and therefore not necessarily applicable in all or specific cases. They are shown below as examples of different indicator types. For each example, there is a brief presentation about the formula used, reference values when possible and what type of data is needed for making the indicator.

Indicator Name:	Total Enterprises Performance TEP
Formula:	TEP = Total Turnover / (Total Costs including Financial Cost and Cost of Accumulated Depreciation)
Reference Value:	TEP > 1
Input Data:	Turnover, Cost of Material (import and domestic), Labour Costs, Administrative Costs, Overhead Costs, Financial Costs, Depreciation
Comments:	This rough indicator gives an over-all indication how a group of selected enterprises (sector, region, etc.) is performing.
Indicator Name:	Profit Margin Indicator PMI
Formula:	PMI = 1 – (Total Cost including Financial Cost and Cost of Accumulated Depreciation) / Total Turnover
Reference Value:	PMI > PMI Set Target Value
Input Data:	Turnover, Cost of Material, Labour Costs, Administrative Costs, Overhead Costs, Financial Costs, Depreciation.
Comments:	This indicator gives an over-all indication of the profitability for a group of selected enterprises (sector, region, etc.) is performing. It should be noted that PMI = 1 – 1/TEP.
Indicator Name:	Labour Productivity Indicator LPI
Formula:	LPI = (Total Turnover – Total Material Costs) / Total Labour Salary
Reference Value:	–
Input Data:	Turnover, Cost of Material, Total Labour Costs
Comments:	This indicator gives an over-all indication of labour productivity for a group of selected enterprises (sector, region, etc.). A common measure of labour productivity used to be sales revenue per employee or number of produced products per employee. These measures have,

however, disadvantages because they, in the first case, do not reflect the value of work, only the value of output, and in the second case, compare physical output with value of input.

Indicator Name:	Capital Turnover Indicator CTI
Formula:	CTI = Total Turnover / (Total Assets - Depreciation) / Inflation factor
Reference Value:	–
Input Data:	Turnover, Assets, Depreciation
Comments:	This indicator gives an over-all indication of how capital is utilised to generate revenue. Efficiency indicator.
	The inflation factor is included for those situations where inflation is significant and would distort the result if not included. The factor uses the official inflation rate p and calculates the average inflation according to the following formula: $1 + p / 200$.
Indicator Name:	Year-end-Outlook Indicator YEO
Formula:	Regression Analysis
Reference Value:	YEO / Estimated Result >1
Input Data:	Accumulated sales revenue from year begins. Estimated sales revenue for the whole year.
Comments:	This indicator is used to predict, based on accumulated history data from year start, and elaborated by means of the Minimum Square Root method, the sales result at year-end for a group of selected enterprises (sector, region, etc.). It should be noted that the predicted result will be statistically more significant after some months.
Indicator Name:	Customer Service Indicator CSI
Formula:	CSI = 1 – Number of Defect Customer Shipments / Total Number of Customer Shipments
Reference Value:	Should be as close to 1 as possible
Input Data:	Number of defect and total shipments
Comments:	This indicator shows customer service level for a group of selected enterprises (sector, region, etc.).

Specific indicators (for Manufacturing Industry)

Indicator Name:	Production Capacity Utilisation Indicator PCU
Formula:	PCU = 1 – Actual Capacity Utilisation / Maximum Capacity
Reference Value:	As close to 1 as possible
Input Data:	Actual Production Capacity Utilisation, Maximum Production Capacity
Comments:	This indicator shows production capacity utilisation for a group of selected enterprises (sector, region, etc.).
Indicator Name:	Production Quality Index PQX
Formula:	PQX = 1 – Total Defects/Total Production
Reference Value:	PQX > PQX set target value

(continued)

Input Data:	Total volume of production, total defects in production
Comments:	Products may not be accepted for various reasons, ranging from missing functionality to cosmetic deviations. From a total quality perspective, however, all defects should be treated in a similar way and result in scrap, re-work or other appropriate measures. The ultimate goal for any enterprise must be 0 defects and management should actively strive for reaching this target. This indicator shows production efficiency for a group of selected enterprises (sector, region, etc.).
Indicator Name:	Maintenance Productivity MNP
Formula:	MNP = Total Planned Maintenance Hours / Total Maintenance Hours
Reference Value:	As close to 1 as possible.
Input Data:	Total Maintenance Hours on Emergency Repair, Total Maintenance Hours
Comments:	The MNP indicator should be as close to 1.0 as possible! MNP in the interval 0.75 – 1.0 is acceptable and means that 25% or less of all maintenance work is spent on emergency repair. MNP around 0.50 means that 50% of all maintenance work is spent on emergency repair. Studies show that in a majority of enterprises in developing countries, emergency repair represents over 80% of all maintenance work. One serious consequence of low planned maintenance work means that production planning and scheduling to meet market demand becomes extremely difficult as no one knows when a machine will break down or stop.
Indicator Name:	Added Value Grade AVG
Formula:	AVG = (Total Turnover – Total Cost of Material) / Total Turnover
Reference Value:	–
Input Data:	Turnover, Cost of material
Comments:	Added value is the amount by which the income of a business exceeds the cost of its inputs—i.e., the sum of its operating costs plus its profit. Added value is an important parameter as it indicates how much market value is produced within the company. This indicator shows production added value as a share of total turnover for a group of selected enterprises (sector, region, etc.).

Specific indicators (example: Textile Industry)

Indicator Name:	Man per Machine Indicator MMI
Formula:	MNI = Number of Workers / Number of Machines
Reference Value:	Present international reference value = 1.6 Workers / Machine
Input Data:	Number of machine operators, Number of textile machines

The use of these and similar indicators is presented in the following section as an example of an ambitious project aiming at assisting company managers in performance monitoring with the means of suitable indicators. The project was initiated by the United Nations Industrial Development Organisation (UNIDO) to improve productivity and performance in industry firms in ten Latin American countries. The name of the project and the computer-based indicator software resulting from the project was BEST, an acronym for Business Environment Strategic Tool-kit.

BEST—AN INDICATOR SYSTEM FOR BUSINESS PERFORMANCE MONITORING

BEST was designed to assist managers in the evaluation of business performance, and seeks to translate strategic objectives into a coherent set of performance measures (indicators). It identifies and highlights those indicators that fall outside pre-set reference frames. In the design of the software, certain assumptions were made about a typical setting for its application. For example, that certain types of input data are not readily available, that benchmarking is not a suitable method for comparing performance when statistical branch data is missing or unreliable, that business/sales planning is often kept at a rudimentary level, and that managers in general lack sufficient understanding about how to measure business performance.

BEST was thus specifically designed for use in a business environment where predictability is modest and where the firm is exposed to external contingencies. In the model described in Figure 7.6 above, this corresponds to an imperfect knowledge about the process. In companies with poorly developed means to measure business results (e.g., in most companies where measurement is based on traditional accounting systems), the companies tend to resort to pre-made rules and rituals for their control (behaviour control). In most situations, this means that the company's possibility of adapting quickly to changing market needs is very limited.

With the possibility to measure results in a more direct way (output control), which was supposed to be facilitated by BEST, important information can be conveyed to managers for appropriate action. A crucial question is of course to what extent the indicators are representative enough for the actual business situation, and to what extent the managers can interpret the indicators correctly. This is crucial for the usefulness of indicators.

BEST—A Brief Presentation

BEST has 24 indicators in the form of simple arithmetic expressions. The indicators are presented as graphics (curves, bars, etc.) to allow continuous monitoring of the company's performance. The graphics can be combined with target values for easy comparison between expected and actual performance.

The BEST philosophy is based on the idea of continuous improvement. Continuous improvement implies that the manager concentrates on those issues that need the most attention. This requires not only that priority issues can be quickly identified but also that the most proper actions be taken. The BEST graphs are tools by which the manager can distinguish urgent areas from less urgent ones. By monitoring the indicators, the manager is able to concentrate on the unstable and varying ones that may need immediate action.

The BEST philosophy is furthermore to provide the user with adequate information to get an impression of the actual situation of the whole enterprise and in what direction it is moving. Detailed information of mathematical accuracy has no or very little relevance for this purpose. Instead, the goal of BEST as a decision support system is to create a holistic impression rather than picking details for isolated study. The intention of BEST is therefore to provide the user with indications and impressions as input to decisions. The actual business decision, however, is the task of the manager himself.

BEST has four modules. The Operations Management Assistance is primarily for short-term business operations. It has a set of indicators for the measurement of vital characteristics such as customer service and sales performance.

Strategic Management Assistance is for more long-term performance measurement such as productivity development, maintenance efficiency and competitiveness, and through it the manager has a good overview of the situation through five basic indicator graphs that can be further expanded into sub-groups of additional indicator graphs. The manager is advised how to react if an indicator is out of range or has a negative trend, aided by options to select and combine graphs in various ways.

Investment Assistance has three alternative investment models to be used for short-term investments such as acquisition of new production equipment. The system recommends the most appropriate of the three models, depending on the investment situation.

Product Monitoring Assistance has two functions: Price Setting Simulation and Product Profit Analysis. The latter ranks the profitability of the company's products in accordance with bottleneck situations that are all characteristic for enterprises in developing countries.

BEST is revenue/market oriented in the sense that sales revenues measure performance of the enterprise rather than production volumes. The opposite was for a long time predominant in many regulated economies; performance was measured by how much the company managed to produce. In many companies where the adaptation to this market oriented view is a slow process, BEST has the potential to be a learning tool for moving towards this new approach.

BEST in Action

The first installation of BEST was in pilot enterprises in ten Latin American countries. After about one year, it was observed that the usage of the installed system varied significantly between enterprises. While some users claimed benefits in getting a better grip of their business process, others seemed not to use the system in their daily operations, claiming various reasons such as missing data, lack of consistency with normal working procedures, and lack of appropriate training. Some users reported too many options in the system functions and, hence, difficulty in selecting the most suitable and adequate functions for their respective operations.

The findings justified a closer analysis to evaluate the scattered picture of the usage of the indicator software. Two alternative explanations were set up as hypotheses about why enterprises had shown reluctance to use the indicator system:

1. BEST is adequate and relevant, but managers are not fully aware of its potential as a powerful support tool in monitoring their businesses.
2. Managers appreciate the potential benefits of the system but BEST is, for different reasons, not fully appropriate as a business monitoring tool.

Testing of BEST at the Company Los Espinos

A study to analyse the applicability of BEST was carried out at the company Los Espinos S.A. in Chile, a company producing plastic bottles of different types and for various fields of applications (Lind et al., 2000). The production process was based on plastic extrusion with modern equipment.

Findings

During the data acquisition phase, it was obvious that some of the data required by BEST were not collected on a regular basis in the company and were therefore not readily available. This lack of data meant that certain indicators could not be utilised. More precisely, the following findings were the most significant ones:

- The Company's information system was primarily geared toward the financial accounting needs.
- The Company's production was totally driven by direct customer demand. As there were no attempts at making forecasts about future customer demand, there was no production plan; because of this, there were no data available for production planning.
- The Company's notion of its production costs was entirely based on cost estimates for material usage, machine times, etc. No data was

collected about actual production costs (actual material cost per product, etc.).

- The Company did not monitor or register any time or resources spent on production re-work, scrap rates, etc.
- The Company did not register or monitor time or resources spent on maintenance in general or on the division into planned and non-planned maintenance.
- The Company did not register or monitor data on customer shipments or data about defective shipments leading to complaints or compensation claims.
- The Company did not register or monitor the accumulated customer order value.

The absence of planning data constituted a major obstacle in the use of BEST because many of the indicators measure performance as ratios between actual and planned data. However, the data that was available was re-arranged and adapted as best estimates. For example, instead of monthly results, a monthly average was calculated, based on year totals. It was obvious that one of the strengths of BEST (and similar systems)—i.e., to continuously monitor performance—could not be adequately utilised.

Based on the input data available, the output provided by BEST was analysed and assessed. In the analysis and validation of output information, the quality, the approximation and, in particular, the absence of vital input data was taken into consideration. In spite of this, the analysis of the various indicators (graphs) showed tendencies (ups or downs) that were explained by what actually happened in the company. Again, lack of reliable input data made too far-reaching interpretations hazardous. The result of the study can be summarised as follows:

- The information structure of the Company was not well suited for a system like BEST, designed for a broad range of input data. By implementing a new information structure, more consistent with the information structure of BEST, the company should be better able to benefit by the system.
- In the actual test, a number of functions available in BEST to support managers in business operations, both in the long run (strategic) and in the short, daily type of operations (decisions, etc.), could not be utilised due to lack of appropriate input data. Certain indicators were therefore not activated—for example, those indicators related to production quality, customer service and maintenance productivity
- In spite of the partly poor quality in input data, there were indicators that came close to estimates made by the Company management. As a matter of fact, the indicators gave a plausible picture of the performance of the Company at large, both in respect to short- and long-term

operations. In addition, certain indicators provided the possibility of deeper understanding of business processes.

Analysis and Conclusion

In analysing the findings from Los Espinos, the model in Figure 7.6 above was used, in which knowledge of the business process and the possibility to measure results are the two basic parameters. If the knowledge of the process is perfect (e.g., the manager has perfect knowledge of the tasks of his subordinates), then behaviour control or personal surveillance is a relevant mode of control. If, on the other hand, there is a need to communicate results to others in the company but also to use formal measures as legitimate evidence of satisfactory performance, then output control, or formal control, occurs. Conversely, if the possibility of measuring results is low and if there is imperfect knowledge about the process, then the enterprise has to resort to rituals and ceremonies that are based on *a priori* knowledge, according to Figure 7.6. Such rituals are, for example, reflected in a firm's behaviour towards customer and clients that are more based on general ideas and conceptions than on feedback from its own close customer contacts.

The findings from Los Espinos motivate the necessity to distinguish between financial and non-financial information. Knowledge about the financial process through the internal accounting system seems to be satisfactory as the possibility to measure financial results is good. One should, however, bear in mind that the accounting system is based on formal rules with parameters that summarise financial data for previous periods. Such data cannot provide a broad view of the more general business situation of the company. The understanding about the financial process and the possibility to measure financial results is important for management of limited value for overall performance assessment.

When it comes to the other set of variables used in BEST and tested at Los Espinos, viz. non-financial variables, it is obvious from the findings that there is limited knowledge about the business process, and also limited possibility to measure results, simply because there are no reference values set.

The findings were summarised in the following table:

Table 7.2 Summary of BEST application at Los Espinos

Limited knowledge of process	Limited possibility to measure results
No data for production planning	No production plan
No data for actual production costs	No cost targets
No data on scrap rates and rework	No target for scrap rates
No data on emergency repairs	No targets for maintenance hours
No data on customer satisfaction	No reference value on customer orders

The table shows that it is simply not a management principle to set goals or targets for significant variables such as scrap rates, costs or maintenance. Without such targets, there is no reference frame for comparison with actual data, which in turn makes performance monitoring hazardous. Lack of targets in critical areas such as production and sales makes it difficult to measure results and performance. Lack of input data from these areas justifies the question to what extent there is enough management knowledge about the process to effectively control, and manage, the process. The findings from Los Espinos indicate that indicators used for performance monitoring require certain conditions for beneficial use.

Concluding Remarks

The analysis of BEST at Los Espinos shows that the information structure of BEST was not fully compatible with that of the company. That is to say, certain functions available in the software were not utilised since they were not demanded. For example, the customer service indicator, showing the number of faulty customer shipments related to total shipments, was not utilised because there was no tracing of faulty shipments to customers. But incompatibility between structures could also be explained by the fact that there are functions demanded by the company but not available in the BEST system. (The more trivial situation, when functions were neither demanded by the company nor available in BEST, was not analysed.)

More generally, we may conclude that in the match between functions available in the computer solution and functions demanded by the company, the following four situations can occur:

1. Information structures are the same.
2. Functions available in the system are not demanded by the company, which means there is an unused potential in the system that could be utilised once the company's information structure is modified accordingly.
3. Functions that are demanded in the company are not available in the system, which means that the system does not provide the necessary support.
4. The company does not demand functions that are not available in the systems.

The four situations are illustrated in Figure 7.7:
Now we return to the two hypotheses set up earlier:

1. The indicators of BEST are adequate and relevant, but managers are not fully aware about their potential as powerful monitoring tools for managing the business, or

THE COMPANY

Function demanded   Function not demanded

	Function demanded	Function not demanded
Function Available	Full Match	Unused Potential
Function not Available	Insufficient Support	Not relevant

BEST

Figure 7.7   Match between functions demanded and functions offered

2. Managers appreciate the potential benefits of the available indicators, but they are not, for different reasons, considered to be fully appropriate as business monitoring tools.

The first hypothesis comes close to functions available in Figure 7.7, the second hypothesis to functions not available. In the first case, managers fail to realise the potential usefulness of the indicators provided and do not ask for them because of ignorance or lack of awareness about their significance for the business. In the second case, managers may appreciate the provided indicators as technically attractive, but the lack of functions or inadequate design reveals that the software designers and developers have not sufficient understanding about managers' requirements of business support tools.

This is experience from one company using indicators for business performance monitoring. It is certainly not representative for all users of indicators for the same purpose, but the example shows clearly that a number of fundamental conditions must be fulfilled in order to utilise relatively simple indicators. Reasons for lack of benefits vary between rudimentary management commitments, lack of data or unreliable data and lack of organisational routines needed for continuous use. In the UNIDO project, the BEST software was implemented in all together one hundred enterprises in ten Latin American countries. The same result as with Los Espinos was reported from the other firms as well, more or less for the same reasons!

CONCLUSION

The discussion above about indicators refers to their use as tools in business performance monitoring, which is just one area of indicator application. Other application areas are in industrial production and in accounting, but also in medicine and health service—for example, the Body Mass Index (BMI), which measures the ratio between size and weight of a person and compares it with certain standard values. Indicators can thus be defined differently, depending on application area, from simple ratios between numbers to more elaborated expressions like the human development index (HDI) and the Gini index applied in economic and social development contexts.

As illustrated in the example from Los Espinos and the criteria from Figure 7.7, an important condition for successful use of indicators and for choosing an appropriate indicator relies on good understanding about the business process and what is important for organizational performance. However, what is considered important often depends on which measures have been decided by management to use for monitoring performance! In practice, and this leads back to the earlier discussion about models—some indicators that would be important are simply not possible to construct since there are no explicit data available. Indicators such as staff morale or work ethic may be impossible to quantify.

Indicators for performance measuring can also lead to contradictory incentives such as neglecting defect production because of the operator's ambition to fulfill production quota. For example, measuring the productivity of a software development team in terms of source lines of code encourages copy and paste code and over-engineered design, leading to bloated code bases that are particularly difficult to maintain, understand and modify.

Indicators as tools for assessing performance are useful for monitoring trends, which may give a clearer view about performance development during a period and thereby also indicate possible future development. The danger of prediction is, however, that historic data can never be any guarantee that a pattern from the past will continue in the same way. The ease of using indicators in combination with sophisticated computer software can lead business astray.

The simple criteria when indicators are applicable are presented above and can eliminate situations where the seemingly obvious use of indicators may turn out to be hazardous. In situations in which there are no articulated goals or references for business activities such as costs or revenues or in which such goals or references are unrealistic and not possible to achieve, indicators are less appropriate. An indicator measuring actual result with expected result is useless if the expectation is unrealistic or not even articulated.

REFERENCES

Ansoff, I. (1965) *Corporate strategy.* New York, McGraw-Hill.
Braudel, F. (1979) *Civilization and capitalism, 15th–18th Centuries, the wheels of commerce* Vol. 2. Berkely, University of California Press.
Bennett, S. (1984) *Nicholas Minorsky and the automatic steering of ships.* IEEE Control Systems Magazine 4 (4).

DJS Research Ltd. (n.d.) Monitoring Performance. http://www.marketresearch world.net/content/view/385/53/

Hirschman, A.O. (1970) *Exit, voice, and loyalty: Responses to decline in firms, organizations, and states.* Cambridge, MA, Harvard University Press.

Kahneman, D. and Tversky, A. (1974) *Judgment under uncertainty: Heuristics and biases.* Science, New Series, 185 (4157).

Lind, P., Sépulveda and E., Nuñes, J. (2000) *On the applicability of a computer model for business performance analysis in SMEs. A case study from Chile.* Information Technology for Development, 9 (1).

Orrell, D. (2010) *Economyths.* Ontario, John Wiley.

Ouchi, W. (1979) *A conceptual framework for the design of of organisational control mechanisms.* Management Science, 25 (9).

Ouchi, W. and Maguire, M. A. (1975) *Organisational control: Two functions.* Administrative Science Quarterly (December).

Pagels, H. (1988) *The dreams of reason.* New York, Simon and Schuster.

Pixley, J. (2012) *Emotions in finance.* Cambridge, Cambridge University Press.

8 Methods and Tools for Business Development

Business development is a generic concept, but it is unique to each individual organisation based on development goals and prevailing conditions. It is an ongoing process that has a starting point when the company is set up, but no endpoint. The development goals may look different and vary from economic growth to increased market shares, from product innovation and development to just increased profit. Charity businesses and social entrepreneurships may not be growth oriented in monetary terms, but instead strive to grow benefits within their specific business areas.

Business development goals cannot be set without considering the resource parameters of the organisation, such as employee skills, financial strength, operating history and market place. Such constraints arise from assessment of current resources, such as employee skills and financial strength, but also from the history of the organisation, including its reputation on the market. Organisation structure, but also the structure of the surrounding society in terms of laws and regulations, sets limits on how goals can be formulated. Because separate conditions apply in each case when an organisation is to be appraised, there is a need to find a generic model that identifies the special characteristics of the organisation or firm. In an attempt to identify such properties, Danielsson (1978) suggested a model of five categories or qualities and gave three reasons for their significance: First, it should be possible to use different perspectives, such as viewing the firm from inside or from outside. Second, it should be possible to distinguish between the observer and the observed, and third, it should be possible to distinguish between different types of problems and phenomena. The five categories are:

Phenomenon: Firms may exhibit considerable complexity in their structures and business processes, which become even more complex and less transparent with increasing firm size. Hence it is important to determine which phenomena will be described and assessed. Omitting this step may result in an unclear and poorly articulated focus.

Perspective: It is common to refer to stakeholder involvements to varying degrees with the organisation or firm. It is not obvious, however, to identify a specific stakeholder with a specific perspective. An external perspective sees the organisation or firm in its context, where it is compared and assessed in relation to other actors. On the other hand, from the internal perspective phenomena can be observed that may not be visible from outside.

Structure: Organisations and firms are ideally structured and organised in accordance with their goals and activities, which implies that the structure is not static but adapts to changed goals and activities. At the same time, many organisations are slow to adapt to changes that would be required for performance reasons. For performance monitoring, it becomes important to consider how the organisation structure has developed.

Process: The business process in a firm or the activities within an organisation take place as a process in relation to time. The process also takes place within a structure defined by the surrounding society, with its legal, political and cultural structures. The society structure is more stable through time compared with the business process of the firm, which may therefore hamper the business's flexibility. In the very long-term perspective, the society's structure may be a process in another long-term structure!

Chronology: The process/structure discussion indicates the importance of time. In order to comprehend the behaviour of an organisation today, it is of importance to understand its behaviour yesterday. Any organisation is generally hindered from moving freely because of its history, its structure and its ongoing processes and commitments to different stakeholders. Firms and organisations undergo different stages with varying success. Understanding how the different stages influence the organisational behaviour is of importance when monitoring the business development and performance.

Business development and performance monitoring are mutually interdependent—monitoring calls attention to whether the business is developing according to plans and expectations, and business development can be influenced in response to monitoring findings. Creating customer value and fostering innovations are just two areas in which methods and models have been developed for this purpose. Less flexible or mechanistically structured organisations lack the readiness to change and adapt to monitoring findings, as their focus is on pre-set goals. Openness to change is therefore an additional monitoring parameter of business development.

In the following discussion about methods and tools in business development, four phenomena with central importance in business and in the business development process have been selected. The four phenomena are competitiveness, innovation, added value creation and adaptability to change.

COMPETITIVENESS

Becoming competitive and improving the firm's competitive strength is a purpose in any business development process. Both external and internal perspectives apply. In global business, the competitive setting increases in parallel with more and more firms entering more and more markets, creating a business environment of the survival of the fittest. From an internal perspective, it becomes crucial for management to identify the match between the firm's resources and the market's demand. Competent employment of corporate resources is the essence of the so-called Penrose Effect, which describes how traditional and unreflective utilisation of resources in a firm hampers growth and development. The release and development of potential and sleeping resources provides the opportunity to diversify production, products and services by utilising the firm's collection of competences and capacities (Penrose, 2009). By focusing on knowledge and skills—not only in managers, but collectively in the firm—a company can foster competiveness through its unique and specific skills, creating a distinctive image.

Prominent concepts of competitive forces have been suggested that are in sharp contrast to the resource-based view of Penrose. Porter (1980), for example, suggests that the external environment has a more decisive impact on firms' competitiveness, and Shapiro (1989), by drawing on his research, argues that strategic conflicts and the imperfections of the market create entry barriers for competition. Various scholars argue, however, that in the turbulent and uncertain environments of modern knowledge economies, the resource-based theory is the most appropriate for performance analysis and strategy formulation of the firm (Hamel and Prahalad, 1994; Gold et al., 2001).

Although the past few decades have produced a large number of often contradictory and overlapping terms and concepts relating to the resource-based view, it is possible to differentiate two types of resources: basic assets, such as financial, physical, technological and human resources; and competencies, such as knowledge and skills, organisational ability within the firm to use its basic assets and to recognise opportunities and ability to create knowledge and innovations. The two types may, for simplicity, be referred to as *capacities* and *competencies*. It is then possible to make further distinctions between types of competencies, as some are simpler and thus more easily obtained by competitors, whereas others are more complex by being embedded in a particular social context and created under particular conditions.

There is no consensus about which particular capacities and competencies and, more importantly, which combinations of these are best for successful development of an enterprise. Indeed, recent studies have suggested that the optimum combination of resources required to gain a sustainable competitive advantage are usually country-, industry- or even case-specific (Roper, 1997; Foreman-Peck et al., 2006). Very often the optimum division of resources depends on the strategy chosen by the enterprise: to compete either on price, quality, or innovative products or services.

In a research project, Baumane et al. (2011) found, in line with the resource-based approach, that competencies have more influence on the firm's performance and creation of sustainable competitive advantage compared to capacity. Innovation leaders, when compared to innovation followers, evaluated their innovation facilitating competencies much higher (for example, entrepreneurial orientation and innovation-facilitating culture). The research conclusion was that the innovation process depends on both capacities and competencies, albeit with differences between sectors.

The conclusion above that competencies are generally more important than capacities is a static comment that may be time dependent. In an economic boom when customer demand is high all forms of capacities are needed to meet the demand and utilise the sales opportunities. In an economic recession, however, with fierce competition between firms, high competence is required to produce quality and market effectively. For business development, there is a need to recognize what the economic context is with respect to the state of the market.

Structure and Process

Based on observations of firms, it has been suggested (Chandler 1984; Heracleous 2003) that organisations tend to adapt their administrative structures to accommodate strategies of growth. In other words, structure follows strategy. Entering into partnerships is mostly a strategic initiative, which leads to change in the organisational structure.

The concept of learning has been widely adopted in organisations, with the result of a continuous learning process taking place. Single- and double-loop learning emphasises that organisations must develop the ability to detect and correct error in relation to a given set of reference values. Double-loop learning depends on being able to take a "double-look" at the situation by questioning the relevance of operating norms/reference values. In the business development process, the questioning of established reference values is an important step in adapting to new business opportunities.

Methods and Tools

One method to analyse and assess competiveness is providing a customer survey in which randomly (or consciously) selected customers and clients make up their minds about services and products and other relevant issues about their supplier. Large firms may use external consultants, who specialise in such methods and who will provide structured reports with comparisons to benchmarks.

Simple indicators can be useful as tools when trends are of interest. One such use for an indicator is to monitor the trend of the ratio between added value and total production costs. The rational assumption is that a trend showing increasing added value (meaning customers accept increasing price) produced with the same costs or, alternatively, the same added value produced with lower production costs, would indicate that the firm has a competitive position in the market. For small firms, this simplified method represents a cost-saving way of obtaining a rough estimate of the firm's competitiveness.

FOSTERING INNOVATION

Being innovative is not necessarily the same as developing a successful business, as illustrated in Figure 8.1, where the external demand determines if an innovation will become commercially successful or not. History is full of examples where this has been proven. The Concorde airplane, a technologically highly advanced and sophisticated innovation, never became a commercial success, whereas the significantly less technological and sophisticated innovation of disposable napkins immediately sparked worldwide demand. Another example is two innovations taking place back in 1947, both representing highly advanced scientific research. The hologram, a product of optical science, has so far not found any particular commercial use. The other, the transistor, is today a prerequisite for practically all technical devices. Different dates have been stated as milestones for the transistor development, but the breakthrough at Bell's Laboratory in December 1947 is generally considered the birth of the first commercially available transistor.

Figure 8.1 illustrates the major activities involved in innovation and emphasises its close connection with the firm's strategy and the importance of being geared both to opportunities in the market and internal capabilities (competencies and capacities). Morgan (1997) reminds us that successful organisations evolve appropriate structures and processes for dealing with

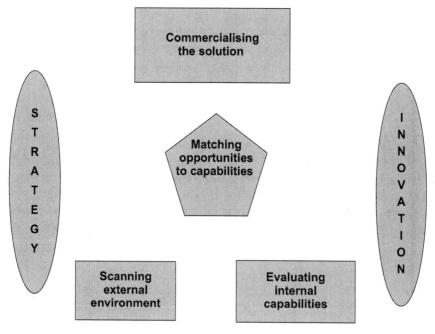

Figure 8.1   Atherton and Hannon's innovation process (2001)

the challenges of their external environment. Scanning the external environment (Figure 8.1) may therefore not be enough unless the significance of environmental changes and their potential implications are clearly perceived. A rule of thumb is still that twenty per cent of information received during a day is of relevance, the remaining eighty per cent of limited importance or relevance. The crucial question is of course which twenty per cent are of relevance to the company and what impact the relevant information will have on the innovation process. It is now generally accepted that innovation is a process rather than a single event (Jones, 2003), subordinated to the organisational structure and to an attitude that is sometimes referred to as *the innovation culture* that can be strong or weak.

For business planning, it is important to distinguish between the two categories of innovations because they may differ in time and resource requirements. Product and process innovations related to goods and services can be oriented to both technology and organisation (Edquist, 2001). Forbes and Wield (2003) argue that though process and product innovations are both important, their importance is different at different stages of industrial development. Process innovation—making things better—is often the first step towards product innovation—making better things. The process innovation step often takes place on the shop-floor, where bottle-necks hinder material flows and the production process. Process innovations are often about small improvements rather than radical leaps and have the goal of cutting costs.

Product innovation is oriented towards the market and to increasing added value in products and services. Edquist (ibid.) points out that some product innovations are transformed into process innovations in a 'second incarnation', but this concerns only 'investment products', not products intended for immediate consumption. For example, an industrial robot is a product when it is produced and a process when it is used in the production process. Product and process innovations are also closely related to each other in many other ways. In spite of this, it is important to make distinctions between different kinds of innovations. In Edquist's taxonomy, only goods and technological process innovations can be considered 'technological innovations' of a material kind. Organisational process innovations and services are 'intangibles'. It is crucial to take these intangible innovations into account as well, since they are increasingly important for economic growth and employment. Figure 8.2 presents Edquist's taxonomy.

Edquist and others use the distinction between process and product innovations to discuss the significance of innovations to employment creation. It is thus assumed that process innovations are labour saving whereas product innovations contribute to creating labour. This one-dimensional view can, however, be challenged within the context of added value and innovations—technological process innovations in production can result in superior products with higher added value, more sales and ultimately even more employment. This is contained in what Schumpeter referred to as *creative destruction* of the

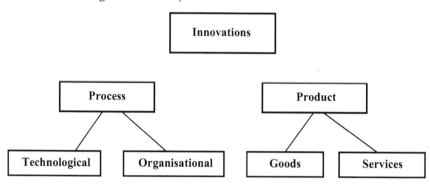

Figure 8.2   Edquist's taxonomy of innovations (2001)

dynamic businessman who starts new production; invests in new technology, in new products, in new markets; and creates and impels development, changing the world and thereby also eliminating old technology and production. Schumpeter used the term to indicate how old and obsolete technology and outmoded economic institutions are replaced by modern product and process innovations (Lundberg, 1994).

Costs of Innovations

The costs incurred by innovations are of different classifications. Technological innovations in the production process require skills and equipment but also implementation efforts that may lead to indirect costs in the form of temporarily reduced productivity. Organisational innovations and changes may result in immediate but temporary implementation costs. Product innovations may require new types of material and equipment and skills to be acquired from outside of the firm. All these costs must be compensated for through a higher sales price. For various reasons, (e.g., competition) the market may, however, set the upper price level. As already discussed in relation to added value strategy, the increase in costs may therefore be higher than the increase in price, which leads to a reduction in profit. In the next section, the implication of this is discussed.

Process and Product Innovations—Some Examples

Process innovations are aiming at cost reduction in the production of services and products. Some examples are:

- Barcodes and scanners in shops and supermarkets for price scanning; products moving along conveyor belts to monitor material flows.
- Production line with robots to eliminate manual work and to increase accuracy, productivity and efficiency.

- Customer order transmitted by information technology directly into the computer-based production plan of the supplier to eliminate administrative work, to speed up order handling and to increase accuracy.
- Tracking information about deliveries, as when clients make inquiries directly into a DHL shipping database to find out expected delivery time and other related information.
- The use of standard components for different but related products, such as standard caps to various forms of bottles.

Product innovations are aiming at the market and increased customer value. Some examples are:

- Low-fuel engines resulting in lower petrol consumption, less pollution and lower fuel costs where governments have introduced tax reduction polices.
- Digital cameras based on new digital technology improving film quality and facilitating manipulation of pictures through editing and copying.
- Cell phones having fundamentally transformed the telecommunication market from a state-directed service to private business, resulting in cost reduction and new functions.
- Microwave ovens with effects on food handling such as storing and cooking.

Service innovations are also aiming at the market and increased customer value. Some examples are:

- 24-hour banking, which has facilitated private administration regarding payment of bills and other financial transactions.
- Online medical diagnosis in which individuals with access to computers and the Internet can inquire about health problems and obtain medical diagnoses.
- Online travel planning that makes it possible to inquire about price and make reservations.
- Weather forecasts updated frequently for ever-smaller regions—of significant importance for industries such as shipping, construction and agriculture.

Innovation Strategies

Figure 8.1 refers to the need to evaluate internal capabilities before framing an innovation strategy. The capabilities include the firm's proprietary capability, which refers to its unique knowledge and skills—for example, intellectual property, such as patents, copyrights and various forms of design. Also included are various forms of specific skills and knowledge, such as deep experience, and familiarity with certain kinds of material and production techniques; highly competent management; and so-called *tacit* knowledge that is not easily copied or possible to communicate to others. Tacit knowledge may be found in sophisticated craft production. A firm has developed tacit knowledge if it can add value ahead of its competitors.

Structure and Process

Innovation structure and process requires a certain amount of redundancy to allow ideas and visions to freely interact and flow. The more potential actors participating in the innovation process, the more variety in ideas and thoughts that can ultimately lead to and become combined in the innovation of a product, a service or organisational change. Consider a system of cogwheels as an example; it illustrates what will happen if there is too little redundancy—it cannot move!

The innovation process is seldom programmable but happens as spin-offs from other activities. It has thus been reported that more than half of product innovations originate from dialogues between suppliers and customers. Innovation as part of business development means to create the necessary facilities in terms of human and financial resources to encourage and foster innovative ideas that can be further developed.

CREATING ADDED VALUE

Added value is one of the more fundamental concepts in business management (Meredith and Shaffer, 2002; Jones and Tilley, 2003). The significance of added value lies in the fact that the value creation is what makes enterprises competitive. Business development therefore ought to take a more conscious stance on what is required for adding value to products and services. Management awareness about the strong relationship between added value, customer value and profit is important and needs to be strengthened even if modern management principles of customer satisfaction and serviceability have been widely accepted among managers today. In practice, however, management is often still conducted in a traditional way, with decisions made incrementally from previous strategies that have been successful but not necessarily taking into consideration newer approaches to business.

Added Value—Definition

The general definition of added value is the difference between a product's market sales price and the cost of input material. The definition points at one important aspect: a product's added value is not determined, or set, by the producer but by the market. Economic theory states that the value of a product is not tied to the cost of production or inherent in the product; that judgment is made by the user and consists of the significance assigned to the satisfaction obtained through its usage or consumption (Menger, 1950).

From a semantic point of view, the definition of added value is inadequate since the production process of goods or services only involves costs (i.e., cost of labour, cost of energy and cost of using machinery and equipment). A better term would therefore be *added costs:* the costs that contribute to the refinement process from input material to finished product since the product does not have a value until a price has been set and accepted by the market.

Manufacturing and Added Value

The importance of the manufacturing sector as a driving force of economic development stems from its integration with other economic activities, generating up-stream as well as down-stream development in other sectors, each sector producing their share of added value.

The significance of added value as an indicator of enterprise performance can be seen from two aspects. Added value, in relation to the usage of material, capital and labour, is a measure of productivity. But its significance also stems from the relationship between what is produced by the enterprise and how its products and services are valued by the market. From economic theory, we know that the value of a product does not depend on the costs of its production. Instead, added value is determined by the market, rather than by the enterprise itself. Value is therefore not inherent in the product but created by user judgment, and it consists of the significance assigned to the satisfaction obtained through its usage or consumption. High added value is thus an indicator of the ability of an enterprise to produce the value that the market is prepared to pay for. If a firm is faced with the situation that its product is considered too expensive by the market, it has two alternative options: to reduce the price (which also means reducing added value) or to increase the customer value by adding new or enhanced functions while retaining or even increasing the price.

Increase in productivity means that the same or more added value is produced with less or the same input (capital, labour), which on the firm level means production costs. Change in added value is the result of a change in output price or material costs, or of both, but not necessarily of production costs. However, with the same production costs, profit may rise with increased added value. Likewise, the refinement cost (i.e. the cost of producing the finished product from the input material) may increase with increasing added value if the added value stems from new product design, new features, etc. As a matter of fact, a number of scenarios involving profit and refinement costs can be imagined as added value increases. One of the scenarios is higher added value but lower profit.

Added Value and Customer Value

In its simplest form, customer value can be defined as perceived benefits of a product or service in relation to perceived sacrifice, such as price and other transaction costs (Naumann, 1995). Customers are interested in quality at acceptable price and they use product and service attributes to evaluate the benefits that will be received (Stock and Lambert, 2001). In a sales situation involving a producer and a customer, it is possible to identify three business strategies, depending on the success or lack of success of the producer's marketing attempts. If the seller (producer) fails in selling the product or service, the following strategies can be expected:

- Strategy 1: Reduce the price to produce a more attractive ratio between product performance and price, hoping that the customer will buy;
- Strategy 2: Improve performance (by adding new functions or providing better service) without increasing the price, in order to become more attractive as a supplier;
- Strategy 3: Improve performance and also increase the price, under the assumption that the improved product performance will, in the eyes of the customer, justify the higher price.

Strategies 1 and 2 may be attractive to the customer, and ultimately even result in a sale. For the seller, however, both alternatives will result in lower profit and are therefore poor alternatives—in the first case because of lower revenue, in the second case because the enhanced performance is likely to result in higher production costs. Strategy 3 is therefore preferable, so long as the increased price can compensate for the added costs incurred by the higher product performance.

To elaborate on the discussion above, we introduce the notion of the *indifference curve*. This is an imaginary optimal price-performance curve representing products and services that a consumer may acquire at price levels that in the consumer's subjective view are reasonable, but just reasonable! An example is illustrated in Figure 8.3. Each point on the indifference

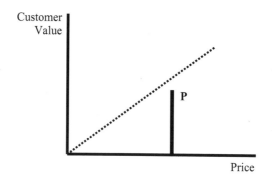

Figure 8.3   Illustration of the indifference curve

curve renders the same level of satisfaction for the consumer. The vertical axis in the diagram below shows the perceived customer value whereas the horizontal axis shows the monetary price of the product or service. Each point in the diagram corresponds to a particular combination of price and customer value. A consumer choosing among products located along the indifference curve would be indifferent among the offerings. Products offering price–value combinations located below the indifference curve yield a lower consumer preference than those along or above the indifference curve.

As customer value does not reach the price-performance curve for the actual price P in the diagram above, the perceived sacrifice (cost) is higher than the perceived benefits. The producer therefore has two options—either to reduce the price of the product (or service) so that the price/performance ratio becomes attractive to the customer (Arrow A in Figure 8.4), or to enhance its performance or functionality so that the customer values the offering more (Arrow B).

Alternative A means reduced price and hence a better performance/price ratio, which is now more attractive to the consumer. If this results in a sale, the producer's income will be lower, and if the costs are unchanged, then the profit will also be reduced.

This well-known scenario of competition based on price reduction has forced many firms out of the market because of financial problems. Lower sales price is expected to result in higher volumes sold, according to traditional price elasticity theory. Higher volumes will, however, lead to more production and higher material costs, more transportation for material input and product outputs and more administrative costs to manage the higher volumes. In addition, additional marketing and sales staff may be required to take care of the new customers.

Lower sales price will cause higher sales volume, which in turn will increase total sales revenue. By definition, the added value is reduced. The cost factor in this business scenario is highly important because both the additional direct costs and the indirect and hidden costs may increase due to the higher volumes, and the total costs may even turn out to be higher than the total revenue. Once the company becomes known on the market for its

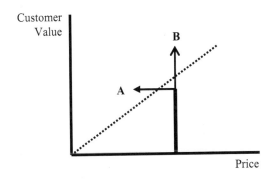

Figure 8.4   Two strategies

low price profile, it may be difficult for it to return to the previous price level in order to restore profit.

In alternative B in Figure 8.4, the producer adds functions and/or features to the product, thereby improving product performance while the sales price remains the same. The new product and service attributes do, however, result in increased costs for the supplier, with the same end-effect—i.e., reduced profit.

In the next alternative (arrow C in Figure 8.5), the consumer value may yield a surplus because the value–price combination, though closer to the indifference curve, is still in the region where the consumer will accept the higher price.

The ability of a producer to increase the price in return for added product and service attributes depends on his success in translating the improvements into financial or other real benefits for the customer. If the producer fails in translating the improvements into customer benefits, he may go unrewarded, resulting in extra costs that cannot be recovered. If the price can be increased to compensate for the extra costs, profit will be unchanged or higher. The variables of price, costs and profit must therefore be balanced.

Many enterprises are caught in a vicious circle from which they do not escape as long as they are trapped in the price competition pattern. When encouraged to embark on an alternative business strategy aiming at higher added value, many enterprises find it difficult to break away from the traditional price competition pattern and instead compensate for higher production costs through increased sales price. Customer value, as well as added value, therefore remains at modest levels, resulting in the following vicious circle:

> Lowest price to get the order ⇒ limited financial scope to develop new products, new materials, new types of service, etc. ⇒ limited use of new skills to enhance present capacity ⇒ limited interest to bring in new employees with new knowledge/ideas and acting as change agents (albeit at a higher cost) ⇒ limited input of new ideas to develop new

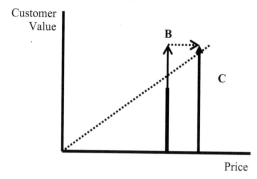

Figure 8.5 A third strategy

business concepts or add new product functions ⇒ little increase in customer value ⇒ price competition remains the primary business strategy ⇒ lowest price to get the order.

The pattern may explain why so many manufacturing enterprises produce a great number of different products in small quantities. As added value is low, these enterprises have few, if any, competitive advantages and therefore have to accept orders that are possible to produce with existing production facilities at a price that the customers are willing to pay. Profits are mostly at low levels, and the margin between profit and loss is often so small that any extra costs incurred as a result of an added value strategy may seem too risky for many firms.

The three alternatives mentioned above describe three business situations that are well known to many enterprise managers. Strategy 1 (price reduction) can be justified if the strategy is to break into a new market. The strategy may be to keep the low price for a period and later revert to the original price. Experience shows, however, that once the market has become accustomed to one price level there is resistance from the market to pay the original (higher) price unless there are obvious changes in the product offering. Often, however, price reduction is not a conscious strategy but more of an act of desperation in an attempt to come out of a competitive situation. Another motivation for using this strategy may be the desire to let the reduced price lead to higher volume sold. Already reduced profit margins may, however, shrink even more if the extra volume results in additional administrative and distribution costs.

In Strategy 2 (enhanced product/service) the decision to add customer value to the product/service at extra cost to the producer is a conscious strategy based on the assumption that the extra benefits will increase attractiveness of the product and lead to increased sales volume. As with Strategy 1, the extra sales volumes may result in additional administrative and distribution costs.

Strategy 3 (enhanced product/service at higher price) is based on the assumption that the extra customer value justifies an increase in sales price, leading to higher added value. Of the three strategies, this strategy is therefore of greatest commercial interest. The crucial question is, however: Will the higher costs incurred by the additional functions and/or service yield enough customer value to justify a higher price? The question is important and relevant—for example, when the additional function relates to better quality. It cannot be expected that customers will appreciate and pay higher prices for ever-increasing quality. Both services and products usually have a lower and an upper quality level, beyond which there is no profit for the producer.

When monitoring performance related to added value, the third strategy seems most attractive compared to the other two but only as long as costs are kept within acceptable boundaries. The assumption that highest added value is always best cannot, therefore, be automatically justified.

Structure and Process

The close connection between added value and customer value demands that costs incurred by increasing added value through enhanced product functions must not lead to a price increase that exceeds the price customers are prepared to pay for the enhanced product, function- or quality-wise. Added value should be in focus for business development but combined with careful cost awareness so that product and service improvement does not result in costs that cannot be covered by revenue.

To retain the forecasted surplus value between sales revenue and production cost, the finished product should reach the customer and be paid for in the shortest possible time, particularly in case of inflation. Revenue value will decrease by a factor $(1 + i/100)^t$ where i denotes the inflation factor and t the time in storage before delivery.

Methods and Tools

By relating the added value to sales value, firms of varying turnover and size can be compared as to production efficiency and productivity. The ratio or indicator is referred to as added value grade and denoted by A. There is a relationship between A and profit margin (P) and refinement grade (R) defined as the ratio between net product cost (the cost of producing one unit less the cost of material) and product cost. The relationship is $P = (A - R) / (1 - R)$. From this relationship can be shown that the value of R equal to $\sqrt{(1 - A)}$ determines how profit margin P will vary with the refinement grade R. For values of refinement grade that are less than $\sqrt{(1 - A)}$, changes in R will have relatively small changes in profit margin, whereas for R-values greater than $\sqrt{(1 - A)}$, even a small increase in refinement grade will cause big changes (increases) in profit margin. The tool is useful in the business development process (see Lind, 2007).

COPING WITH CHANGE

The concept of *change* has links to other concepts such as *adaptation, contingency* and *uncertainty*. Change in technologies and market behaviour becomes a challenge and induces organisations to adapt their operations to act and cope with the new conditions. Originally, however, the organizational response to external changes was more mechanistic (Burns and Stalker, 1961) and regarded as temporary disturbances to be eliminated. As the contingency approach became an influential organisation model, the view that change required alignments within internal procedures and management practice started to dominate, and the need for new types of skills and resources emerged. Organisations that for various reasons do not adapt to environmental changes or undergo incremental changes only run the risk

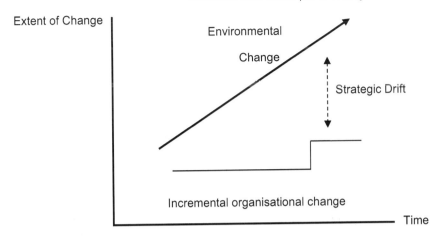

Figure 8.6 Organisational strategic drift and environmental change

of exposing themselves to strategic drift, in which the strategic direction of the organization gradually deviates from the direction in which society is headed based on new technologies as well as other kinds of social changes (see Figure 8.6).

Theory of Change

Change can be described and treated in a variety of ways. Here we shall use the view proposed in 1951 by Kurt Lewin, a German-born sociologist practising in the United States, which is still pertinent today. Lewin's point of departure was that the present condition of a system is a dynamic social equilibrium, which is a state of balance maintained by active driving and resisting social forces. Change consists of altering the driving and resisting forces, thereby facilitating the movement of the system to a new level of equilibrium. Lewin regarded change as a process with three phases:

Unfreezing: behaviour that increases the receptivity of the system to a possible change in the distribution and balance of forces

Moving: altering the magnitude, direction, or number of driving and resisting forces, consequently shifting the equilibrium to a new level

Refreezing: reinforcing the new distribution of forces, thereby maintaining and stabilising the new social equilibrium

Changing the culture of an organisation is one of the most difficult tasks facing all its individual constituents. It is very much like trying to change all that you as an individual believe in, or have been brought up to believe in. To energise change requires an 'unfreezing' of the status quo, change to be effected, and a 'refreezing' or consolidation of the new state. Lewin argued that organisations existed in a state of equilibrium that was not in itself conducive to change. This equilibrium was the result of opposing forces that constantly acted upon the organisation and its individuals. These were forces for change (driving forces) and forces against change (restraining forces) (Lewin, 1951).

Figure 8.7 shows a typical set of these forces. Lewin called the process of balancing driving and restraining forces a '*quasi-stationary equilibrium*'. This is because a true equilibrium assumes that no change takes place at all, given a perfect balance between opposing forces. In the world of organisations, of course, this is unrealistic. There is change happening all the time. The point is that the opposing pressures of driving and restraining forces will combine to constrain change to a minimum and mitigate any degree of further and future changes.

Imbalance occurs when the number of driving and hampering forces is not the same. This is, of course, not a mathematical equation but rather a psychological imbalance. After moving the situation to a new position where the driving and hampering forces are again in balance, the 'refrozen' state will remain until a new imbalance occurs, the new position unfreezes, and the organisation is moved again to a new position. The change process is thus open-ended. On the other hand, no organisation can constantly change; it must have periods of stability between changes. In order to promote the right conditions for change, there has to be an unfreezing of this situation.

An imbalance must be created between the driving and restraining forces. This means removing restraint or fuelling drives. Lewin argued that there was an optimal way of configuring this process. First, the restraining forces should be attended to and selectively removed. The driving forces will automatically push change forward because removing the restraining forces will have created an imbalance in the quasi-stationary equilibrium. Ideally, an increase in the number of driving forces or an increase in the potency of the existing set will achieve a greater degree of change. Refreezing the new

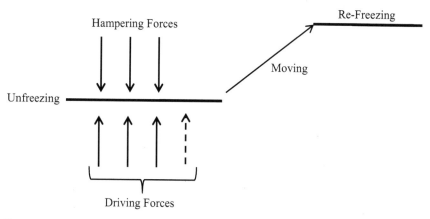

Figure 8.7   The Lewin change model (1951)

Table 8.1 Driving and hampering forces for change—examples

Driving Forces (for change)	Hampering Forces (against change)
Changing markets	From individuals:
Shorter product life-cycles	Fear of failure
Changing values towards work	Loss of status
Globalisation	Habits
Social transformations	Fear of the unknown
New technology	Loss of friends and colleagues
Increased competition	From the organisation:
	Strength of culture
	Rigidity of structure
	Reduced budget means
	Lack of competence
	Contractual agreements

situation is the final stage. This sequence is essential, according to Lewin (ibid.). If attention is first given to driving forces, then the result will be a commensurate increase in the number or potency of restraining forces, and the status quo will remain. No change will occur.

With reference to Table 8.1, one must remember that not all changes coming from outside (changing markets, social transformations, etc.) are of significant value, and hence they are not all driving change! Psychologists claim that merely twenty per cent of all impressions that we receive during a day will be of any significance and contribute to the creation of our mental landscape. It also means that eighty per cent of all impressions have little lasting impact. The critical issue is to distinguish the important twenty from the less important eighty per cent.

Creating a Change Climate in the Organisation

For business development to be successful, it is imperative to understand both the formal and informal structure of the organisation to ensure optimal match between demand and resources. The traditional understanding of an organisation is the common hierarchical structure with the leader at the top and employees further down in the hierarchy. An organisation is, however, much more than a static diagram, which does not reflect the variety, the dynamics between individuals and, most importantly, how the organisation can adapt to new business opportunities. Alternative descriptions of organisations have been suggested using metaphors (Morgan 1997). Organisations can thus be described as:

- Machines with rules and routines describing their functions and features. For machines, we also use words like *efficiency* and there are guidelines to help operate them. As with the machine, the organisation defines specified job objectives.

- Organisms or species adapting to the environment and developing interdependency among humans, machines and organisational needs. As with organisms, the organisation is contingent on the environment, and we can also refer to a natural selection and a life cycle within which an organisation is born, lives and dies.
- Brains or information processing systems that are part of the organisation and contribute to the decision-making capacity and are necessary for control and communication.
- Political systems built on social hierarchies in which there is competition among interest groups that may lead to corruption and bribery.
- Cultures that can be likened to geographical cultures, each with its specific value system, heroes, rituals, symbols, traditions and myths. Most of these are also present in organisations.
- Prisons, where individuals feel trapped because of formal and informal repression systems restricting their behaviour and exposing them to various forms of penalty systems.

Not only do individuals within an organisation experience restrictions that the organisation puts on their behaviour, but also the organisation itself is bounded by and depends upon factors beyond its control. Changing an organisation is thus restricted by the following three external factors—the legal system; the political system; and traditions, culture and values. These three factors define a structure that is stable, at least during a relatively long time period over which the change process takes place (see Figure 8.8). Within this structure, a change process is possible that may focus on changes in management (leadership style, organisation structure), employment (competence and skills, career, promotion) and strategy (goals and plans, short/long term objectives, products and skills, collaboration).

Cultural Aspects of Change

Change processes take place in environments characterised by local value systems, and the organisation in which change is taking place is therefore a product of an organisational culture that has developed particular attitudes towards change. These attitudes may be consciously adopted as a

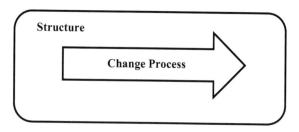

Figure 8.8   Organisational boundaries

management style for or against change, or they may be the result of historic sediments settled during the lifespan of the organisation. But the organisation is also characterised by its geographical context and the different cultural value systems that influence and form organisational behaviour in different parts of the world.

In a number of influential studies—for example, Hofstede (1991), Schwarz (1992) and Trompernaars (1993)—cultural aspects of managerial and organisational behaviour have been presented and explained. Hofstede (ibid.) refers to two types of cultural behaviour that may have impact on the change process in organisations. Firstly, Uncertainty Avoidance, which can be defined as the extent to which the members of a culture feel threatened by uncertain or unknown situations. Change processes are by nature uncertain because outcome is not known beforehand, and in countries with a high rating of the Uncertainty Avoidance index there seems to be a stronger resistance to change.

The second type of cultural behaviour with impact on the change process is Power Distance. Power Distance is defined as the extent to which the less powerful members of institutions and organisations within a country expect and accept that power is distributed unequally. In countries with a low Power Distance index, members of organisations expect to be consulted as stakeholders in the change process, whereas in high Power Distance countries, members expect to be told what to do.

Change and the Employee

Change can have its origin in employee reactions (mistrust of the current organisation and work, a feeling that organisational performance could be better) and also have impact on employees (fear of the unknown, loss of organisational security). In both situations, the role of the manager is important.

Traditionally, the manager's role in the change process has not been explicitly focused upon. With the advent of the present organisational paradigm, in this book referred to as Organisational Culture, emphasis is on the individual and focusing on the employee during the change process is therefore vital. Without support from and dialog with the employees, the change process risks being at stake. In addition to the more traditional role of the manager—i.e., to make use of the employees to achieve organisational goals—the additional role that has come into focus in learning organisations and in organisations open to change is *the mentor* role, in which the manager makes use of the organisation as a resource to assist employees in achieving their own individual goals.

In a change process, the employees should be involved in accordance with modern leadership philosophy insisting on employee participation. Hirschman (1970) identified four different stereotyped reactions, depending on the employee's attitude towards the organisation and the change process.

The very loyal employee is probably supportive of the change process and actively takes part in the creation of a better and more efficient organisation. The less loyal employee is participative and creative but with a critical approach, observing problems and questioning the implementation of the change process. Managers involved in the change process will have most support from the two creative types of employees, whether loyal or not. Less creative but loyal employees are not necessarily contributing to the process; the less creative and less loyal employees will probably sooner or later leave the organisation because of lack of stimulation. (This typology has also been discussed in Chapter 7.)

The Learning Organisation

For a learning organisation, two elements come into the foreground—learning from others and learning from internal mistakes. Analysing mistakes that have been made inside the organisation offers important input into the business development process. From the discussion about backgrounds for initiating change, we notice from Table 8.1 that unhappiness to infer displeasure with employee performance is one of the driving forces for change. Change is thus closely related to learning. Change is an opportunity to learn!

All organisations have clients. Regardless of whether the organisation is a private business with a solid customer base or a government organisation with the long-term objective of improving road safety or reducing industrial pollution or developing new methods for weather forecasting—there are always those who will benefit from services provided by the organisation. The reversed situation would be depressing: If no one were looking forward to the services or benefiting from what the organisation produces, then what reason would there then be for the organisation to exist at all? The clients are the lifeblood of the organisation, its *raison d'être,* and the objectives for learning should therefore be to better respond to the needs and expectations of clients. If we broaden our view to also include other stakeholders, such as employees and society at large, then the basis for learning is to analyse feedback from stakeholders and to analyse and assess our behaviour in response to clients' requirements and needs.

The Image-Vision Gap between the internal management vision and the image created among clients and outside stakeholders must not be too wide. The same applies to the gap between managers and employees in the organisation—a shared vision is a critical component for organisational success. There is an important difference between a vision built around a charismatic leader—which may be transitory—and what is built around shared goals. For the development of a learning organisation, the building and maintenance of a shared vision offers individuals the support to excel and learn. A learning organisation has a process approach to life in which the continuous improvement translated into the Plan-Do-Check-Act Cycle is a viable strategy. Organisations therefore must have the capacity to sense, monitor, and scan significant aspects of their environment. They must be able to relate this information to the operating norms that guide the operation, and they must be able to detect significant deviations from these norms. They must be able to initiate corrective actions when discrepancies are detected. The two concepts of single-loop and double-loop learning have been introduced to show the two aspects of learning. Single-loop learning rests in the ability to detect and correct errors in relation to a given set of operating norms. Double-loop learning, on the other hand, depends on being able to take a "double-look" at the situation by questioning the relevance of operating norms.

REFERENCES

Atherton, A. and Hannon, P. (2001) *Innovation processes in and the small business: A conceptual analysis.* International Journal of Business Performance Management, 2 (4).

Baumane, I., Lind, P., Simonova, T., Timofejevs, A., Vedina, R. and Wróbel, P. (2011) *Innovation capabilities in tourism and food production SMEs in the Baltic Sea Region.* International Journal of Knowledge Management Studies, 4 (4).

Burns, T. and G. M. Stalker (1961) *The management of innovations.* London, Tavistock.

Chandler, A. (1984) *Strategy and structure.* Cambridge, MA, MIT Press.

Danielsson, A. (1978) *Teori för beskrivning av företag* (in Swedish). Lund, Studentliteratur.

Edquist, C. (2001) *Innovation and employment: Process versus product innovation.* London, Edward Elgar Publishing.

Forbes, N. and Wield, D. (2002) *From leaders to followers: Managing technology and innovation.* London, Routledge.

Foreman-Peck, J., Makepeace, G. and Morgan, B. (2006) *Growth and profitability of small and medium-sized enterprises: Some Welsh evidence.* Journal of Regional Studies, 40 (4).

Gold, A.H., Malhorta, A. and Segars, A.H. (2001) *Knowledge management: An organizational capabilities perspective.* Journal of Management Information Systems, 18 (1).

Hamel, G. and Prahalad, C.K. (1994) *Competing for the future.* Boston, Harvard Business School Press.

Heracleous, L. (2003) *Strategy and organisation.* Cambridge, Cambridge University Press.

Hirschman A. O. (1970) *Exit, voice, and loyalty: Responses to decline in firms, organizations, and states.* Cambridge, MA: Harvard University Press.

Hofstede, G. (1991) *Culture and organisations.* London, McGraw-Hill.

Jones, O. (2003) Innovations in SMEs in Jones, O. and Tilley, F. (Eds.) *Competitive advantage in SMEs.* London, Wiley.

Jones, O. and Tilley, F. (2003) *Competitive advantage in SMEs.* London, Wiley.

Lewin, K. (1951) *Field theory in social science: Selected theoretical papers.* D. Cartwright (Ed.). New York, Harper & Row.

Lind, P. (2007) *Competiveness through Increased Added Value: A challenge for developing countries.* Journal of Comparative International Management, 8 (1).

Lundberg, E. (1994) *Studies in economic instability and change.* Stockholm, Centre for Business and Policy Studies.

Menger, C. (1950) *Principles of economics.* New York, The Free Press.

Meredith, J. and Shaffer, S. (2002).*Operations management for MBAs.* New York, John Wiley & Sons.

Morgan, G. (1997) *Images of organisations.* London, Sage.

Naumann, E. (1995) *Creating customer value: The path to competitive advantage.* Cincinnati, OI I., Thompson Executive Press.

Penrose, E. T. (1959) *The theory of the growth of the firm.* Oxford, Oxford University Press.

Porter, M. E. (1980) *Competitive strategy.* New York, The Free Press.

Roper, S. (1997) *Product innovation and small business growth: A comparison of the strategies of German, U.K. and Irish companies.* Journal of Small Business Economics, 9 (6).

Schwarz, S. (1992) *Universals in the content and structure of values: Theoretical advances and empirical tests in 20 countries.* Advances in Experimental Social Psychology 25.

Shapiro, C. (1989) *The theory of business strategy.* RAND Journal of Economics, 20 (1).

Stock, J. and Lambert, D. (2001) *Strategic Logistics Management.* New York, McGraw-Hill.

Trompenaars, F. (1993) *Riding the waves of culture.* London, The Economist Books.

9 Information Systems as Business Monitoring Tools

Monitoring business performance is a continuous activity utilizing various sources of data, ranging from loosely structured observations or perceptions—even intuition—to more prescribed and structured information. For the monitoring of business performance, accounting data historically represented formal information, and pre-defined parameters such as liquidity and profit margins were used to facilitate the monitoring. These parameters were simple and well defined and did not require the vast information processing facilities offered by computers, which, as they arrived, were rather used for the processing of large amounts of data and routines for invoicing and bookkeeping.

The use of computers as monitoring tools dates from the process industry, where temperatures, pressures and similar physical and technical parameters were monitored. With reference to the discussion in Chapter 3 (comparing models in natural and social sciences) we may claim that those early monitoring principles were based on simpler models with fewer and more well-defined parameters than is the case in business performance monitoring.

Let us therefore begin this chapter by making a very basic statement: Computer programs are based on models of reality. A computer program is not a model in itself. This distinction is important to make here because we will be concerned with the two steps, from reality to model and from model to computer program, that literally determine the applicability and usefulness of formal information handling systems. As an illustrative example, one may chose accounting—an application area where computers are used extensively. Broadly defined, accounting practice is concerned with the collection of data relating to the economic activities of an organisation and its use of resources, with analysis of that data utilized for (corporate) decision-making purposes and control over the use of the resources.

To perform his task the accountant needs a model: a simplified picture of the enterprise that highlights those specific areas that the accountant is interested in analysing, such as cash flow. The model may also describe the pattern for decision-making as well as the control structure of the enterprise. The model is, of course, less complex than the enterprise itself in order to be manageable. It has therefore been deprived of most variables except for those considered most essential. For example, most models have been deprived of dynamism because they are to be used repetitively. Therefore, they reflect a static situation. Furthermore, accounting models, like many other models of economic or social realities, often represent different schools of thought. There may then be different, even competing, models for the same reality, each model having its own view on cause/effect relations.

A computerized accounting system is built around a computer program residing in a computer with routines for data acquisition and data dissemination. The accounting program is based—i.e. designed and constructed—on an accounting model, using one of many programming tools. Already at this stage we may ask to what extent the selected model is appropriate: For example, is it too simplified or too static to be a relevant description of a particular situation? Also, does the computer language manage to interpret the model as an administrative tool in spite of its simplified false-true grammar? These are all questions to which we shall return in the following discussion.

The word *model*, the common dominator in the two steps above, has two meanings, which were outlined in previous chapters. One meaning is similar to 'mapping' or creation of an image of reality or part thereof. The other meaning is 'something worth imitation.' For example, in the 1960s 'The Yugoslavian model' was regarded as an interesting socio-economic experiment between socialism and capitalism, whereas 'The Western model' has been, and is still to some extent, a concept in development theory and in political science.

The failure to distinguish between the two meanings leads to confusion. A computer program of an accounting model, for example, is often referred to as a *computer model* and regarded as something scientific, contextually neutral and therefore of high value. As a matter of fact, a computer 'model' is a transcription in a simplified language of an image that has been subjectively interpreted and created by somebody. Confusion may arise if computer 'models' are discussed from the second perspective above, as something worthy of imitation, rather than from the first perspective, in which the question of usability and applicability of the theoretical model belongs. It is not enough that a computer solution is formally correct; it must also be practically useful.

In the next two sections, we will scrutinize the two steps, from reality to model and from model to computer program, in more detail. In doing this, we will show that the steps from reality to computer programs are much more controversial than is often realized. In the context of applicability of computers in developing countries, this cannot simply be ignored.

FROM REALITY TO MODEL

The interpretation of reality for a model is affected by three factors: what is the conception of reality, who has the conception, and what is the purpose of the model. If there is a conception that reality is predictable, then the purpose of the model may be to find just those variables that make prediction possible. But conceptions of reality differ among interpreters, and the design of models is therefore influenced by the interpreter's own world-view.

To make things worse, our conception of reality may be based on other images, or models, that we create or which are created for us by others. It is therefore a tendency, if seen in a wide time perspective, that certain models and conceptions of reality amplify each other into solidified basic models. Such a basic model appears in the Western view on certainty and predictability. The relationship between the model and our conception of reality means that to adopt a model is also to adopt a world-view or a conception of reality.

FROM MODEL TO COMPUTER PROGRAMS

The step from model to computer program means, as in the step from reality to model, a further simplification. In the first step, this was deliberate because the model should be a simplified, yet trustworthy, image of reality. In this second step, however, the transformation becomes a simplification because the computer technology sets limits. This simplification is therefore not deliberate.

A major limit is, of course, the computer program itself that must be designed in accordance with a pre-defined logical structure to fit with the technological constraints. Ambiguity in the model, implicit or unavoidable if the model is to reflect a social system with human integration, is not allowed in the computer program simply because the computer program cannot by itself judge whether a conclusion arrived at in the program is reasonable or not. Every situation that may appear in reality must therefore be a priori foreseen in the model to be reflected in the program; otherwise it will not be recognized at all. It is thus a simplification and also a limitation in the usability of the model, that all forms of ambiguity must be avoided in the computer program.

Models help us to understand the world around us and to communicate this understanding to others via textbooks, discussions, articles, etc. This communication is based on language, albeit the language is sometimes inadequate to express specific phenomena and subtle meanings. As long as the communication takes place in a cultural domain with a common frame of reference for abstract reasoning and metaphors, these difficulties can be overcome. But as soon as this common reference frame can no longer be assumed as a basis (for example, in communication between different cultural domains with different value patterns and intellectual traditions), communication may become distorted and meanings become defective or misleading.

In this respect, computer language can be regarded as an expression of a specific culture in which the language is based on formal logic and deprived of inexactness and ambiguities. In this culture, exact wording in language and semantic accuracy are cornerstones. We can therefore say that the computer language is too straightforward to serve as an interpreter of the conceptual thinking behind many models.

Models can be regarded as a type of intellectual tool that helps to understand the world around us. One and the same reality can be interpreted by different models, each model having its perspective and highlighting particular phenomena. But one and the same reality can also be interpreted differently by different interpreters and thus produce different models. Such models often represent different schools of thought and show thereby the inexactness and uncertainty in our attempts to describe reality. General models are therefore no more general than the underlying world-view of their originators. In other words, no model can claim absolute credibility.

However, when a model is transformed into a computer program it has a tendency to become a generalization. There are primarily two reasons behind this. First, a computer program is regarded by many as the result of a consensus decision where the most appropriate model has been selected to be transformed into a computer program. The second reason is that those suppliers who invest in producing this particular computer program promote their product as being as generally applicable as possible in order to maximize the volume of sales. As long as the model can be traced back to the originator, validation of the model can be done by evaluating the arguments of its originator. In the computer program, the bridges back to the underlying model and its originator are, in general, blurred. The transfer from model to computer programs is therefore also a step of impersonalization. The view of a computer program as an expression of formalized logic has contributed to the conception of a higher veracity. This gives us reason to take a brief look back in time to see how mathematical logic developed into computer programs.

Model and Computer Program—A Time Perspective

In the middle of the seventeenth century, the scientific development towards more accuracy in measurement created needs for artificial modes of expression based on mathematics. Leibniz (1645–1716), one of the first to use an axiomatic structure to describe thinking, based his theories on a method in which sentences could be described in a formal language and conclusions could be drawn, as in solving an equation.

A century later, Boole (1815–1864) presented his logical algebra with a further systematizing of the analogy between thinking and algebraic operations. Boolean algebra was first used in set theory and in probability theory, and not until the end of the 1930s was the most important application area realized: mechanical computation. It was Shannon who unified the two development paths (formal logic and mechanical computation) by proving that what happened when electrical components (e.g., switching relays) were connected could be interpreted by Boolean algebra. From then on, the development into today's computer technology evolved. This formal logic is thus to a great extent realized in today's computer technology and perhaps even more in the systematic approach to problem solving (e.g., flow-charts) that is also the structure of computer programs.

MONITORING BY MEANS OF AN INFORMATION SYSTEM

The computer as a management tool allows the extraction of information from raw data emitted by the business process to support monitoring and analysis decisions. Figure 9.1 illustrates an information flow in which various types of signals are emitted from operations and activities. The signals may convey, for instance, messages that material is missing for production or that deliveries to a customer have been delayed. Signals are detected provided there is a suitable interface—e.g., a reporting procedure.

After computer processing of the signals by means of a suitable application model, the output data are compared with pre-defined plans and reference values.

Under the assumption that the interface is adequate for detecting and retrieving the signals, and provided that the computer's application programme is capable of making relevant comparisons with target values of the plan, the information is ready to be used for decision making. The distinction in Figure 9.1 between data and information should be noted!

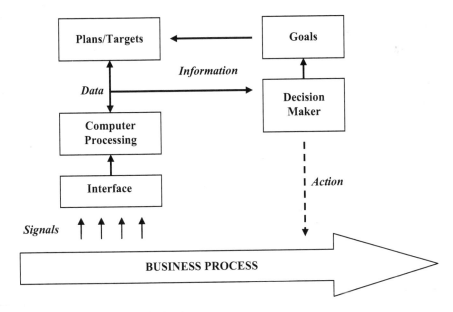

Figure 9.1   Monitoring the business process

In this context, it is important that the goals and plans are not only consistent and realistic but also integrated with the information flow. This means that the interface arrangement in Figure 9.1 must be designed in such a way that among all signals being emitted from the business process, the only ones being captured are those related to the goals and plans. Often, goals and plans are formulated in accordance with what is measurable or which signals it is possible to retrieve. Certain signals may not be possible to detect, even less possible to retrieve—for example, those about poor working conditions, about a hostile or unfriendly work atmosphere or about lack of trust between employees and managers. These are types of signals that would be important to collect, as they are significant for business and operational efficiency.

ARE INFORMATION SYSTEMS REASONABLE?

To what extent can we expect computers to one day exhibit human creativity, subtlety, sensitivity and wisdom? A classic and probably apocryphal illustration of the limits that seem to exist is the following example from the field of computer translation of human languages, presented by Carl Sagan (1977, 210–11):

A delegation including a U.S. senator was proudly taken through a demonstration of a computer-based translation system, to translate from English to Chinese. The senator was asked to produce an English phrase for translation and promptly suggested, 'Out of sight, out of mind. 'The machine dutifully generated a piece of paper on which were printed some Chinese characters. But since nobody including the senator could read Chinese, the test was completed by letting the computer run the translation in reversed order. The Chinese characters were thus read by the computer and a new piece of paper was produced. The visitors crowded around the new output, which to their puzzlement read: 'Invisible idiot'.

This probably fictitious example still reveals a fundamental weakness of computer-based information systems—their incapability of assessing how reasonable the result of their own work is. Even if there are formal rules that can be applied to assess the plausibility of a result, the information system has to be told which rules to apply. There is no way that the information system is capable of exerting such control by itself. In fact, to do so would require a mental process of great complexity, with so many context- and time-dependent possibilities that a computer model capable of such sophisticated self-assessment would have to be as complex as reality itself!

This introduces a dimension in the discussion about information and information systems that deserves more attention than is generally the case—namely, the integration between semantics and technology. Two aspects will be mentioned in the following discussion: The first is the semantic variety in the human language to express and explain things, which is in contrast to the simplified syntax of computers. The second is the dialogue between the systems analyst and the user, a place where syntax and semantics often come in conflict; the user wants to do things that the computer syntax cannot accept.

The Myth Surrounding Information Systems

In pace with advances in technology and as information systems have become more powerful, we tend to be more and more affected by computers and information systems in our homes, at work and in society at large. As information technology can convey information faster, more reliably and, not least, in bigger volumes, new and more demanding applications have been added to the already vast number of information systems, which have thus become an integrated part of society.

The quantitative capacity of today's information systems was unimaginable only few years ago. This unprecedented development has led to and created a mythological perception of information technology as representing a new and different kind of technology, in particular because of its integration with human mental processes. The myth can be observed through the rhetoric surrounding information technology, highlighting mediocre achievements as significant breakthroughs. One such perceived breakthrough was the paperless office, a myth that never came into being. The belief that more information also leads to better decisions is another widespread myth that was excessively cultivated for a long time, until space shuttles crashed and stockbrokers created turbulence on the stock market. In the late 1990s, the so called 'new economy' was to a large extent the child of information technology in alliance with the globalisation story, an alliance that formed based on the vast amounts of market information that could be collected, stored and disseminated with the help of the new technology.

There is a syndrome related to the use of information systems that could best be described as the *as if* syndrome—viewing or interpreting the world through the pictures created by information technology as if the picture were reality itself. Forecasting, for example, is a concept used in business, and forecasting systems try to predict future events as if the future were predictable. This rhetoric of information technology has its roots in the scientific worldview that has been predominant in the development of Western societies for the last four hundred years. Rhetoric can be used effectively to take the sting out of critical voices. Rhetoric may thus prevent the emergence of alternative perspectives that would otherwise contribute to less bias and truer pictures of phenomena.

The Danish author Hans Christian Andersen's story, *The Emperor's New Suite*, can be seen as a good illustration of this type of rhetoric: The Emperor's behaviour *as if* he can see his fancy new dress (which in fact does not exist) resembles the *as if* syndrome in information technology.

The story illustrates the power of rhetoric and how far from common sense that rhetoric is capable of taking us. In the vast literature on information technology, the use of clichés such as 'the Information Society' and 'the Information Revolution' has contributed to the rhetoric that is also reinforced by politicians and policy makers, as well as the information industry itself. Without reflecting upon background, context and meaning, the clichés lead to a jargon, another characteristic of the 'Information Society'! Using the clichés, however, in the ambition to convince ourselves that profound changes have taken place in society and reshaped values and behaviour patterns, reveals a lack of understanding of what the mechanisms are that do create profound changes in society and human behaviour.

Like the Emperor and his ministers who pretended they saw what was not to be seen and who did not dare to reveal they had been taken in, one cannot avoid observing a similar attitude when it comes to Information Technology. By refraining from posing critical questions about Information Technology and its usage, the necessary but important discussion about its applicability and true contribution, in a wider context, will continue to be absent. The billions of dollars that have been invested in 'computer-in-school' projects around the world is just one example of how perceived benefits tend to be increasingly obscure, as some in-depth analysis and critical questions reveal the opposite (e.g. Greenfield, 2010; Toyama, 2011).

Still, however, we need more evidence before we are in the position to claim that the Emperor is naked—that information technology is partly primitive and immature. Has it not proved to be an extension to human intelligence and ability? Would it not be right to admit that the recent development in information technology has been, and is, exceptional? Most probably from a technological point of view—but as an extension to human intelligence probably not, as was illustrated in the Viking space shuttle example presented next.

The Viking Space Shuttle

On the 2nd of July in the year 1976, an event took place that marked a further development of formalised intelligence, and the seemingly successful enhancement of human brain capacity. As the Viking space shuttle that day landed on the planet Mars, a real achievement of human creativity and, in the language of political rhetoric, another milestone on man's way from the cave to the super-technological society had been reached. The Viking Mars Mission, a US programme intended to collect as much detail as possible about the planet, and in particular to look for any sign of life, was indeed a remarkable technological venture!

The technical set-up that was to guide and control the voyage through space until it reached the final destination, the planet of Mars, was indeed a new token of how far man had managed to make science its servant. A significant part of the onboard technique and technology in the spacecraft shuttle was to be used for communication and navigation. The onboard computers, the brain of the Viking spacecraft, represented the very latest in information system technology at the time. The computing capacity installed to analyse the enormous volume of incoming signals, and to instantly convert data into valuable information, was amazing for the time and so was the capacity to store the large amount of data generated from onboard instruments as well as from the earth stations. The brain of the Viking space shuttle on its voyage into the unknown, the computer-based information system, was indeed a triumph of man's ingeniousness!

If we, for a moment, however, disregard the rhetoric and try to assess the amount of 'brain ware' or 'intelligence' represented by the 'Viking' information (or computer) system, it may be illuminating to use a scale that ranges from the most primitive form of life to the more advanced forms, represented by the human being. On this scale one would find that in the evolutionary development of higher and higher forms of life and intelligence, the level of 'intelligence' represented by the 'brain' of the Viking space shuttle had been surpassed already more than hundred million years ago!

How relevant is this comparison, and what could be a measure of intelligence in this context? Firstly, the computers on board were stored with pre-programmed instructions amounting to millions of bits (binary digits, the basic unit of information in computing). The enterprise of not only sending the shuttle into space, but also making it land on a planet millions of miles from earth, was at the time considered a tremendous human achievement that also marked the latest achievements in the development of computer technology. Comparing the amount of brain ware of the Viking information system with that of living beings, the information stored in the onboard computers was of the size of the genetic information stored in the DNA molecules of live beings, which contains the genetic instructions for life.

In the human genetic DNA code, the amount of stored information is approximately equal to two million ordinary pages of printed text, an enormous library of information that would count ten thousand books of two hundred pages each. A tower of these books would be almost as high as the Eiffel Tower in Paris, for one individual only. The genetic information stored in a human being is many times larger than the amount of information that was kept in the computers on board the Viking. Again, if we use the evolutionary scale to determine where the various forms of life can be placed according to their capacity of storing genetic information, we should find that the Viking space shuttle had slightly more 'genetic information' than a bacterium, but significantly less than an alga.

Intelligence is not, however, primarily related to stored information, neither in a computer nor in humans. Intelligence is associated with the brain and its ability to combine bits of information into meaningful information. The tools used by the brain to carry out mental activities are the so-called neurons, switching elements containing a large number of synapses that resemble the device we use to switch on and off a lamp. The switching capacity in the human brain is of a magnitude that is hardly imaginable! The human brain, characterised by around ten trillion synapses (a ten followed by thirteen zeroes) is thus capable of ten trillion different mental states, or thoughts. Some of these synapses are involved in cognitive interaction with other synapses; others are concerned with non-cognitive functions, and some may be just waiting for new information to flutter through. We may thus conclude that the human brain has a considerable over-capacity for mental activities.

In his book *The Dragons of Eden*, Carl Sagan points out how the great variation of possible mental states leads to the unpredictability of human behaviour:

> (the number of different states of the human brain) is an unimaginably large number, far greater, for example, than the total number of elementary particles (electrons and protons) in the entire universe. It is because of this immense number of functionally different configurations of the human brain that no two humans, even identical twins raised together, can ever be really very much alike. These enormous numbers may also explain something of the unpredictability of human behaviour and those moments when we surprise even ourselves by what we do. Indeed, in the face of these numbers, the wonder is that there are any regularities at all in human behaviour. The answer must be that all possible brain states are by no means occupied; there must be an enormous number of mental configurations that have never been entered or even glimpsed by any human being, in the history of mankind. From this perspective, each human being is truly rare and different and the sanctity of individual human lives is a plausible ethical consequence. (Sagan, 1977, 42)

In situations where people interact, both with other people and within organisations, the irregularity in human behaviour complicates any attempt at formalising and predicting such interactions.

> Why then, when we seem to have such effective thinking in the technical area, do we seem to make so little progress in the more human area: we still have wars and crime and inhuman behaviour; we still have poverty and ignorance. Is it simply that the type of thinking that is so very successful in the technical area is of much less use in the human area? Space exploration is relatively easy to deal with because nothing changes. The gravitational pull of Mars can be calculated centuries in advance and will not have altered by the time a space probe gets there. It could be that human matters are so complicated by interactive change and feedback loops that our ordinary linear thinking is unable to cope. (de Bono, 1988, 17–18)

Is it therefore so that technical situations, such as the landing of a space craft shuttle on a distant planet (e.g., the Viking), is paradoxically significantly easier, since the landing is a predictable situation and possible to describe and articulate in words and technical terms beforehand? It is possible to store different levels of commands in the onboard information system before they actually they have to be executed, each level pre-programmed and thus ready when the next hierarchical level is to be activated and involved.

As a contrast, in the interaction between humans it is significantly more difficult to predict which rules and commands to apply. In sophisticated technical systems, as in the Viking example above, the human interaction with the technical system has to be kept to a minimum in order not to jeopardise the predefined rules. In social interaction between humans, new commands and rules have to be invented in an ad hoc manner to cope with new and unexpected or unpredicted events.

Hubert Dreyfus, one of the pioneers working with the concept of artificial intelligence systems, concluded that in order to translate a natural language more is needed than a mechanical dictionary—no matter how complete—and the laws of grammar—no matter how sophisticated. The order of the words in a sentence does not provide enough information to enable a machine to determine which of several possible parsings is the appropriate one, nor do the surrounding words—the written context—always indicate which of several possible meanings is the one the author had in mind" (Dreyfus, 1972).

In language communication, there are ways of structuring sentences, of stressing and combining words and of using punctuation, to have the desired effect. Words alone may not be enough to convey the intended meaning of a sentence, as was pointed out by Dreyfus. The use of punctuation—for example, hyphenation—can radically change the meaning of a sentence, as the following example illustrates:

> 'The sun was shining on the hot-dog eater' is not the same as 'The sun was shining on the hot dog-eater'.

The two sentences, having the same set-up of words, convey two very different meanings. As, however, the semantic content of a sentence is of absolutely no meaning or relevance to a technical information system, it is only through the hyphenation that the two meanings can be distinguished. With the help of the brain, we are able to conclude from the actual context whether we have to do with an innocent Sunday stroller enjoying a sausage in the sun or with an abnormal consumer of dogs. The computer programme, however, is not able to make this kind of conclusion from the context, and would therefore be at loss for not knowing how to hyphenate the sentence.

Heinz Pagels, former Director of the New York Academy of Science, considered that

> "Brains understand what things mean, how they function; they are sensitive to semantics. Computers just obey rules or syntax; that's why they

are such good calculators, but poor at the things in which humans excel. Unlike a computer's world, the real world is unlabelled, and yet our brain can organise its experience, memorise and recall parts of it. Brains evidently do have pattern recognition hierarchies. In the visual field they organise texts into objects, objects into scenes, and these into abstract concepts. Existing computers can do none of this". (Pagels, 1988, 115)

CHARACTERISTICS OF INFORMATION SYSTEMS

The reference to 'systems' creates the perception of something orderly, rational and well defined, and from the definition of systems this may well be true: A system is a set of interrelated elements striving towards a common goal, and it should be clear if an element belongs to the set itself or not (in that case, to its complement). Each element is directly or indirectly connected to every other element. Describing something as a system is both relevant and illustrative when the definition can be applied. A system of cog-wheels or a shoal of fish has all the characteristics of a system. Since the system is an interpretation of reality, it is also a model, but with specific characteristics described above. A system is a model of an observed situation (an organisation, a shoal of fish), not the situation itself.

Experience tells us that situations we encounter are often not specified well enough to be regarded as systems in a strict meaning. Information we receive about a situation may be incomplete, or we may even be uncertain how to describe what we see. In our desire for an orderly and rational world, it is therefore tempting to view a collection of things as a system even if the things do not comply with the definition. Viewing a configuration of elements as a system rather than, for example, as a 'manifold of elements' is a choice the observer makes.

It is essential to point out that information systems are generally not systems in a strict sense. That means there is not a set of interrelated elements that have a common goal, and it is not meaningful to determine if an element belongs to the set itself or to its complement. Typical elements of an information system are procedures and routines, hardware, data, and the organisation of data. Tasks that are the result of the Information System, as well as individuals assigned to these tasks, must be regarded as elements of information systems because they become increasingly integrated with the organisation. But since many of these tasks, and not least the individuals, are also elements of other sets or systems, they conflict with our definition of a system as elements that cannot belong to both the set itself and its complement. Therefore information systems are hardly systems. So what are they?

System in *information system* refers to the systematic way of organising data and making information available. This would make the concept of information systems more intelligible and probably reduce some of the ambiguity of where the 'beginning' and the 'end' of the information system are. This would have direct and significant impact on how costs related to information systems could be determined.

Information Systems and Information Technology

In the following discussion, the terms *information systems* and *information technology* will be used consistent with the very general notion that *information technology* is about techniques whereas *information systems* refers to applications. With this very broad definition, it cannot be avoided that the terms will sometimes be used interchangeably; there is overlap between the two. Somewhat more precisely, *information technology* refers to the techniques developed essentially for hardware, software and telecommunications networks. It is both tangible (e.g., with servers, PCs, routers and network cables) and intangible (e.g., with software of all types). Information technology facilitates the acquisition, processing, storing, delivery and sharing of information and other digital content. To the information technology definition we may also include intellectual infrastructure, such as the accumulated knowledge, research results and patents, as well as organisational affiliations working with and developing information technology.

Rather than trying to define information systems, others have referred to the domain of study of information systems, which involves the study of theories and practices related to the social and technological phenomena, which determine the development, use and effects of information systems in organisations and society. Although technology is the immediate enabler of information systems, the latter is actually part of the much wider domain of human language and communication, and will remain in a state of continual development and change in response both to technological innovation and to its mutual interaction with human society as a whole, (Ward and Peppard, 2002).

The Formality of Information Systems

Information systems have a high degree of formality and restrictions imposed upon them by their basis in technology and its technique. Some of the limits have been gradually reduced in pace with technological advances and innovations. This happens, for example, to communication speed and data storing capacity. But there are other limits that cannot be reduced or eliminated simply because they are intrinsically interwoven with the mathematical-logical principles constituting the foundation of information technology design.

The formality of information systems has its background in these mathematical-logical principles and formal rules:

- There are rules on how to handle data; these rules need to be strictly followed in the design and development of information system software.

- The design of information systems must follow a strict structure to ensure technical functionality of the system. The organisational functionality of the information system, however, can generally not be guaranteed because the structure of the information system does not necessarily tally with the dynamism and operational structure of the organisation, which is usually less formal and more ad hoc.
- There is a formal language for the rules and the structure. The language is a linguistic simplification of human language, guided by a grammar with few but very strict rules. The language does not allow ambiguities of any kind, which makes it basically alien to human communication practices, such as the frequent use of so-called language games, a concept introduced by Ludwig Wittgenstein, the philosopher who showed how the original meanings of words can be deliberately changed but still be intelligible. As information systems tend to become more integrated with organisational structures, and thereby also increasingly used for communication between individuals, their inability to cope with the richness of human language is a severe limitation to their wider usage of in organisations.

Information System Applications of the Analysis Type

An important aspect of analysis applications is the cause-effect pattern of the studied phenomenon that must be known in order to understand what gives rise to certain observed effects, and which effects should be expected if certain events happen. Revealing this cause-and-effect relationship is fundamental as it helps us analyse the mechanisms behind observed behaviour and also speculate about the future. Unfortunately, however, most cause-effect patterns are complex and do not provide us with the entire picture.

A way out of this dilemma can be to resort to simplified analysis that does not require the cause-effect relationship to be explicitly known. One may therefore distinguish between simple and advanced analysis, depending on the degree of accuracy when creating the picture. Simple analysis means there is generally no need to go beyond and ask what the specific mechanism behind certain behaviour is. As an example, we may take sales analysis in a firm in which the focus is on who the customers are and when and what they buy. In this simple situation, there is no need to know the mechanisms behind the customers' preference attitudes. In other words, the cause-effect relationship between customer and product does not need to be explicitly known to do simple analysis.

In far more complicated situations—for example, when analysing customer preferences for certain ranges of products—it may be necessary to simulate market behaviour. In such situations, the cause-effect pattern must be articulated and known. This complex analysis is more controversial because it requires sophisticated models of markets and market behaviour based on predefined parameters. A complication is here that the more complex the computer model is in relating effects to causes, the more sophisticated the input data that is needed—and that may or may not be available or possible to retrieve!

Analysis results with diagrams and tables that are provided in the form of computer output are often credited with a high degree of confidence. This is the case even if the reliability of input data is uncertain. As advanced analysis involves manifold parameters and relationships, it is a complicated task to identify essential signals from the operations, to capture these signals and to measure them by quantitative methods. A pre-condition for such analysis is therefore that the analysis model is articulated and developed close to the user, that the application is well known to the developer of the model and that the data available really supports the computer model. If the correspondence between reality and model is weak, then the usefulness of the results is limited.

In the following discussion about information and information systems, one should have in mind the conflicting views between the unpredictability of human behaviour, on the one hand, and the need for information systems to work in predictable environments, on the other.

CLASSIFICATION OF INFORMATION

Land (1985) classified information that is used in organizations into three basic types: descriptive information, probabilistic information and qualitative information.

Descriptive Information

Under this category, Land (1985, 212–213) distinguishes three different types of information:

> Description of rules that govern or constrain the affairs of the real world: Most organizations of any size function on the basis of a formalized set of rules and such organizations developed large-scale data processing systems at an early stage in the history of computing in order to undertake some of simpler rule-following activities. However, in only a few cases are such rules as inviolate and unchanging as the laws of nature, and the legislation or regulations under which an administration operates will need interpretation from time to time. Thus far computers have been less good at this task. As the line between rule compliance and discretion is not always clear or easy to draw, computer-based information systems that incorporate legislation or regulations run the risk of not allowing interpretation and discretion and thus becoming dysfunctional. It should also be noted that in organizations rules can be felt to exist widely and uniformly applied, but are not to be found

anywhere in a neat encoded form. Rather they are informal, either as commands from the organizational hierarchy, or as norms which are part of the organizational culture. The systems analyst will find it useful to explore such descriptive information in terms of pragmatics, semantics and syntactics.

Regarding the description of the state of the real world: The data files or the accounting record books of an organisation contain a great deal of such information, such as, for example, the records on the stock available in the warehouse or the employee records in the payroll system. But computer files and databases will often present an incomplete or inaccurate picture of the part of the world that they try to describe. There may be many reasons for this; for example, the data files may not be updated frequently enough, or they may not include accurate descriptions of real but non-legitimate (unrecognized) practices. In any case, the formal data systems in all organizations are always complemented by the informal knowledge, observations and communications of the employees. While the computer records of an airline reservation system may show no availability of seats for a certain flight (with the number of booked passengers equal to or greater than the number of available seats), the airline clerks may know that a number of booked customers will not turn up, and they may still sell seats to new customers. They are using their informal knowledge ahead of their formal, computer-based source. It is quite easy to see how this practice complements the limitations of the computer-based system, but it could get out of hand!

Regarding the description of the changes in the state of the world: This refers to the recording of events or transactions taking place as the organization functions. For example, banks record their customers' transactions during the day; this information is used at the end of the day to update the customers' accounts. In a similar way, the computer-based information systems of the stock exchange try to follow with great timeliness and accuracy the changes in the traded shares' prices. However, the real information system of the stock market is much more sophisticated, and relies on many professionals observing a great many different events and trends, from the success of crops in various places of the world to changes in the balance of power in the Middle East, all of which eventually result in changes to share prices.

Probabilistic Information

Probabilistic information refers to information on the basis of which a description of a part of the world can be inferred or guessed (Land 1985, 212–213). It includes the following types:

- Predictive information: Organizations make use of various types of forecasts and may apply statistical forecasting techniques. Such forecasts may deal with phenomena that are very regular and therefore for which there is a high degree of certainty that the forecasted information is correct. Others involve many assumptions and are used to exhibit alternative scenarios rather than to predict a future state. Managers and other professional experts make many predictions without formal statistical support. In fact, in most organizations, strategic decisions depend to a great degree on informal forecasts by expert managers rather than on formal forecasting techniques.

- Inferred information: Information that attempts to describe the world by means of inferences from a limited set of observations or measurements of the world. This is the case where a statistical sample is used to infer a general pattern, as, for example, when a sample of customers' opinions is used to make marketing decisions.
- Information derived from a model of the world: Models simulating the behaviour of the world can be built and are used in many decision-making situations. Models, however, are always approximations of real world phenomena. They make assumptions, may use statistical techniques on data samples, and can be built to serve particular interests. Consider a supermarket company trying to obtain planning permission from a local council for a new store. What would they put into a scale model of the building that was to go on show in the town hall? A full car-park or an empty one; mature trees or saplings; litterbins full, litterbins empty or no litterbins at all? Apart from such formal models, decision makers will often have their own perceptions of the world which can be thought of as informal models and according to which they make decisions—for example, decisions concerning which formal techniques and models to adopt.

Qualitative Information

Qualitative information refers to the explanations that lie behind the description of how the world is now or is expected to be (Land 1985, 214). This category of information is less likely to be found in a formal system; it is conveyed by a great variety of signs, often in accompanying descriptive information. For example, the tone of somebody's voice may convey a message more important than the content of the verbal expression.

Explanatory information is information that sets out to interpret other acts and signs (Land 1985, 214). Qualifying and qualitative information moderates descriptive information of a formal system. Patterns and norms determine how things should be done and the values according to which evaluations and judgements are made. Judgemental information is based on subjective or intuitive appreciation of a situation. Information about values, attitudes and power is often important for understanding the motivating forces in organizations.

Land (ibid.) also points to the coexistence of formal and informal information, even of the same type. This is particularly significant for the development of computer-based information systems, which is a process of developing a formal information system, in terms of data required, their format, and their processing. The behaviour of a computer-based information system is decided mainly by the analysis and design tasks, and its functioning is in this way fixed to a great degree before it starts operations. However, as Land reminds us, any such designed system is only a part of a broader system involving people who tend to develop informal practices complementing, or even overriding, the fixed, formally functioning system. Analysts must therefore be able to appreciate the informal aspects of a work environment within which a new information system is intended to operate. They need to be careful not to destroy vital informal practices with rigidly formal decision-making or other work procedures. They should equally carefully consider how designed rule-following systems can be used in situations in which human intuition and judgement appear to play a significant role. This last point may be considered as rather controversial and worthy of a bit more debate. Consider the advantages that have stemmed from auto-pilots in commercial airliners, or the improved quality in motor cars that come from an automated factory with welding done by robots.

ACHIEVEMENTS OF INFORMATION SYSTEMS IN BUSINESS

How does your organization measure and communicate the value of contributions from information technology? This was the question asked some years ago to a number of international CIOs (Chief Information Officers) by the CIO Forum, a UK-based consulting organisation. The responses varied from silence to confusing responses filled with jargon. It was rare to receive a clear and coherent response. This was not as one might have expected if one assumed that businesses receive significant benefits from information systems. The starting point for a discussion about gaps between expectations and results in the use of information systems in business is an indicator of why these gaps may be of a specific nature (and also more critical) for information technology and its applications.

In the 1999 World IT Census conducted by the London School of Economics and Compass, 659 chief executives of the world's largest companies were asked their opinions concerning the contribution of IT to business results. The overall conclusion was that IT achievement falls considerably behind managers' expectations. Some comments from the interviewed CEOs:

"We always seem to be one year away from achieving high value— sometimes high values do not happen at all";

"The high cost of undelivered promises is a continuing and increasing problem";

"We see the value of IT all right. We can't just, as yet, find the way to realise it";

"We cannot evaluate IT investments because the returns depend on other non-IT factors. Too often, an IT project just enables other projects".

Some seemingly contradictory standpoints can be noted among the comments— for example, despite the failure to meet expectations, the chief executives of the major organisations have even higher expectations for the future. In spite of the obvious disappointment, one out of four managers thus considers information technology very important for the business results, and one out of three refer particularly to improvements in efficiency.

In the time period following the survey, improvements in information systems and technology have had positive impacts on and benefits for management. The rhetoric in the IT sector is still, however, obscuring some of the actual facts, making assessment of benefit hazardous.

Three central issues were raised in the survey to reflect CEOs' expectations, achievements and future requirements concerning IT. Table 9.1 shows the three issues. (Note that score figures were established by subtracting the number of low from high responses; low and high responses reflect the three importance levels identified by respondents.)

For example, managers in the survey do not think that IT contributes to better cost control, but they have great hopes that this will be the case in the future! Managers furthermore expect that IT will increasingly contribute to improve competitiveness despite the fact that managers today do not see any

Table 9.1   Expectations, achievements and future requirements among 650 chief executives in large firms, 1999 (Compass World IT Census 1999)

Issue	Expect	Achievement	Requirement
"What was your expectation of IT's contribution to performance improvements, what was achieved and what are your future requirements?"	31	12	37
"What was your expectation of IT's contribution to cost management, what was achieved and what are your future requirements?"	1	–8	9
"What was your expectation of IT's contribution to competitive advantage, what was achieved, and what are your future requirements?"	7	–28	33

significant contribution. This is because information technology is today so broadly disseminated that only those enterprises who are first can claim a competitive advantage, and then only as long as the competitors have not yet caught up.

Finally, the more confidence that managers show towards information technology, the more positive they tend to be towards existing IT investments. There are two interpretations here: Either the corporate culture is very positive to information technology in general, and thus sets higher-than-average values on its impact, or these enterprises have learnt to make better use of information technology.

A number of international surveys in the 1990s regarding investments in computers and information technology reveal quite substantial gaps in a number of situations as noted by Heeks (1998):

- "The relationship between results and investments in information technology in US firms is acquiring a slightly negative bias." (as cited in Heeks, 1998)
- "Twenty per cent of all IT expenditures is wasted, another thirty to forty percent leads to no net benefits accruing" (as cited in Heeks, 1998)
- "Despite spending more than USD 200 billion on Information Systems in the last 12 years, there is little evidence of meaningful returns." (as cited in Heeks, 1998)
- "As many as seventy-five percent of all large systems may be considered to be operating failures." (as cited in Heeks, 1998)
- "Despite various attempts to co-ordinate investment, improve procurement practices and develop complementary human resources, computerisation has not resulted in any measurable increase in public sector productivity." (A World Bank investigation of more than USD 500 million spent on IT by Turkish Government, 1993)

From these assessments, it seems clear that there is a gap between plans for and reality of IT applications. The next question we need to answer is, therefore: To what extent may this be specific to information technology?

What Makes IT Gaps Special?

Is information technology unique in comparison with other types of technology, such as production technology (e.g., lathes, drills) or transport technology? At least two reasons would support the uniqueness of information technology in this comparison. First, it is applied in practically all sectors and in combination with other types of technology. Second, its focus is mainly on hardware when it comes to investments, whereas functionality and application is closely related to the software. As the costs of hardware are mostly easy to estimate and budget for, the costs for making hardware together with software an integrated function in the organizational context are not as easy to estimate. This has a number of implications, such as:

- It becomes difficult to distinguish whether perceived effects come from IT alone, or from another technology, or in a combination of the two;
- There is a special psychology of expectations around information technology;
- The often-complex integration with the organisation makes it difficult to distinguish costs and benefits both in time and in space;
- Training in IT has no clear boundaries; how much is application and how much is technology?

The costs for an IT-based application are primarily costs for software and its implementation (adaptation, training, etc.); the price for the software package is often well known, but the implementation costs are often difficult to estimate, or even to know ex post!

The uniqueness of information technology is probably its duality: It is shaped by organisational needs, but it also creates new forms of organisational structures and behaviour. This makes investment in information technology very complicated because traditional investment analysis models are intended for well-defined and less integrated investments. Traditional methods such as cost/benefit analysis therefore have limited value as assessment tools for IT investments.

Costs/Benefit Analysis and Information Systems

A general aspect of the problem related to cost/benefit analysis was formulated in a research report by Land (1998), summarized as follows:

> 'Everybody does cost benefit analysis on a project. Most of them are fictional. The saddest part is that it is not just the benefits that are fictional but the costs as well. They don't begin to assess what the real costs of the system are. They do cost benefit analysis to get money. We have trouble convincing ourselves of value of business terms. We cost justify new systems on the basis of lies and overstatements, we don't measure the true business value'. Land (ibid.) mentions several problems and difficulties in estimating costs and benefits for information system projects:

- "A significant proportion of costs are fixed and independent of utilisation. Allocating costs to specific information system projects may therefore be arbitrary" (19);
- "Lifetime costs are difficult to estimate because the life of new systems is uncertain—technological obsolescence and changing requirements make it increasingly hazardous to provide a reliable estimate of the system's life" (20);

- "The project champions tend to have a strong attachment to and belief in the ultimate worth of the system under review. Hence champions have a tendency to underestimate costs or fail to add contingencies—in order to increase the chance of the project being accepted" (20);
- "Many applications are targeted at second order effects—such as better information" (21);
- "In many cases, the change which has to be evaluated is a major reorganisation in which information technology plays an important role—but it is the investment in the reorganisation as a whole which adds value and has to be evaluated" (21).

A common tool for cost/benefit analysis is the Net Present Value (NPV) method (or variants thereof). The method compares the value of the investment with the net cash flows, discounted to the present value, that are expected to arise in each year during the foreseen lifetime of the machine. If the NPV value is greater than zero, then the investment can be considered economically justified.

Investments in computers are seldom exposed to formal investment analysis like the NPV method. The reason for this is twofold: It is difficult to estimate the benefits, particularly within a given time frame. It is also difficult to estimate costs for the process of adapting software to the organisation, or the reverse. Investments are therefore often justified by referring to more intangible returns such as 'the importance of keeping path with the technological development' or 'to stay competitive', etc. It is obvious that this approach to justifying an investment differs significantly from other more 'conventional' investments in, for example, a lathe or a truck.

In the NPV method, a significant parameter is the interest rate that defines the cost of capital. This rate is related to how fast the investment should be depreciated. The longer is depreciation time, the lower the interest rate, and the easier to justify an investment. In today's IT race, where a new product becomes obsolete within a very short period of time, depreciation time is short (a few years only), which results in a relatively high interest rate. Most managers know that using the NPV method to analyse IT investments is likely to result in a negative value that would not justify the investment. As there may be a variety of reasons behind a decision to invest in IT (business strategy, psychology, prestige, etc.), managers may therefore feel tempted to refrain from more structured analysis.

An indirect measure, on the macro level, of the gap between benefits and cost is to compare the accumulated cost of computers and information systems (e.g., costs for import of IT) and growth in, say, manufacturing added value. As a majority of IT investment goes to industry, it should be possible to observe a correlation within a fixed time period (e.g., a ten-year period) between the annual growth in manufacturing added value (MVA) and import value of computers. No such correlation can, however, be observed from statistical data.

REFERENCES

Compass World IT Census (1999) London: London School of Economics.

Dreyfus, H. (1972) *What computers can't do*. New York, MIT Press.

Heeks, R. (1998) *Information systems without information technology*. Information Technology in Developing Countries, 8 (3).

Heeks, R. (1998) *Information systems and public sector accountability*. University of Manchester, Institute for Development Policy and Management.

Land, F. (1985) *Is an information theory enough?* The Computer Journal, 28 (3).

Land, F. (1998) *Evaluating information systems*. Proceedings Working Conference, Asian Institute of Management, Bangkok.

Pagels, H. (1988) *The dreams of reason*. New York, Simon and Schuster.

Sagan, C. (1977) *The dragons of Eden*. New York, Random House.

Ward, J. and Peppard, J. (2002) *Strategic planning for information systems*. New York, Wiley & Sons.

World Bank (1993) *Turkey: informatics and economic modernization*. World Bank Country Studies.

10 Going Astray—Business Models and State Bureaucracies in an Unholy Alliance

Monitoring business performance has been the main theme throughout this book, focused essentially on market oriented firms in the private business sector and other organisations in which stress is placed on organisational performance. As, however, business models have increasingly been adopted as attractive models for public sector institutions, this final chapter will seek to analyse the appropriateness of applying business models in state organisations. Such analysis may be called for since many questions have been raised about an alliance in which models developed for one context are applied in a different context with different characteristics and conditions.

Even if the concept of a *business model* is not very well defined, it gives the impression of something rational and effectual and therefore also attractive to apply in seemingly less efficient and bureaucratic state organisations. The transfer of models between different institutional groups is, however, not trivial; this point was emphasized in earlier chapters' discussions about models as mappings of different realities. The spectrum of business models is quite significant, ranging from the explicit and articulated commonly found in larger firms to more implicitly applied models in smaller firms (which account for about ninety-nine per cent of all firms). Since small- and medium-sized firms differ from large firms as to risk taking, financial strength, long-term strategies and business endurance, the business models, articulated or not, must respond to different needs. Consequently, there is not *one* business model, but a wide variation adapted to different conditions and scenarios.

In contrast to the traditional organisation structures with many levels between top and bottom, between top management and the shop floor, modern organisations strive to achieve a flat structure with fewer layers of middle management. The number of levels in public organisations, which are based on the bureaucratic school of Weber and Fayol (see Box 10.1), creates structures that often differ from private firms. The traditional bureaucracy model assumes that task responsibility is confined to the level where the task is being performed or carried out. The responsible employee is judged by the ability to perform the task and not expected to go beyond the responsibility area. Business models in the private sector, however, encourage employees to take appropriate personal initiative for benefit to the organisation and to the business. The two realities are thus quite different.

Public organisations occasionally bear the stamp of political bias, which implies that decisions follow a partly different pattern compared to decision making in private firms. Learning is an important aspect of business development and attitude improvement and, hence, also an important aspect of the business model. Learning from mistakes is generally considered a basic condition for improvement. In organisations dominated by decisions with a political bias, learning from personal mistakes can be more controversial because admitting that mistakes have been made in political decisions may jeopardize political credibility and open opportunities for the political opposition. Such an aspect of learning is hardly a salient feature of the private sector.

With the increasing use of business models in the public sector and with the great variation of business models, it is relevant to ask which models are being adopted and how are they are being implemented and used.

WHAT IS A BUSINESS MODEL?

Value creation is a fundamental strategic goal for organisations wherein the benefit meaning of value may vary for clients or owners, employees or other stakeholders. A business model is constructed with the purpose to support and foster the implementation of a business strategy and is built around a core of qualities such as strategic objectives, clients, products, available resources, financial conditions, owner aspirations and assessment of business potentials. As long as the business model is based on assumptions that correctly match the strengths and weaknesses of the firm, it should be able to contribute to competitiveness and corporate ability to respond to business opportunities. In spite of the obvious significance of business models, there is, however, a variety of definitions and interpretations.

Variations of Business Models

Organisation theory and practice describe business models vaguely as part of a business strategy aiming at a comprehensive approach to create value for customers and owners. In a broader perspective, business models of today should preferably also shoulder responsibility for social values such as philanthropy and ethics, and this new responsibility has not made the concept much clearer. Literature provides a great variety of business model definitions and different interpretations that have manifested themselves in various models. Over the years, models have come and gone; some have stayed for a period while others disappeared swiftly after having enriched business consultants and made students confused, as new business models were waiting around the corner. *Management-by-walking-around, one-minute manager, Theory X and Y, zero-based costing*, and *re-engineering* are just a handful of business model examples out of an extensive list.

It is clear that there is not just one business model; paradoxically, the one size-fits-all approach is common for most models, and no single model claims to be useful or applicable for one specific purpose only. With the application of business models in the public sector, it is therefore intriguing to ask which models have been of particular interest and from which private sector examples have they been adopted—from large firms or from the small business sector, from formal or informal firms?

BUSINESS MODEL PROTOTYPES FOR THE PUBLIC SECTOR

Large organisations are generally developed with a long-term perspective and therefore involve activities that are recurrent and repetitive. They favour the distribution of authority and create positions that tend to become patterns for other organisations, not least in the public sector. Large firms tend to be structured in such a way that corresponds with the business strategy (Chandler, 1984).

Informal organisations are mostly born out of social relations where people come together through acquaintances. Important conditions for sustainability are trust, dependence and liking between owners and partners. This may be characteristic of small firms, which develop informal communication channels and communication patterns facilitating the exchange of views and reactions in a less formal and more direct way.

One might, therefore, expect that the business models that appeal to public sector organisations stem from large formal firms representing the successful users of the various types of business models available and promoted. But a report in *Harvard Business Review* (Girotra and Netessine, 2013) shows that failures occur for large firms using formal business models for various reasons. This is especially true for business model innovations—when the new idea is not a product, service, or technology but a different method of engaging with customers while earning revenue from them. Large organizations, in particular, struggle to implement such innovations. In this regard, three common problems have been identified in executing or rolling out a new business model in large organizations. The following are extracts of the identified problems.

1. Lack of top management support and attention:

Unlike other innovations, implementing a business model innovation often requires changes that affect multiple parts of the organization. And while the R&D department can sponsor and push through a new product or technology, rolling out a business model innovation requires direct support from the top management.

2. Reluctance to experiment:

Even the most brilliant business model innovation idea is just that: an idea. It relies greatly on assumptions and judgments and, in the absence of a crystal ball, the best tool we have is experiments, but established companies are surprisingly bad at experimenting.

3. Failure to pivot:

Even when the company experiments with a new business model, it often fails to interpret test results correctly and adjust an implementation plan accordingly. A large failure rate is nonetheless unacceptably high because so far too many large firms have not shown enough commitment and flexibility in the way they develop the business models and roll them out.

Even if business models adopted and used in the public sector tend to be brought from the large firm segment of the private sector, there is no guarantee that they should be particularly relevant and well adapted to their intended purposes in their new environments. The three common problems mentioned above in executing a new business model in large private firms are considered below for the public sector:

1. Lack of top management support and attention:

Implementing a business model requires changes that affect multiple parts of the public organisation. Thinking and behaving in accordance with private business concepts and principles like profit, competition, customer response, and service quality are not ideas that easily inspire and imbue the public organisation that has a deeply rooted culture and has been shaped in a bureaucratic mould. More than top management support would be required for successful implementation.

2. Reluctance to experiment:

As already suggested above, even the most brilliant business model innovation idea is just an idea. Experimenting with private business models in the public sector relies on assumptions and evaluations of how previously untried models can be implemented without coming in conflict with political commitments and violating the political public system. Efficiency in public organisations is not primarily about growth, profit and competitiveness but more about complying with the political agenda, handling taxpayers' money efficiently and responding to expectations and wishes of the population.

3. Failure to pivot:

Even when public organisations experiment with new business models, there is an apparent lack of evaluation as to relevant usefulness and reasonableness in adopting models that were originally developed for very different contexts. Owing to the political rhetoric and disinclination to confess failures in decisions already taken, any acknowledgement of such failure will be unlikely.

NEW MODELS IN PUBLIC SERVICES

The trend to modernise public sector organisations was first observed in the 1980s in the most advanced countries, but it has not been uniform across an international perspective. The root of new ideas in organisation theory can partly be ascribed to the change from mass production industry to what has been referred to as knowledge-based industry with ideas from Japanese manufacturing that had begun retreating from the pure bureaucratic form of organisations (Oliver and Wilkinson, 1992). The ideas gradually spilled over to public administration, where concepts like goal orientation and process approach soon met with interest and sympathy by decision makers and politicians. The period coincided with the public sector expansion during the 1960s and 70s, resulting in escalating costs that could not be covered simply by increased taxation.

The alternative to increased government income through taxes was to reduce costs in the state budgets. The most attractive approach seemed to be to make the public bureaucracy more efficient by adopting suitable models from the industry sector; huge amounts of money were invested in the new programmes. Deregulation of selected former public organisations and also delegation of responsibility to private actors required new approaches for retaining degrees of public control and to monitor performance. The hypothesis was that the introduction of private business concepts like market, manager, and measuring and control would lead to cost-effectiveness and organisational efficiency. Initially, the new ideas for public management were generally not considered to bring any significant negative side-effects.

With reference to the discussion in Part 1 of this volume, where models are viewed as pictures of reality and the usefulness of the model depends on how well reality (or a part thereof) is pictured in the model, the question arises of which parameters have been identified as being important and relevant when adopting the new models. For a business model in a private firm to be useful, there are a number of *a priori* parameters to be identified that are related to, for example, customers and markets, production and products, employees and owners. If the model is applied in another context, such as in the public sector, it cannot be taken for granted that conditions in the two contexts are similar enough for the model to forecast the same result. For example, a private firm knows its established customers, and the firm may campaign to find new customers who are suitable and relevant for the products and services being offered. A public organisation does not have the privilege of selecting people profiled to match the type of public service for which the organisation has responsibility.

Budget Driven and Market Driven Organisations

In earlier chapters, there was a discussion about performance and how to measure performance. In spite of the awareness that economic measures such as accounting are not enough to create a picture of organizational performance, the financial flow is one of many other indicators to show performance. Public organisation activities may be financed via a budget that is controlled by government while most private organisations are financed through the revenue from sales. A third category is those public organisations where activities are financed both from the state budget and through income from internally generated services.

Danielsson (1997) distinguished between budget and market driven organisations and emphasised that there is a fundamental difference between the two types based on the possibility of controlling the financial flow. A public organisation is usually financed through public means and the inflow of capital is therefore not directly related to performance as it is in a private firm, where quality and service directly influence sales revenue and thereby also the financing of operations. The necessary capital for running a budget driven organisation is generally channelled through the government budget structure indirectly from political decisions. Figure 10.1 illustrates schematically a budget driven organisation in the example of a public university.

The government allocates financial resources through the State budget for higher education that may be channelled via a university board. The resources are used by the individual university to employ faculty and staff and for purchasing materials. A second input is young people enrolled as students to take part in the education, leaving as graduates after training. Faculty and other staff fulfil a range of duties, such as research, training, and official duties. The labour market does not pay the university for graduates;

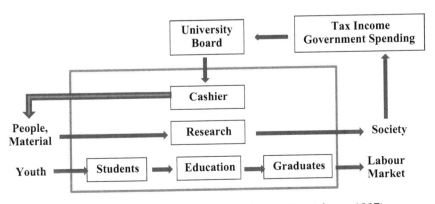

Figure 10.1   A budget driven organisation—university (Danielsson, 1997)

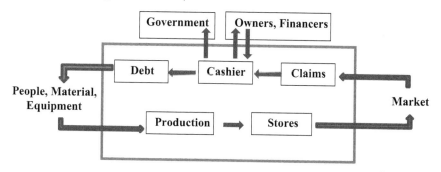

Figure 10.2 A market driven organisation—manufacturing firm (Danielsson, 1997)

neither do society nor other beneficiaries pay directly for research results. Such benefits rendered to society are returned to the State through taxes and other charges, which in turn provide capital for the university board in accordance with political decisions. Performance of the university in terms of student qualifications and quality in research results has no obviously direct impact on allocated funding, at least not in a short-term perspective. In most cases, poorly performing state organisations can continue long before there is a political consensus for changes.

In a market driven organisation, such as the example of a manufacturing firm in Figure 10.2, owners or other financiers provide starting capital. Starting capital is used to acquire the necessary facilities and services for production such as personnel, machines and material. Finished products are sold to the market at a price that generates revenue and flows back into the firm. If the revenue from sales is greater than the costs, there is a financial surplus, and part of the surplus is paid to the government as tax, part as dividends to owners and financiers. The market is sensitive to the performance of the company in terms of reliability and quality of products and service. Declining performance is often observed within a short time period through reduced market demand.

The market oriented firm in Figure 10.2 makes use of the financial flow as an indicator of performance—poor performance leads to negative customer response, reduced demand and reduced input of money. This, in turn, justifies a quick reaction to attend to weaknesses in the organisation in order to improve the response from customers and increase sales revenue. A budget driven organisation like the example in Figure 10.1 does not have the same possibility to react based on reduced flow of input capital because the provision of capital is not directly related to performance, but to political decision.

PUBLIC AND PRIVATE—TWO DIFFERENT REALITIES

What distinct differences exist between the two realities? Public sector organisations operate in accordance with an agenda that is basically set in a political context that is coloured by ideology and therefore strives to influence reality with political means. The agenda of the private firm is set according to market demand and represents an operating strategy the firm can successfully adapt to reality.

Central governments are structured in ways that reflect their core societal activities—for example, industry, trade, economy, and culture. This implies a need for political stability so that the public core organisations can operate and develop with a long-term perspective. Bureaucracy in the social system creates inertia in the decision process, which to some extent characterises the reality of the public sector. While inertia, therefore, may have a hampering effect on efficiency, it may sometimes be necessary to elucidate different perspectives in a complex decision process. Private business models are, however, geared to speed in decision making while avoiding complex decisions that would risk slowing down the business process.

A priority objective of the public sector is administration of the state, which is a complex task, bearing in mind the expanse of scattered and partly contradictory aspects of society. A model to handle complexity and diversification in society must accumulate the most vital aspects and interpret messages and views on a macro level. Attention to societal messages and views, which is the responsibility of the public sector, is sometimes filtered through political bias that may not always seem rational from a micro perspective, but simple and awful relations in economic, technical and social systems where individuals interact may easily lead to complex, hazardous and even completely unpredictable situations. Pagels (1988) claims that in systems with three or more parameters, which is not at all unusual even for simple systems, the combination of parameters may lead to chaotic situations under certain conditions. Instead of accepting that a model is not completely reliable unless it equals reality in complexity, and hence is of no use as a model, the desire to make reality intelligible and manageable leads to unjustified simplifications in attempts to interpret reality. By introducing the principles of competitiveness in public sector organisations there is an overwhelming risk that complexity is addressed by simplification.

Exposing public organisations to competition is, however, one of the driving forces behind the trend to implement private business models in the public sector. The underlying assumption is that competition contributes to increased efficiency through benchmarking with other actors and organisations from the private sector. By studying and analysing best practices among competitors and other types of seemingly successful organisations and firms, the criteria for comparison must first be identified and selected. Benchmarking is a process, and each step in the process spells out what is to be done in a generic manner. When applying a generic model in a specific situation (a specific firm or organisation), we cannot know to what extent the 'best practice' example is best practice from a sustainability perspective, taking into account the effortful learning process. Benchmarking is a simplified model that provides a useful way of understanding important steps to improve business performance. To what extent it is also a useful model for a specific firm with a specific culture is another question (see also Chapter 6).

A number of pre-conditions must thus apply for competitiveness to become a cogent argument—for example, the process leading to a competitive strategy is a change process that must permeate the organisation and influence employee attitudes. Focusing solely on management and formal methods borrowed from business does not create enough awareness among employees, which widens the vision–culture gap, the misalignment that develops when management moves the organisation in a strategic direction that employees do not understand or support (for detail, see Chapter 6).

Public perception, as opposed to the reality of private business, is broader and more committed to the development of society. Steven Lukes, an American political and social theorist, claims that government control happens in three ways: through decision-making power, through non-decision-making power and through ideological power (Lukes, 2005). Lukes arranges public issues according to three categories. The first comprises the most common issues on the political agenda; the second, those issues that are *not* on the agenda but have been removed or eliminated for various reasons. The third, and most important, issue is the power to influence people's wishes and thoughts: the power of thought. Governments have the power to focus on the three issues, and the way they do so will reveal how they perceive reality and in which way their political power will be used in the service of society development. None of these issues are considered in business models of the private sector.

HIERARCHIES AND LEARNING IN PRIVATE AND PUBLIC SECTORS

The trend towards flatter organisations has been part of organisational change for the last fifty years and characteristic of the structure of private business firms. Reducing middle management and organisational levels has been an ambition to simplify administration and shorten communication distances as well as cut costs. In the process of delegating responsibility and encouraging employees to suggest initiatives for improving productivity and working conditions, various kinds of reward systems have been introduced as methods within human resource management.

Employees taking initiatives with the ambition to improve performance require adequate knowledge about their own job as well as an understanding of how different units within the organisation work together for optimisation. Learning has always been a precondition to carrying out a task, but a more recent approach to learning has drawn the distinction between the process of learning and the process of learning how to learn (Morgan, 1997). Learning how to learn implies acquiring the ability to question whether standard norms applied mechanically in response to situations are

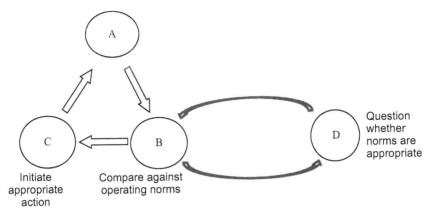

Figure 10.3 Questioning operating norms (Morgan, 1997)

still appropriate or whether they are ready for change. Circle A in Figure 10.3 illustrates the processes of sensing, scanning and monitoring the environment for situations and activities of interest and relevance for the organisation. Circle B encompasses the process of comparing information from A with current operating norms to decide if action is required. In Circle C action or no action is taken depending of the outcome of comparison in Circle B.

A decision to act or not to act in C depends on the comparison with current norms in B. If, however, it would turn out in D that a current norm is obsolete or no longer valid or relevant and therefore can be modified to a new standard norm, the comparison in B might now recommend action to be taken in C. While questioning current norms ("learning to learn") should be a continuous task for managers in the private sector, and indeed in the business model, the corresponding situation is different in a public sector organisation. Questioning and changing current norms has not been a tradition in the bureaucratic models.

While learning to learn is the essence of improving performance in private firms, one does not find the same attitude in most public organisations. One reason may be that norms are established in accordance with political decisions and can hardly be changed unless there is a political decision. Another reason may also be prestige—changing norms could be seen by the political opposition as a sign of mismanagement or mistakes in previous decisions. This can be observed on regional levels, where local authorities and local governments share with the local business community the ambition of local economic growth. Central-government-directed national programmes for supporting small firms mostly have a set of norms for a uniform regional treatment, which is not always suitable for the conditions of small firms in a particular region. Different perspectives often lead to the chicken-and-egg problem: Whereas local governments like to see prosperous business firms generating jobs and tax income that would contribute to the financing of improved community service, the business community wants to see local government commitment to infrastructure programmes as preconditions for a prosperous business sector.

BOX 10.1 MINI-ENCYCLOPAEDIA: FAYOL AND WEBER

The Administrative School—Fayol

Henri Fayol was the founder of the Administrative Organisation School and based his theories on his experience in the mining industry in France. The Administrative School emphasises that responsibility must be related to authority and that authority must take responsibility. Therefore, each business goal must not have more than one manager, and that one manager has the responsibility to see that the goal is achieved. Fayol also underlined the importance of clear directives between manager and employee, which include complying with discipline norms. Information should be vertical and formal through the hierarchy, and direct horizontal communication should be avoided. Fayol encouraged initiatives. He introduced the organisational concept of control span, which defines the number of employees controlled and managed effectively by one manager without too much effort. In a normal situation, the optimal control span should cover six to eight employees, but in the case of extremely standardized tasks, the control span may cover thirty persons.

The Bureaucratic School—Weber

Max Weber was the founder of the Bureaucratic School, which distinguishes between power and authority. While power coerces to obedience, the authoritative person is obeyed by free will. Weber maintained that efficiency is achieved through formal rules, reports and communication channels. Organisations must be hierarchical and have impersonal communication channels following the hierarchical structure. Weber's theory emphasises the importance of suppressing the informal authorities and highlighting those who are authorities due to their formal positions. The advantage of bureaucracy is that conflicts can be reduced through reference to formal rules. The theory is particularly relevant for organisations working in a stable environment with the need for safety and control, which applies to public organisations.

MODELS LEADING ASTRAY

Questionable results of major reforms in the public sector in several countries have created growing uncertainty among the public about the State's ability to cope with the ever-increasing complexity of society. Privatisation of vital public institutions like health care, education and infrastructure systems has strongly reduced the responsibility of the State for important public service areas through delegation to private actors. Reforms of the public sector used to be based on solid knowledge and analysis that preceded the reforms, whereas radical changes in social functions take place today ostensibly without the same thorough analysis. Instead, the legitimacy of the reforms is achieved with the help of post evaluations that are geared and adapted to previously set goals. Statistics provide the seemingly objective support for evaluations, which can claim that goals have been met. For example, the police can carry out traffic controls when there is less traffic for an easy collection of statistical credits by fulfilling measurable goals.

The Polish-British sociologist Zygmunt Bauman claims that science about humans and society only slightly differs from magic, and many of the models used in science have similarities to incantations in primitive cultures (Bauman, 1992). Models are based on assumptions about reality, and the less one knows about the aspect of reality to be described, the closer the assumption comes to guesswork—or perhaps incantation? Since reality is not easily bounded in time and space, a generic model can only become fragmented and incomplete—in some cases, it can even become an incorrect description of reality.

The more comprehensive the reality to be captured by the model, the more complex the model itself must be. At a high hierarchical level at which no details can be discerned, the complexity may seem manageable; relations between models can be formulated and cause-effect chains can be presented in a credible and trustworthy way. It is not until such hierarchical models are confronted with the reality defined by everyday life of people that the explanation power of the models is questioned.

The central theme in the attempts to modernise and improve efficiency in public sector organisations by adopting models from industry is New Public Management, a concept originally coined by Hood (1991) and based on the hypothesis that market orientation, business management and the use of indicators and other measuring tools will ultimately make the public sector as efficient and productive as the private business sector.

New Public Management is about measuring quality and other business principles with simple quantitative measures such as economic indicators. The possibility of measuring outcome becomes of primary importance and is therefore decisive for the design of models and the assumptions made. The *result goal* is semantically as well as from a content point of view an incomprehensible concept where the present and the future coincide as the future hypothetical outcome rather than the actual starting point determines the goal. With the *result* and the *goal* being the same then the outcome is always achieved, a self-fulfilling prophesy!

The primary objective of New Public Management is accountability to the system itself and not to a civil servant or department in a public organisation. In a recent book, Dahler-Larsen (2012) presents a critical reckoning with the "evaluation society" and claims there are no objective evaluations but rather exercises of power. Concurrent with the growing focus on simplified and one-dimensional evaluations, one can notice how reality is gradually adapted to how evaluations are performed. From this it follows that there is a risk that goals are replaced by criteria that can later be formally evaluated. Political initiatives are chosen under the condition that they can be evaluated. Professional authorities run the risk of being undermined and weakened. This risk has been particularly highlighted in the academic context and in higher education.

New Public Management in the Academic Context

Applying New Public Management principles in academic environments follows the same pattern as in other areas—namely, measuring academic quality in education by means of simplified quantitative methods. A more strict government control of academic research focused on economic yield has resulted in a new vocabulary in which research is synonymous with *innovation*, which is primarily associated with the development of new techniques and products. Although this may be a laudable aim when seen from a national economic perspective, it means in reality that the purpose of higher education and research is being redefined.

The modern European university has been modelled in accordance with liberal principles for more than a hundred years in the spirit of Wilhelm von Humbold. The basic idea has been that higher education should foster intellectual ability among individuals for the benefit of both individuals and society. Currently, higher education is increasingly focused on professional education for which knowledge has become synonymous with techniques and abilities to foster economic growth.

Recent research maintains, however, that exerting control on research and higher education has not led to any measurable effect on economic growth (Rider, Hasselberg and Waluszewski, 2013). The authors point out that it is not possible to predict to what extent research considered detached from worldly affairs can become relevant and important twenty years from now.

CONCLUSION

New Public Management has become a symbolic expression in the process of adopting business models from private to public sector organisations. The privatisation of public service sectors like transportation, health care and education has created the need for standardisation in order to make the services as comparable as possible to facilitate their sale to private firms. For political correctness, the politicians responsible for the sales require quality assurance and certification as appropriate from the service firms.

The measures of quality and certifications constitute one of the cornerstones in new public management: evaluation of outcome. Standardisation defines which reference values are to be determined for later evaluation and since the public organisations to become privatised receive the same reference value, to facilitate comparison, the emphasis on measures and evaluation is more important than the service itself.

The ambition of this final chapter has been to analyse the appropriateness of applying business models in organisations belonging to the state. With the relatively thorough discussion about models in this volume, we have chosen to regard models as pictures of reality; the more complex the reality, the more uncertain becomes the picture. Public sector organisations with their mission and responsibility to carry out directives from political authority operate in a world of highly complex reality. It would be remarkable if business models designed for significantly less complex business environments could be applicable and useful in a very different context.

REFERENCES

Bauman, Z. (1992) *Intimations of postmodernity*. London, Routledge.
Chandler, A. (1984) *Strategy and structure*. Cambridge, MA, MIT Press.
Dahler-Larsen, P. (2012) *The evaluation society*. Stanford, Stanford University Press.
Danielsson, A. (1997) *Företagsekonomi—en översikt*. Lund, Studentförlaget.
Girota, K. and Netessine, S. (2013) *Why large companies struggle with business model innovation*. Harvard Business Review, September 27.
Hood, C. (1991). *A public management for all seasons*. Public Administration, 69 (1).
Lukes, S. (2005) *Power: A radical view*. London, Macmillan.
Morgan, G. (1997) *Images of organisations*. Thousand Oaks, CA, Sage.
Oliver, N. and Wilkinson, B. (1992) *The Japanization of British industry*. Oxford, Blackwell.
Pagels, H. (1988) *The dreams of reason*. New York, Simon and Schuster.
Rider, S., Hasselberg, Y. and Waluszewski, A. (2013) *Transformation in research, higher education and the academic market: The breakdown of scientific thought*. Heidelberg, Springer Science.

Index

Note: Page numbers in *italics* indicate tables, figures, and boxes.